Early Pithouse Villages of the Mimbres Valley and Beyond

Papers of the

PEABODY MUSEUM OF

ARCHAEOLOGY AND ETHNOLOGY

HARVARD UNIVERSITY

CAMBRIDGE, MASSACHUSETTS, U.S.A.

VOLUME 83

Early Pithouse Villages of the Mimbres Valley and Beyond

The McAnally and Thompson Sites in Their Cultural and Ecological Contexts

Michael W. Diehl and
Steven A. LeBlanc

With contributions by
Roger Anyon, John W. Arthur,
and Paul E. Minnis

PEABODY MUSEUM OF
ARCHAEOLOGY AND ETHNOLOGY
HARVARD UNIVERSITY
CAMBRIDGE, MASSACHUSETTS, U.S.A.

2001

Cover art by Ron Stauber
Project supervision by Joan K. O'Donnell
Design and production by Bruce Taylor Hamilton
Printing and binding by Thomson-Shore, Inc.

Copyright © 2001 by the President and Fellows
of Harvard College
ISBN 0-87365-211-8
Library of Congress Control Number 01-131185
Manufactured in the United States of America

Contents

Appendix: Tree-Ring Dates from Upland Mogollon Pithouse Villages 121

References 129

Figures

Tables

Acknowledgments

The authors wish to express their appreciation to the many people who contributed to the completion of this research in varying ways. These include Mimbres Foundation board members Jay T. Last, Laura Stearns, and Tony Berlant. They also include the McAnally and Thompson families and many other individuals in the Mimbres region who provided support and encouragement. Other individuals and institutions that played a role in conducting or supporting the research are listed below.

We would like to thank Ron Stauber, who produced the site and unit drawings for the book, and June-el Piper and Lynne Sebastian, who edited the text. The Mimbres Foundation provided field and artifact photographs, and Michael Diehl, Steven LeBlanc, and Paul Minnis took the environmental photos. Jacquelyn Honig gave invaluable assistance to Steven LeBlanc in the preparation of the volume. Joan K. O'Donnell managed the editorial process and supervised production of the finished book, which was designed and produced by Bruce Taylor Hamilton. Donna Dickerson of the Peabody Museum Press provided production assistance.

Finally, we thank Bruce Huckell, Stephen Lekson, and an anonymous reviewer, who all made useful suggestions for the manuscript. We appreciate their generosity and advice.

ARCHAEOLOGISTS, 1975–1976 SEASONS

Roger Anyon
Michael Blake
Carl Halbirt
Robert J. Hard
Bonnie Kranzer
Mark Lindley
Steven LeBlanc

Ellen McCann
Paul E. Minnis
Margaret C. Nelson
Laura Owens
David Stailey
Robert Schiowitz

INSTITUTIONS

The Arizona State Museum, Tucson
The Arizona State University Department of
      Anthropology, Tempe
The Field Museum of Natural History, Chicago
The Laboratory of Anthropology, Museum of
      New Mexico, Santa Fe
The Maxwell Museum of Anthropology,
      University of New Mexico, Albuquerque
The Mimbres Foundation, Pasadena
The Museum of Northern Arizona, Flagstaff
The National Science Foundation
      (Grant No. DBS 9219848)
The Santa Fe Institute, Santa Fe

1 Introduction

The McAnally and Thompson sites are two prehistoric villages located along the Rio Mimbres in the heart of the Upland Mogollon region of the North American Southwest. As Early Pithouse period villages, these sites contain architecture, artifacts, and detritus of the earliest relatively sedentary horticulturists to occupy the region. The lifeways of these people—their subsistence practices, including foraging and growing crops, their knowledge of construction and of the manufacture of stone tools and pots, and their rules for social interaction—provided the foundation for nine centuries of continuous occupation and use of the Mimbres Mogollon area.

Despite their generative role in the Mogollon cultural and historical sequence, Early Pithouse period villagers have received comparatively little attention from archaeologists in the last 30 years. Instead, the legacy of these early inhabitants has been overshadowed by studies of their descendants, the Classic Mimbres pueblo dwellers, who are famous for their black-on-white decorated bowls (Brody 1977; Brody et al. 1983; LeBlanc 1983).

Since the conclusion of Paul Martin's excavations in the Pine Lawn Valley of New Mexico during the 1940s, there have been several interpretive syntheses of Mogollon Early Pithouse period occupations (Hunter-Anderson 1986; LeBlanc and Whalen 1980; Lekson 1992a; Wheat 1955), two major excavations of Early Pithouse villages (Fitting 1973;

Lightfoot 1984), and several comparatively small excavation projects (Berman 1978; Duncan et al. 1991; Gilman et al. 1991; Kayser 1973; Wills 1991a). The partial excavations of the Thompson and McAnally sites by the Mimbres Foundation during the 1970s, reported preliminarily in LeBlanc (1975, 1976a) and LeBlanc and Whalen (1980) and discussed in detail in the present volume, added to the number of sites that have been excavated.

After this manuscript was completed, the report on the Wind Mountain site in the Mangas Creek area became available (Woosley and McIntyre 1996). Although this site consists primarily of a Late Pithouse component and a smaller Classic Mimbres occupation, there is some evidence for a minor Early Pithouse occupation. Because this useful addition to the available information on the Upland Mogollon pertains to later periods than our primary focus, our inability to include it in this discussion was disappointing but not critical. In fact, examination of this work suggests that it provides additional supportive information for many of the inferences made here and does not refute them.

Prior efforts in the archaeology of pithouse villages are most interesting because they offer divergent characterizations of subsistence, settlement, and social organization. Many of the interpretive differences may be attributed to the fact that most scholars have different areas of methodological expertise. Moreover, most scholars initiate research from different intellectual perspectives, and these begin with manifestly different assumptions. Often, heuristic divergence begins with basic questions, such as, "What constitutes an Upland Mogollon pithouse village?" and "Where should we fix the approximate beginning and ending dates for the Three Circle phase?"

In writing this volume, the authors share two primary goals. The first is to synthesize information about Upland Mogollon Pithouse period (A.D. 200–1000) occupations throughout the region. A current synthesis for this period is necessary because improvements in middle-range theory have promoted the generation of new interpretive results from recent studies of museum collections. The second goal is to present a complete account of the excavations of and artifacts obtained from the Thompson and McAnally sites. This book provides the primary descriptive and contextual data for these two sites, superseding preliminary accounts given in LeBlanc (1975, 1976a) and LeBlanc and Whalen (1980).

BACKGROUND TO THE MIMBRES FOUNDATION EXCAVATIONS

The Mimbres Foundation research began in 1974 as a rescue operation, with the goal of trying to recover information about the Classic Mimbres period before all the sites were completely looted. We envisioned a basically synchronic project and had little immediate interest in the other prehistoric periods in the area. In the 1970s the gross chronology and cultural history of the Southwest, one of the best-researched areas of the world, were considered reasonably well understood.

Both the foundation's approach and its use of the then-accepted cultural sequence were severely tested within the first few weeks of our first season, and the research design evolved rapidly. It soon became clear that the larger Mimbres sites were heavily damaged. Although an occasional small roomblock could be encountered that was relatively intact, it was very unlikely that broad-scale intrasite research would be fruitful. On the sites available to us, we would not be able to carry out a modern program of research on the scale of earlier excavations at the Swarts Ruin or Cameron Creek Village. Subsequently, Harry Shafer was able to undertake such broad-scale excavations on the NAN site, and the NAN Ranch study complements the diachronic approach we employed (Shafer 1982, 1990, 1991a, 1991b, 1991c, 1995; Shafer and Taylor 1986). In addition, recent systematic surveys

and excavations of sites located east of the Black Range along tributaries to the Rio Grande have added much to our knowledge of Classic Mimbres phase and subsequent Puebloan occupations in southern New Mexico (M. Nelson 1999).

Almost immediately after the initiation of the Mimbres Foundation research in the 1970s, the overall picture of the cultural sequence was determined to be very incomplete, if not inaccurate. The foundation initiated a reconnaissance survey to try to find Classic period sites. The methodology was flexible enough that sites of other periods were discovered and recorded as well. This rather casual initial survey was expanded in subsequent years, and a systematic stratified sampling approach was adopted, along with both opportunistic surveying and landowner interviews. The results of this work are summarized in Blake et al. (1986).

At the outset of the Mimbres Valley survey, the McAnally site was discovered directly across the river from the Mattocks Ruin. It was obvious that it was "Pine Lawn" in time period and earlier than the Harris site that Haury (1936a) excavated a few miles upriver and the pithouses that Nesbitt (1931) excavated at the Mattocks Ruin. The potential for diachronic samples that spanned the Pine Lawn phase through the Classic Mimbres phase and that were obtained from essentially the same location was obvious. Test excavations at the McAnally site began almost immediately. Although we had encountered extensive looting on the Mattocks and other sites, we were recovering good botanical, faunal, and pollen samples, as well as artifact assemblages that could be securely placed in time. Even as we discovered the limitation of doing synchronic work, we recovered information that could be very useful in diachronic studies. The McAnally site provided a spatially controlled sample that would likely increase the temporal span of our information by several hundred years.

A similar revelation about the post-Mimbres sites was also taking place. The nature of these sites was not at all what one would expect from the literature, and excavations within the Mimbres Valley were begun on the post-Mimbres phases as well (Nelson and LeBlanc 1986). Post-Mimbres phase sites located east of the Black Range were the focus of subsequent studies by Margaret Nelson (1999), who was an early contributor to the Mimbres Foundation's efforts. These later periods are considered only briefly in this volume, but they are relevant in interpreting settlement patterns and subsistence strategies for the entire sequence (e.g., Minnis 1985a).

The initial work on the McAnally site was intended to provide a comparative framework for later periods. We had neither the intent nor the resources to undertake broad-scale excavations. As work began, we immediately discovered that the ground was exceedingly hard. Virtually every square meter of soil had to be loosened with a railroad pick. Given the effort required to climb the McAnally hill, the incredible hardness of the soil, and the need to abandon the hill frequently to avoid lightning storms, every piece of information was well earned. The excavation strategy of the McAnally site is considered in detail in chapter 10.

As the survey and excavations continued, it became clear that one could put the prehistoric sequence into five analytically useful temporal intervals: Early Pithouse period, Late Pithouse period, Classic Mimbres period, Black Mountain phase (Animas), and Cliff phase (Salado). These intervals are not all analytically equivalent. The Late Pithouse period may be subdivided, and the Early and Late Pithouse and Classic periods clearly represent a cultural continuum. In contrast, the Black Mountain and Cliff phases are not continuous with the preceding occupations, at least not in the Mimbres Valley, and the exact nature of these latter intervals is another subject of interest and debate. Nevertheless, for the purposes of looking at settlement location, population size, and subsistence strategy, these five divisions provide a useful taxonomy for discussing the prehistoric occupations in the region.

Although we recognized the broad utility of the five intervals, the Mimbres Foundation research indicated that spatial variation was also important. The Mimbres Valley can be farmed effectively along a vertical gradient of some 2,000 feet, ranging from relatively mountainous terrain to the almost flat Deming Plain; these areas were heuristically divided into the upper, middle, and lower valley zones based on their elevation and macro-ecological contexts.

Studying the cultural sequence through excavations in one place was not nearly as interesting and informative as doing so in several localities along this elevational and topographical gradient. The research became an effort to obtain comparative samples from each of the five intervals in the upper, middle, and lower valley. We did not expect always to have the good fortune of finding temporally discrete sites in very close proximity, as we did with the Mattocks and the McAnally sites, but we felt we could obtain samples within each of these three portions of the valley in sufficient proximity to make useful comparisons.

Efforts to select sites for this purpose had to account for other concerns, including logistics, permissions for access, site security, and the quality of deposits.

Our goals were only partially met. Our lower valley Cliff phase site was completely bulldozed by looters just before we were scheduled to begin excavations. Two nearby Late Pithouse and Classic sites were also thoroughly damaged before we could work on them, obviating any attempts to excavate there. Nevertheless, we came close enough to fulfilling our site sample that an analytical framework was developed.

The second Early Pithouse period site reported here, the Thompson site, was excavated to help fulfill the research strategy. In terms of the broader elevational gradient, this was the lowest Early Pithouse site that we could excavate. Although our goal was limited to obtaining comparative and datable material, the extreme shallowness of the site was discouraging, and only limited effort was expended. The conditions at the Thompson site generally prevailed at the other sites that we selected for excavation, and resources were not available to locate suitable substitutes. Only the Black Mountain phase site was really productive. Although the Thompson site was of considerable interest, therefore, practical and depositional constraints greatly limited what could be learned.

It is our opinion that because of the hard soils, steep slopes, and inaccessibility of many Early Pithouse period sites, efforts moving beyond the type of excavations and information recovered to date will require a vast supply of research money and a large pool of labor. Alternatively, one could seek a site situated on a typical landform (hilltop) and overall setting (overlooking a major drainage) for the Early Pithouse period that may yield well-preserved deposits and that offers soil conditions compatible with less destructive excavation techniques.

CULTURE HISTORY SUMMARY

A very brief synopsis of the temporally broad prehistoric occupation sequence of the Mimbres Valley is provided here simply to orient the reader. It has been covered in more detail elsewhere (Blake et al. 1986; LeBlanc 1983; Minnis 1985a). This volume presents important revisions to the Early Pithouse and Late Pithouse sequences. Owing to the complex and technical nature of these revisions, as well as the need for a full discussion of the systematics of Upland Mogollon pithouse sites, an extensive discussion of the Pithouse period sequence is reserved for chapter 2.

The preceramic occupation of the Mimbres area is poorly documented, and in fact so little evidence is available that a discussion of the preceramic occupations of the Mimbres Valley is not warranted. Beginning about A.D. 200, a number of sites were occupied that may be assigned to the Early Pithouse period, which is the focus of this volume. These villages are virtually all located on hilltops or other isolated locations. Around A.D. 600, there was a marked shift in settlement pattern from hilltops to river terraces, where later pithouse villages and subsequent pueblos may be found. The term "Late Pithouse" period recognizes the importance of this shift in the locations of settlements. As is discussed in chapter 2, the Late Pithouse period has been divided into a number of temporally sequential phases that are marked by changes in architecture and ceramic styles.

The subsequent and commonly recognized Classic Mimbres phase marks the end of the prevalent use of pithouses as residences in the Mimbres Valley and is characterized by aboveground cobble-walled rooms (in effect, "pueblos") and the famous black-on-white pottery. It begins around A.D. 1000 and terminates with a significant occupational discontinuity that occurs around A.D. 1130 to 1150. The nature of this discontinuity and the reasons that it occurred are the subject of ongoing research and scholarly debate. The subsequent interval, roughly A.D. 1150 to 1300, is termed the Black Mountain phase in the Mimbres Valley and seems to be related to the better-known Animas phase in Hidalgo County. Similarly, the Mimbres Valley Cliff phase seems to be an expression of the Salado phenomenon that is better known in Arizona and spans much of the fourteenth century A.D. (Nelson and LeBlanc 1986). The Black Mountain and Cliff phases have distinctively different architecture, site layouts, and pottery; the extent to which they represent new people or simply new styles is an open question. Estimates of the relative population sizes for these time periods suggest that the population increased severalfold from the Early Pithouse period through a maximum that occurred during the Classic Mimbres period. A population decline followed during the Black Mountain phase. Cliff phase populations approximated those of the Early Pithouse period.

After approximately A.D. 1400, the valley ceased to be occupied by pottery-making pueblo dwellers. Although permanent (sedentary) farming villages did not occur again until the historic period, Apache uses of the Mimbres Valley during the nineteenth century are well known, and the Apaches' use of that area as a home range may extend back into the seventeenth or even sixteenth centuries. Owing to the ephemeral character of Apache sites, scholars are unable to assess accurately the protohistoric Apache population density or the nature of their use of the area.

THE ORGANIZATION OF THIS VOLUME

This book is organized into two sections. The first section (chaps. 2 through 9) synthesizes information about changes in Upland Mogollon pithouse villagers' ways of life over eight centuries, from A.D. 200 through 1000. In the second section of this volume, chapters 10 and 11 describe the excavated deposits and the artifact assemblages that were recovered from the McAnally and Thompson sites, so that other scholars interested in the archaeology of the Mimbres Valley might use this information.

Since an understanding of these changes requires knowledge of the temporal and environmental contexts of these sites, the culture-historical sequence and environmental contexts of Upland Mogollon pithouse sites are described and discussed in chapter 2. Critical shortages of hard evidence have not prevented scholars from offering descriptions of Upland Mogollon lifeways; given the dearth of evidence, it is not surprising that some of these descriptions differ from one another. Accordingly, chapter 3 reviews prior scholars' studies of Mogollon prehistory and their largely hypothetical descriptive accounts of the pithouse dwellers' life-styles.

Culture history is not the ultimate goal of most American archaeological research; instead, archaeologists seek to identify systemic relationships among different facets of culture and environment. In this book, the substantive analytical chapters (chaps. 4 through 9) specifically address the question of how people organized their subsistence efforts: What did they eat? For how long were sites occupied? What tools were used to process foods? Are there any relationships among changes in the diet, changes in the intensity of site use, and changes in tool shapes and sizes? We focus on these questions because, despite more than half a century of archaeological research, these basic questions have not been adequately addressed. A full account of subsistence change is a necessary prerequisite for understanding other changes in Upland Mogollon lifeways.

Chapter 4 analyses the amount of effort invested in pithouse construction and remodeling between

A.D. 200 and A.D. 1000. The analyses presented there indicate the existence of a trend. As time passed, Mogollon pithouse villagers invested, in relative terms, ever-greater effort in the construction and maintenance of their dwellings. We suggest that these changes are symptomatic of longer occupations of pithouses on subannual and perennial scales.

Chapter 5 describes the amounts of different charred plant remains that were recovered from the McAnally site. Increases in the amounts of maize suggest that agricultural plants may have become increasingly important through time. The results of the paleobotanical analyses appear to support the trend observed independently in the ground stone data in chapter 6; however, they are weakened by low macroplant recovery rates in the McAnally and Thompson samples and by the absence of a comparable suite of data from other Early Pithouse period sites.

Chapter 6 describes the ground stone artifacts that were recovered during the excavations at the McAnally and Thompson sites. Manos and metates from McAnally and Thompson are included in an analysis of grinding stones from many other Mogollon pithouse villages. The analysis indicates that the efficiency of maize-grinding tools increased throughout the first millennium A.D. We argue that these changes were driven by a need to process ever-increasing amounts of grain, and that the changes are symptomatic of the increasing importance of maize in the diet of Mogollon pithouse villagers.

Chapter 7 discusses the uses to which Early Pithouse period ceramics from the McAnally and Thompson sites were put and the insights that this information provides about the kinds of foods that were prepared in the vessels. Chapter 8 describes the faunal remains found at the McAnally site. Since there are virtually no comparable data from other Upland Mogollon Early Pithouse villages, no comparative analyses were attempted. The osteofaunal data presented in chapter 8 indicate, in an unsatisfactory way, some fraction of the range of animal resources that were used by Mogollon pithouse dwellers. Chapter 9 describes the chipped stone data from the Thompson and McAnally sites and places these data in the context of a regional analysis of spatial and temporal variation in the composition of Mimbres Mogollon chipped stone assemblages.

Chapter 10 describes the excavation units, depositional contexts, architectural details, radiocarbon dates, miscellaneous artifacts, and ceramic frequency distributions from the McAnally and Thompson sites. Chapter 10 is not a comparative study. This volume is the only source for the archaeological information obtained from these two sites, and it must serve as the site report for the research conducted there by the Mimbres Foundation.

In chapter 11, we close with a discussion of the relationship between the McAnally and Thompson sites in the context of the Mimbres Valley, emphasizing temporal changes in subsistence, demography, and social organization. Although many aspects of our discussion here are little more than well-informed hypotheses, they serve as a basis for future research.

Finally, the appendix to this volume provides a comprehensive summary of tree-ring dates from Upland Mogollon pithouse villages. These have been compiled from a number of sources and are important for establishing the basic facts of the Upland Mogollon Pithouse period chronology described in chapter 2.

2 The Environmental Context and Culture-Historical Framework of the Upland Mogollon Region

The McAnally and Thompson sites are Early Pithouse period villages occupied by the earliest agriculturally based people of the Upland Mogollon region. By describing artifacts, and by assigning them to specific intervals in space and time, archaeologists construct categories that are useful for compacting a great deal of information into a few commonly accepted descriptive terms. The term "Upland Mogollon" distinguishes the artifacts produced by the occupants of the Thompson and McAnally sites from artifacts manufactured by neighboring groups, including the people of the Anasazi culture area to the north, the Jornada Mogollon culture area to the south and southeast, and the Hohokam culture area to the southwest (Cordell 1997). The designation "Early Pithouse period" resulted from studies that contrasted the artifacts and settlement patterns of Upland Mogollon villagers during the interval from A.D. 200 through A.D. 600 with those of later pithouse villagers. A date of A.D. 550 was previously proposed for the end of the Early Pithouse period (Anyon et al. 1981; Anyon and LeBlanc 1984; LeBlanc and Whalen 1980), but new information and a reassessment of previous dates point to A.D. 600 as a better working date.

This chapter introduces readers to the cultural and historical framework that defines the occupational sequence of the Upland Mogollon Pithouse periods. Our focus here is historical because the analyses pre-sented in subsequent chapters of this book modify existing models of Pithouse period lifeways. These analyses make temporal comparisons that are achievable only by combining data from different "branches" within the Upland Mogollon area. For a detailed discussion of the branch concept as it has been applied to the Mogollon region, see Wheat (1955). For those who are unfamiliar with the concept, it is sufficient to define a branch as a geographic subdivision of the Mogollon culture area. Most often, branches are named after centrally located towns or drainages.

THE UPLAND MOGOLLON REGION AS IT IS DEFINED IN THIS VOLUME

Upland Mogollon pithouse villages span a wide geographic area. They have been found in the Forestdale Valley (east-central Arizona), the Pine Lawn Valley (in the vicinity of Reserve, New Mexico), the Mimbres River valley (southwest New Mexico), the middle to upper Gila River valley (from Duncan, Arizona, to the vicinity of the Gila Cliff Dwellings, New Mexico), and in the vicinity of the Gallo Mountains and east of the Black Range, New Mexico (Anyon and LeBlanc 1984; Bradfield 1931; Bussey 1975; Fitting 1973; Haury 1936a, 1940; 1936a; Kayser 1973; LeBlanc 1975, 1976a; LeBlanc and Whalen 1980; Lekson 1990; Martin and

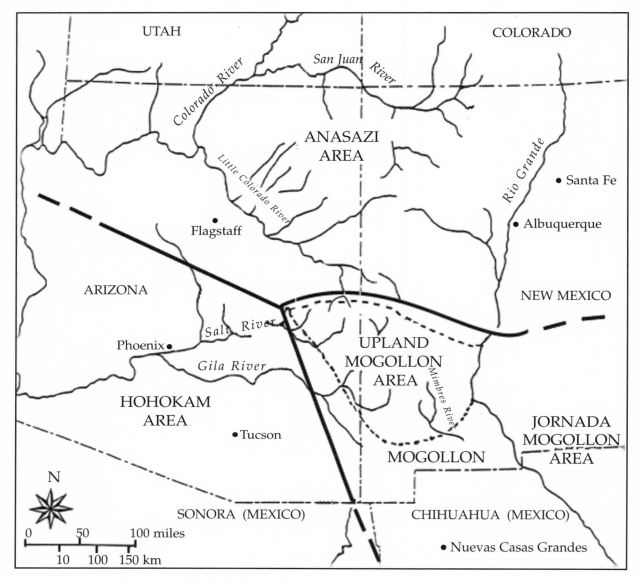

FIGURE 2.1. *The Upland Mogollon region of the greater American Southwest.*

Rinaldo 1950; Minnis and Wormser 1986; M. Nelson 1986a). Our definition of the Upland Mogollon region excludes the Jornada and San Simon branches of the greater Mogollon culture area for reasons that are discussed below. The Upland Mogollon area is illustrated in figure 2.1, above.

For the purpose of analysis, we feel that it is acceptable to group sites from all branches of the Upland Mogollon region. Based on scales of land use attributed to Pithouse period occupants of the Mimbres, Reserve, and Forestdale branches, all of the areas included in the Upland Mogollon in this volume

had access to the same suite of resources within the greater Upland Mogollon culture area. The primary environmental contrast in rainfall, physical geography, and biotic provinces is between that experienced by the low desert occupants of the Jornada, San Simon, and northern Chihuahuan branches, and that of the branches located in the foothills and mountain regions of the rest of the Mogollon area.

Some archaeologists feel that regional syntheses are inappropriate, however. From their perspective, the different branches must be kept analytically distinct owing to three conditions: (1) microclimatic differences in the immediate contexts of different archaeological sites, (2) perceived (but interpretatively ambiguous) differences in the decorative style of black-on-white painted pottery and perceived (but, we believe, not real) differences in architecture, and (3) perceived (but, we again believe, not real) differences in the timing of major ceramic horizons.

In this chapter we demonstrate that there are no substantive objections to broad syntheses of the changes that occurred throughout the Upland Mogollon region during the Pithouse periods. We first review the range of environments available to the occupants of different sites. Our environmental discussion takes into consideration extant models of Pithouse period subsistence and settlement strategies; as a consequence, we consider a much greater area around sites than is usually considered by advocates of the Mountain Mogollon versus Desert Mogollon dichotomy. We show that the case for substantial environmental differences between Mimbres sites (considered by a few archaeologists to be one of the Desert Mogollon branches) and Mountain Mogollon sites is only supportable if one assumes that prehistoric pithouse dwellers rarely strayed more than a few kilometers from their residences.

Second, we review the history of archaeological research in the Upland Mogollon area. We note that most of the distinctions between different Mogollon branches rely on differences in the style of black-on-white painted pottery and the timing of its occurrence throughout the area. We show that despite slight variability in late ceramics and in early architecture, there exists a broad suite of changes in material traits that occurred in all of the Upland Mogollon branches. Furthermore, we agree with the widely accepted contention that a separate culture-historical framework is required for the Jornada branch, since broad changes in architecture and pottery types that occur throughout the Upland Mogollon region do not correspond with the sequence of events in the Jornada Mogollon area.

Questions about the timing of major ceramic horizons are inextricably linked with the consideration of stylistic differences. We show that the proliferation of phase names in the Upland Mogollon area is largely a historical consequence of the use by archaeologists of ceramic seriation in the absence of absolute dating methods. Phase chronologies for Upland Mogollon branches often differ subtly in their assessment of the timing of major changes, such as the introduction of black-on-white painted pottery. When one considers

the tree-ring and radiocarbon dates that are available from Upland Mogollon sites, however, one must conclude that there is no independent basis for suggesting that all major horizon changes did *not* occur simultaneously throughout the Upland Mogollon area. This sort of discussion is not new for most Southwestern scholars. A similar argument was made for much of the Anasazi area almost two decades ago by Cordell and Plog (1979). Their compelling paper helped bring about a renaissance in the study of Anasazi archaeology, but unfortunately no comparable changes occurred in the study of Upland Mogollon pithouse villages. This assessment does not demean recent efforts in the excavation of pithouse sites; Upland Mogollon pithouse villages simply have not been studied nearly as intensively throughout the region, or in any particular branch, as have contemporary Anasazi sites. We hope that with this volume we may stimulate a resurgence in the study of Upland Mogollon pithouse villages.

UPLAND MOGOLLON AS A PREHISTORIC RESOURCE USE AREA

The concept of a distinctive "Mountain" Mogollon that includes only the Forestdale, Point of Pines, and Reserve branches is primarily based on differences in the immediate microclimatic contexts of "Mountain" sites as compared with "Desert" sites. Mountain Mogollon residential sites are surrounded by conifer woodlands and the other botanical and faunal resources endemic to those woodlands. In contrast, the immediate biotic surroundings of the Duncan site, Mogollon Village, the upper Gila River sites, and sites located in the central and southern Mimbres Valley, which are all classified as "Desert," are arid grasslands and riparian communities. Essentially, the case for the existence of substantial environmental differences between, for example, the Promontory site (in the Reserve branch) and the McAnally site (in the Mimbres branch) rests on casual observation. A person standing in the middle of the Promontory site would probably note that the nearest tree is a piñon pine, or possibly a ponderosa pine. The same observer standing in the middle of the McAnally site would note that the nearest tree is a juniper, although ponderosa pines may be seen along the Rio Mimbres just a few kilometers to the north. Most of the Mimbres Valley within a kilometer of McAnally is covered with grasses, juniper, and, along the riverbed, deciduous

TABLE 2.1
BIOTIC PROVINCES WITHIN 60 KILOMETERS OF UPLAND MOGOLLON BRANCHES OR SITES

Branch/Site	Biotic Province									
	121.3	122.3	122.4	123.3	133.3	141.4	142.1	143.1	153.2	154.1
Duncan site[a]	—	x	x	Trace	Trace	—	x	x	x	Trace
Mogollon Village[b]	Trace	x	x	x	—	x	x	x	x	Trace
Reserve branch[c]	Trace	x	x	x	—	x	x	—	—	—
Point of Pines branch[d]	Trace	x	x	x	Trace	—	x	x	—	x
Forestdale branch[e]	Trace	x	x	x	Trace	—	x	x	—	Trace
Winn Canyon[f]	Trace	x	x	x	Trace	—	x	x	Trace	—
Mimbres branch[g]	Trace	x	x	x	—	—	x	x	x	—
Upper Gila[h]	Trace	x	x	x	Trace	x	x	x	x	—
Diablo Village[i]	Trace	x	x	x	—	x	x	x	—	—
San Simon branch[j]	Trace	x	—	x	—	—	—	x	x	Trace

Biotic province codes (after Brown, ed. 1995):
121.3 = Rocky Mountain (Petran) Subalpine Conifer Forest
122.3 = Rocky Mountain (Petran) and Madrean Montane Conifer Forest
122.4 = Great Basin Conifer Woodland
123.3 = Madrean Evergreen Woodland
133.3 = Interior Chaparral
141.4 = Alpine and Subalpine Grasslands
142.1 = Plains and Great Basin Grasslands
143.1 = Semidesert Grassland
153.2 = Chihuahuan Desertscrub
154.12 = Sonoran Desertscrub, Arizona Upland Subdivision

Biotic provinces located within 60 kilometers of:
[a] Duncan, AZ
[b] Glenwood, NM
[c] Reserve, NM
[d] Point of Pines, AZ
[e] Fort Apache, AZ
[f] Silver City, NM
[g] Mimbres, NM
[h] Cliff, NM
[i] Gila Forks (confluence of the West and Middle forks), NM
[j] San Simon, AZ

trees. Within one kilometer of the Promontory site, one observes mostly piñon and ponderosa pines (Martin 1943:115).

Is it appropriate to base such a critical distinction (and the corollary implication that one ought not compare Mimbres Valley sites with Mountain Mogollon sites) on a casual observation, especially one that is devoid of any theory to support its use as a typological construct? We suggest not. Instead, we feel that far too much emphasis has been placed on the *immediate* microclimatic contexts of archaeological sites, since the occupants of most Mogollon branches had access to the same broad suite of resources.

Studies of the scale of land use in the Forestdale, Mimbres, Point of Pines, and Reserve branches of the Mogollon show that people made use of vast territories outside of the immediate locations of their residential sites. Wills (1996a) has linked Late Archaic to Early Pithouse period changes in the use of caves on the plains of San Agustin with land-use changes in the Reserve branch, more than 60 km distant. Minnis (1985a) noted that Late Pithouse and Classic Mimbres

period land-use strategies incorporated ecological zones as diverse as the low Chihuahuan desert of the Deming Plain and the conifer woodland forests in the northern Mimbres Valley, and the foothills of the surrounding mountain ranges (an area about 110 km long, south to north). Vast land-use areas have been suggested for other Mogollon branches, as well. Rice (1980) suggested that prior to A.D. 1000, pithouse villagers in the Forestdale branch engaged in "extensive" subsistence practices that used a wide variety of wild and horticultural products garnered over a sizable area.

Expanded scales of residential mobility and resource use have been offered as models for subsistence and settlement in other areas and for other time periods in the Upland Mogollon area. For the Jornada area, Whalen (1981) presented an essentially closed-system model of land use during the Mesilla phase (the first few centuries A.D.; see also Whalen 1994:23) in the Hueco Bolson, an area of about 50 kilometers along a line drawn east-west through the widest part. Wills (1996b) posited that major changes in Late

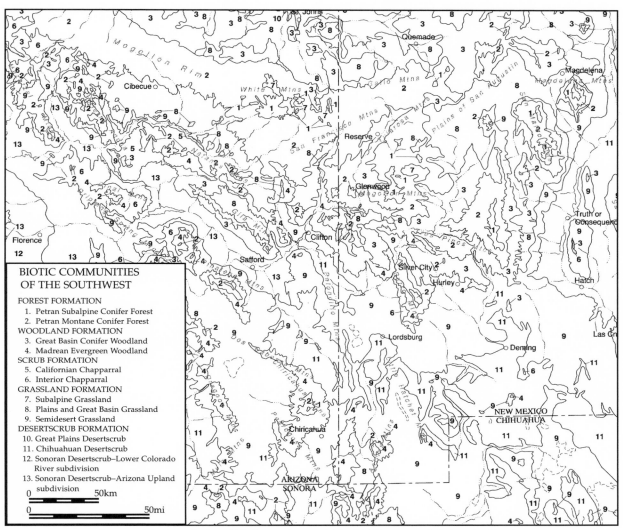

BIOTIC COMMUNITIES
OF THE SOUTHWEST

FOREST FORMATION
  1. Petran Subalpine Conifer Forest
  2. Petran Montane Conifer Forest
WOODLAND FORMATION
  3. Great Basin Conifer Woodland
  4. Madrean Evergreen Woodland
SCRUB FORMATION
  5. Californian Chapparral
  6. Interior Chapparral
GRASSLAND FORMATION
  7. Subalpine Grassland
  8. Plains and Great Basin Grassland
  9. Semidesert Grassland
DESERTSCRUB FORMATION
  10. Great Plains Desertscrub
  11. Chihuahuan Desertscrub
  12. Sonoran Desertscrub–Lower Colorado
      River subdivision
  13. Sonoran Desertscrub–Arizona Upland
      subdivision

FIGURE 2.2. *Boundaries of biotic provinces within 60 kilometers of the McAnally site.*

Archaic period (roughly 1500 B.C.–A.D. 200) subsistence in the vicinity of Reserve, New Mexico, were stimulated by competition from hunting parties who maintained residential base camps in the low deserts below the Mogollon Rim. For the Mimbres and upper Gila valleys, Lekson (1992a) offers a characterization of Classic Mimbres phase (A.D. 1000–1150) land use that encompasses vast areas, comparable in scale to historical descriptions of Apache mobility (in effect, tens of thousands of square kilometers). Although some researchers do not agree with the extremes of scale involved in some of these models, the arguments these days seem to contrast estimated land-use diameters of around 60 km against *larger* scales of analysis (for a Tucson Basin example, compare Diehl 1997, Huckell 1995, Roth 1992, and Wills 1996b).

There is room for disagreement over the exact sizes of territories used by pithouse villagers. Yet there are also compelling *general* reasons to assume that the resource-use strategies and subsistence-settlement practices of Upland Mogollon pithouse dwellers promoted access to multiple resource zones—and to the same suite of resource zones, regardless of the immediate microecological contexts of residential sites. Based on cross-cultural research, Gilman (1987) proposed a general model of pithouse occupations that entails the use of winter residential villages and numerous distant summer occupations. In an archaeological application, Gilman (1986) found archaeological evidence for a two-season land-use pattern that incorporated broad resource areas in the San Simon branch. Ethnographic studies show that the Apaches (Basehart 1974) made use of vast territories surrounding their winter residential villages.

FIGURE 2.3. *Petran Subalpine Conifer Forest.*

Combined evidence from archaeological, ethnohistorical, and historical sources indicates that the Zunis and Hopis made use of huge territories around their pueblos and outlying farmsteads (Schroeder 1979).

Up to this point, we have demonstrated only that the typological approach defined primarily by local, microenvironmental differences does not accord well with the strongest theoretical models of land use around pithouse sites. We have not yet demonstrated that the microenvironmental vision is inaccurate, however. We shall now consider the environments to which the occupants of different Mogollon branches had access, and we shall show that the Mountain versus Desert environmental distinction does not correspond to substantive environmental data.

A DESCRIPTION OF BIOTIC PROVINCES WITHIN 60 KM OF UPLAND MOGOLLON SITES

In this reconstruction of Upland Mogollon environmental diversity, we assume a land-use radius of 60 km around sites. This assumption is consistent with the theoretical studies described above. If our assumption and the theory and models that support it are correct, then the occupants of all branches of the Upland Mogollon had access to the same suite of biotic resource zones. Table 2.1 lists the different biotic provinces available within 60 km of Upland Mogollon sites located in the Forestdale, Mimbres, Point of Pines, and Reserve branches. We also include 60-km areas centered on sites that some have treated as though they are located in different (albeit, unnamed) branches. These include sites near the confluence of the West and Middle forks of the Gila River (near Diablo Village), the middle San Francisco River (Mogollon Village), and sites near Cliff, New Mexico (Lee Village), Duncan, Arizona (the Duncan site), and Silver City, New Mexico (the Winn Canyon site). The San Simon branch, which we exclude from the Upland Mogollon area, is listed for the purpose of comparison. We direct the reader's attention to the fact that vast tracts of Great Basin Conifer Woodland (commonly referred to as "piñon-juniper zone") are easily accessed from all Upland Mogollon branches and not from the San Simon branch. Most Mimbres pithouse sites, which are concentrated in the middle and upper

FIGURE 2.4. *Petran Montane Conifer Forest.*

Rio Mimbres area, are located within 10 km of the Great Basin Conifer Woodland biotic province. Figure 2.2 illustrates the approximate boundaries of these ecological zones and the major geographic features in the vicinity of the Mimbres Valley. These biotic provinces are described in detail below. The information is largely derived from ecological studies in Brown (ed. 1995).

Petran Subalpine Conifer Forest

The highest elevations of the southern Rocky Mountains in the Mimbres branch are found east of the Rio Mimbres in the Black Range (fig. 2.3) (Brown and Lowe 1995). This high (2,450–3,500 m) subalpine boreal forest receives 635 to 1,000 mm of rainfall annually, mostly in the form of snow, and the frost-free growing season is commonly less than 75 days (Pase and Brown 1995a). Some of the most frequently encountered overstory species include varieties of alder, aspen, birch, cottonwood, fir, madrone, maple, oak, pine, poplar, spruce, and willow (Pase and Brown 1995a; Peet 1988:65–66). Understory shrubs include numerous species of consumable berries. Owing to

their diversity, subalpine forests are frequented by a range of larger Southwestern mammals (bear, mountain sheep, mountain lion, coyote, etc.) and numerous smaller mammals and birds. They are also important summer habitats for mule deer and elk (Pase and Brown 1995a:38). From the McAnally site, the nearest occurrence of this biotic province is roughly 25 km northeast, in the Black Range.

Petran Montane Conifer Forest

The northern and western portions of the Mimbres Valley fall within the Petran (Rocky Mountain) Montane Conifer Forest biotic province (Pase and Brown 1995b). Peet (1988:80) describes the region as Ponderosa Pine Woodland, based on the most obvious plants (fig. 2.4). Area elevations range from 2,300 to approximately 3,000 m, and rainfall typically exceeds 500 mm annually (Pase and Brown 1995a). Ponderosa pine, alligator-bark juniper, Gambel oak, and other oaks are the most obvious trees in the region and would have provided excellent sources of architectural wood. Sumacs, currants, and other berries may be found in the moister areas, and could have been eaten by humans as well as other animals. Larger game animals include elk, mule deer, white-tailed deer, mountain sheep, bear, mountain lion, coyotes, and wolves. Smaller creatures that may have been economically useful include wood rats, squirrels, cottontail rabbits, and turkeys. From the McAnally site, the nearest occurrence of this biotic province is 15 km northeast, in the Black Range.

Great Basin Conifer Woodland

This biotic province is also commonly referred to as the "piñon-juniper zone" (Cordell 1995:43; West 1988). The vegetation and fauna of this province provide the environmental setting in the immediate vicinities of the McAnally site. Elevations range from 1,500 to 2,300 m, and the topography includes high hills and short mountain ridges. Throughout the region, 300 to 500 mm of annual rainfall is common (West 1988:223); Bayard, New Mexico, for example, receives approximately 340 mm of rainfall annually (Brown 1995a:57). The ponderosa pine and alligator-bark junipers of higher elevations occur infrequently in this province, and piñon pine and one-seed juniper are the predominant trees on slopes and hills (fig. 2.5). Cottonwoods grow densely along the Rio Mimbres floodplain. Cacti of the *Opuntia* genus (varieties of cholla and prickly pear) are widespread, as are yucca, and they all produce edible fruits. All of the animals of the higher elevations, except mountain sheep, wander into the lower portion of this province because the grass and browse grow densely and there are numerous berry-producing shrubs.

From the McAnally site, the nearest occurrence of this biotic province is 4 km to the northwest. In some biotic typologies however, juniper *defines* the lower extent of this province, in which there is a gradient of decreasing juniper and increasing piñon as elevation increases (West 1988). If juniper alone is taken as the indicator species for the lower limit, then McAnally is actually situated *within* the Great Basin Conifer Woodland province. It is noted that the Reserve branch sites of SU and Promontory are also situated within this province—an observation that directly contradicts the characterization of the Mimbres branch environment as being fundamentally different than that of the Reserve branch.

Madrean Evergreen Woodland

The Madrean Evergreen Woodland (Brown 1995b) biotic province is centered in the Sierra Madre of Mexico but extends northward into the Basin and

FIGURE 2.5. *Great Basin Conifer Woodland.*

Range region in southern New Mexico and Arizona. For the occupants of the McAnally site, this province could be found to the southwest in the Burro Mountains. The most common overstory species include oaks, one-seed juniper, piñon pine, and a variety of other pines. Other common and potentially important species include varieties of acacia, agave, cacti, sumac, and yucca. Major large game are presently limited to bear and deer. Of the Upland Mogollon branches considered in this study, only sites located in the immediate vicinity of the Gallo Mountains do not have access to this biotic province. From the McAnally site, the nearest occurrence of this province is 5 km to the west.

Plains Grassland

East of the Black Range, occupants of the Mimbres branch had access to a high-altitude grassland that is essentially a vast southward extension of the plains of San Agustin (fig. 2.6) (Brown and Lowe 1995). The Plains Grassland biotic province of the American Southwest is the southwestern-most extension of the shortgrass prairie of the western Great Plains (Brown 1995c:115–116). Southwestern Plains Grasslands average 250 to 300 mm of annual precipitation; the town of Hillsboro, for example, receives an average of 274 mm annually, about half of which falls from June through August. Mammals common in the area include elk,

FIGURE 2.6. *Plains Grassland.*

mule deer, and pronghorn antelope. Bison may have inhabited the region as far south as Casas Grandes, Chihuahua (Wallace 1883, cited in Brown 1995c). Commercial bison ranchers have to provide mineral supplements for their herds, however, leading one to question the long-term viability of nondomesticated bison populations in the area. The prehistoric density of bison in the southernmost extent of this biotic province was probably never very great. From the McAnally site, the nearest occurrence of this biotic province is 25 km east-northeast, on the east slope of the Black Range.

Semidesert Grassland

This biotic province includes low-elevation arid grasslands between 1,600 and 1,800 m and has a mean annual rainfall of about 250 mm. Presently, Semidesert Grasslands include grasses and shrub-infested zones where creosote bush, Mormon tea, rabbitbrush, and saltbush grow densely on the heavily overgrazed landscape (Brown 1995d; Sims 1988) (fig. 2.7). Along the Rio Mimbres floodplain, cottonwood continues to grow densely, along with mesquite, oak, and walnut. In prehistoric times, the region away from the floodplain was probably an open savanna, consisting mostly of grasslands and a few one-seed junipers. Elk,

mule deer, antelope, and coyotes frequent the region, along with jackrabbits and the occasional mountain lion.

Access to this resource zone may be the primary consideration for advocates of the Mountain versus Desert Mogollon dichotomy, since only limited areas of this province lie within 60 km of the Point of Pines branch, and none of it is immediately accessible to occupants of the Reserve branch or of sites in the vicinity of the Gallo Mountains. This province provides the immediate context of the Thompson site, and it is accessible from the McAnally site within a few kilometers to the south.

Chihuahuan Desertscrub

At the lowest elevations in the vicinity of Deming, New Mexico, and on the margins of the Rio Grande, the landscape of the Upland Mogollon region consists of low rolling hills and flat basins dominated by the Chihuhuan Desertscrub biotic province (fig. 2.8). Total annual precipitation in this province ranges from 200 to 300 mm, and more than half of the rain falls from May through September, when the ground surface is hottest and the moisture evaporates quickly (Brown 1995e:170). To make matters more complicated, areas that receive 500 mm in an unusually wet year may

FIGURE 2.7. *Semidesert Grassland.*

FIGURE 2.8. *Chihuahuan Desertscrub.*

receive as little as 50 mm in the following year. In moist areas where springs augment the river flow, cottonwoods and oaks may be found growing on the floodplain. Away from the drainage, cacti, creosote bush, grasses, Mormon tea, saltbush, shrub mesquite, sumac, yuccas, and herbaceous plants (amaranth, snakeweed, and the like) provide the ground cover (Brown 1995e; MacMahon 1988). Prehistorically, grasses were likely more widespread, since modern livestock grazing has promoted the growth of shrubs at the expense of grasses (Sims 1988:280). Antelope, coyotes, jackrabbits, javelinas, and roadrunners share the arid landscape with mice, wood rats, and various snakes, lizards, and other reptiles.

In terms of area, Chihuahuan Desertscrub is the second *smallest* biotic subdivision within 60 km of the McAnally site (see Brown and Lowe 1995). Thus the characterization of the Mimbres branch as "desert oriented" or as a Desert branch is inaccurate. This biotic province occurs in small patches within 10 km south of McAnally, but true open desert is not encountered until one travels 19 km south. It is particularly noteworthy that occupants of the McAnally site had more immediate access to Petran Conifer Forests and to Great Basin Conifer Woodlands than they had to Chihuahuan Desertscrub.

Summary of Biotic Provinces

The characterization of the Mimbres branch as a lowland or Desert branch that is fundamentally distinct, environmentally speaking, from Mountain branches, such as Reserve and Point of Pines, is factually incorrect. Virtually all of the landscape within 60 km of the town of Mimbres, New Mexico, is characterized by (in decreasing order of surface area) conifer woodlands, grasslands, and alpine forests (Brown and Lowe 1995). Since prehistoric humans were capable of frequent and far-ranging hunting and gathering trips, as well as seasonal residential migrations, all occupants of the Upland Mogollon area had access to the same suite of resources provided by this topographically and biotically diverse region.

THE UPLAND MOGOLLON REGION AS A CULTURE AREA

As previously noted, some researchers might feel that the stratagem of lumping analytically all of the Upland Mogollon branches is inappropriate for reasons of interbranch variation in material culture and variation in the timing of cultural changes. The authors of this volume recognize that variation in material culture is analytically interesting. We do not feel, however, that such variation as has been documented in the Upland Mogollon region and has been used to distinguish between different branches is significant enough to prohibit diachronic studies that use data from the entire region. There are no compelling reasons to suspect, for example, that the pithouse dwellers of the Reserve branch practiced widely different customs with respect to religion or social organization than did the occupants of the Mimbres branch. We also note that interbranch stylistic variation in ceramics is only recognized for two of the nine centuries of pithouse occupation in the Upland Mogollon region and that the interpretive significance of Upland Mogollon ceramic variation has not been well established. Furthermore, differences among branches in architecture, particularly in the sizes (surface areas) of houses, are only apparent when the SU site is treated as the representative site for the Reserve branch, and in any case these differences are not statistically significant. Finally, there exists a broad suite of changes that occur essentially simultaneously (given the extant corpus of dendrochronological and radiocarbon dates from pithouses) throughout the region. Each of these issues is discussed in detail below.

Ceramic Variation, A.D. 900–1000

The claim that the Mimbres, Forestdale, Point of Pines, and Reserve branches are different analytical entities that mandate the use of local phase sequences is partly the consequence of an historical accident. The technique of ceramic seriation was made *possible* by the existence of stylistic variation in local ceramic production by prehistoric people. It was made *necessary* by the absence, for the first several decades of the twentieth century, of any reliable means of absolute dating for archaeological sites. Relative dating was the only means available for ordering and comparing archaeological sites within any single drainage. The existence of different branches of the Upland Mogollon is thus partly a simple consequence of the techniques available to archaeologists before the widespread availability of dendrochronology and radiocarbon analysis. Had scientists discovered absolute dating techniques before seriation was used to order the archaeological record, we might be faced with very different chronological and spatial classification schemes than those that are currently fashionable (for a related and more detailed discussion, see Cordell and Gumerman 1989 and Cordell and Plog 1979).

Moreover, it may be inappropriate to impose rigid limits on comparative analyses based on interbranch stylistic variation in ceramic decorations, since that variation has only been established for two of the nine centuries of pithouse village occupation. For the ninth and tenth centuries A.D., researchers recognize the existence of several different black-on-white painted wares for the Reserve (Reserve Black-on-white) and Mimbres (Boldface Black-on-white) branches. On the early end of the Upland Mogollon temporal continuum, however, the case for interbranch stylistic variation is not compelling. The Early Pithouse period (A.D. 200–600) is represented by ceramic assemblages that include Alma Plain brownware and red-slipped wares that are indistinguishable between branches, along with trace quantities of Anasazi intrusives such as Lino Grey.

Finally, we suggest that stylistic variation alone does not indicate the existence of radically different cultural systems within the Upland Mogollon region. For example, there is no compelling suite of assumptions or middle-range theory that leads one to conclude that the differences between Reserve Black-on-white and Mimbres Boldface Black-on-white are indicative of radically different religious or value systems, social organizations, worldviews, or patterns of resource extraction and use.

We suggest that the existence of stylistic variation does not preclude the inclusion of sites from different Mogollon branches in broadly comparative diachronic studies. Indeed, sophisticated approaches to stylistic analysis suggest that multiple branches may be included in any study of culture change, since the occupants of different drainage systems were socially and economically linked. The study of spatiotemporal frequency variation of different pottery types has generated important insights about the intensity of interaction between occupants of different river valleys (Hegmon et al. 1998; Tainter 1982, 1984). Regardless of the ultimate social or psychological causes of stylistic variation, the movement of vessels out of areas where they were produced necessarily implies the movement of people, and the movement of people from one area to another necessarily implies social and economic interaction between different communities. Although scholars note that the need for further research in this arena of interest is apparent (Hegmon 1992; Rautmann 1993), the observed connections

among settlements in different branches fundamentally obviates any need to treat different Mogollon branches as social or economic isolates.

Architectural Variation, A.D. 200–600

Beginning with Wheat (1955), many archaeologists have noted that pithouses at the SU site appear to be considerably larger than pithouses at contemporary sites in other Mogollon branches. If one were to assume that the SU site is representative of the Reserve area and that there are differences between SU pithouses and those in other branches, one might argue that there was variation in social organization and economic production among the different branches of the Upland Mogollon region, as, for example, Wills (1992) has argued based on differences between pithouses at SU and those at Sabik'eschee Village (an Anasazi Basketmaker site in Chaco Canyon).

Both assumptions can be questioned on the basis of extant data. Wills (1996a) calculated a mean SU pithouse floor area of 38 m². Diehl (1994) arrived at a lower figure of 31 m² (not including ramps), but excluded larger possible "kivas" (structures A, D, and V) and pithouses with ambiguous temporal associations (structures W, X, and Y). While both averages are larger than those for most Early Pithouse period sites, they are not significantly larger than the floor of Feature 39 at LA 5407 (30 m²; Kayser 1973), the mean estimated surface area of McAnally structures (about 27 m²; see chap. 4, this volume), or the Georgetown phase pithouses at Bear Ruin, Crooked Ridge Village, Diablo Village, Harris Village, Mogollon Village, and Winn Canyon (Diehl 1994: app. A).

We recognize that the lack of statistical significance in the comparisons between SU and other Upland Mogollon sites is possibly attributable to the small number of Early Pithouse period houses that can be used to represent other branches. As of this writing, Martin's excavations at SU, more than 50 years ago, remain the most extensive excavations of an Early Pithouse period site. Future excavations may, in the course of increasing the sample sizes from different branches, verify the perceived difference between SU site and other Upland Mogollon sites. It is equally appropriate and cautious, however, to note that *extant data* do not support the contention that SU site pithouses are significantly larger than those from other branches. Furthermore, when pithouses from the Promontory site are included with those of SU, the

TABLE 2.2
MEANS OF MOST RECENT TREE-RING DATES FROM MOGOLLON PITHOUSES

Occupation Phase	Mean "r" Date[a]	Number of Cases	Mean "vv" Date[b]	Number of Cases
Three Circle phase	A.D. 879	2	A.D. 818	11
San Francisco phase	A.D. 742	2	A.D. 757	10
Georgetown phase	—	0	A.D. 624	1
Early Pithouse period	A.D. 505	3	A.D. 447	11

[a] Less than a full section is present, but the outermost ring is continuous around the available circumference.

[b] There is no way of estimating how far the last ring is from the true outside.

mean pithouse floor area for the Reserve branch is even lower (29.4 m^2). Thus, if significant intersite variation in the surface area of pithouses does exist, then the primary point of comparison may be between the SU site and other *sites*, rather than between the Reserve branch and other branches.

Interbranch Temporal Variation in Phase Transitions

Some may question the appropriateness of comparing data from all of the Upland Mogollon branches on the grounds of alleged variation in the timing of transitions between locally defined phases. Most Southwestern archaeologists are familiar with comparative charts that, when interpreted literally, seem to imply the asynchronous occurrence of phase transitions that are associated with major ceramic horizons in the various Mogollon branches.

In fact, recognition of differences in the timing of local phase transitions requires a precision that is not supported by the chronometric (dendrochronology or radiocarbon analysis) methods. One cannot conclusively demonstrate that broadly observed changes did *not* occur concurrently throughout all of the Upland branches of the Mogollon. We must conclude that there are no demonstrable differences in the timing of major ceramic horizons in different branches, and it follows that there is no a priori reason for objecting to the regional syntheses that are generated in this volume.

Our findings in this regard will not surprise most archaeologists. Similar problems have been noted previously, not only for the Upland Mogollon region (Berman 1979) but in other regions of the Southwest as well. These problems may be partially attributable to the manner in which prior generations of archaeologists conducted their fieldwork and analyses (Cordell and Plog 1979, 1981). In our opinion, Bullard's (1962)

critique of Mogollon phase chronologies, which was based on a general lack of adequate chronometric data, remains reasonable, but his substantive conclusion that Mogollon sites may be cross-dated by looking at the frequencies of Anasazi wares on Mogollon sites was incorrect. As Cordell and Plog (1979) demonstrated, the Anasazi chronologies in which Bullard placed great confidence were equally flawed.

Very few chronometric dates are available from Upland Mogollon pithouses. Table 2.2 describes the occupation dates of different phases in different branches and notes the number of tree-ring dates that may be used for each phase. In constructing the table, we assumed that it is inappropriate to use multiple dates obtained from the same house and that the most reliable date comes from the most recent specimen. Tree-ring dates from Upland Mogollon pithouse sites were obtained from a variety of sources, including Bannister et al. (1966, 1970), Dean and Robinson (1978), LeBlanc and Whalen (1980), and notes on file with the New Mexico Cultural Resources Inventory System in Santa Fe (NMCRIS LA 5407). Although they are few, and substantive analyses may be unwarranted, the available radiocarbon dates from archaeological sites do not conclusively support the suggestion that there were differences in the timing of phase transitions between different Upland Mogollon branches. Table 2.3 lists the dates from Upland Mogollon pithouse sites.

Summary

In the preceding discussion we addressed possible objections to the inclusion of the Mimbres Valley sites in broadly comparative, multiple-branch syntheses of Upland Mogollon archaeology. We have established the following facts: (1) a sequence of archaeological horizons throughout the Upland Mogollon area occurs, indicating that the same cultural events

TABLE 2.3
RADIOCARBON DATES FROM UPLAND MOGOLLON PITHOUSE VILLAGES

Site	Sample I.D.	Context	Material	Uncalibrated Age	Calibrated Date
Lee Village[a]	B-61014	Roof beam	Cottonwood, outer ring	1170 ± 80 C-14 b.p.	A.D. 890, 940
	B-61015	Roof beam	Cottonwood, outer ring	1030 ± 70 C-14 b.p.	A.D. 1000, 1010
	B-61016	Roof beam	Cottonwood, outer ring	1150 ± 70 C-14 b.p.	A.D. 900–980
	B-61017	Roof beam	Cottonwood, outer ring	1200 ± 70 C-14 b.p.	A.D. 820–870
	B-61018	Roof beam	Cottonwood, outer ring	1120 ± 70 C-14 b.p.	A.D. 900–980
McAnally[b]	UCLA-2153A	Roof beam	—	—	A.D. 580 ± 60
Mogollon Village[c]	B-32287	—	—	1140 ± 50 b.p.	A.D. 706–992
	B-32288	—	—	1190 ± 50 b.p.	A.D. 709–977
	B-32289	—	—	1550 ± 60 b.p.	A.D. 264–603
	B-47208	Feature 44	—	1870 ± 60 b.p.	B.C. 4–A.D. 244
	B-47209	House 12	—	1360 ± 80 b.p.	A.D. 529–779
	B-47210	Roof	(2 samples)	1470–1580 ± 60 b.p.	A.D. 426–610
	UCLA-1953D	Roof beam	—	—	A.D. 545 ± 60
SU[d]	B-25543	Extramural pit	—	1470 ± 40 b.p.	A.D. 493–639
	B-26135	Extramural pit	—	2020 ± 50 b.p.	B.C. 170–A.D. 67
	B-24309	Extramural pit	—	1530 ± 140 b.p.	A.D. 200–790
Winn Canyon[e]	N-1555	Pithouse	—	—	A.D. 310 ± 75
	N-1556	Pithouse	—	—	A.D. 350 ± 170

Sources:
[a] Diehl (1994:53).
[b] This volume and LeBlanc and Whalen (1980:514).
[c] Duncan et al. (1991:23–26); Gilman et al. (1991:104–106).
[d] Beta-analytic analysis sheets in Wills (1991a).
[e] James Fitting (personal communication, 1976).

affected the occupants of all of the Upland branches; (2) within the limits of detection, these horizons occurred simultaneously; and (3) the occupants of all branches had access to the same suite of resources. Accordingly, we hold that there are no substantive objections (based on observable facts or even well-reasoned speculation) to the inclusion of the Mimbres branch in synthetic studies that also include the Forestdale, Point of Pines, Reserve, and upper Gila branches.

THE UPLAND MOGOLLON CHRONOLOGICAL SEQUENCE USED IN THIS VOLUME

Upland Mogollon pithouse villages were occupied from A.D. 200 through 1000. The term "Pithouse period" is used to distinguish between pithouse village occupations and subsequent surface "Pueblo period" occupations in the same area. The Pithouse period is further subdivided into the Early Pithouse (A.D. 200–600) and Late Pithouse (A.D. 600–1000) periods. Finally, the Late Pithouse period is divided into three

phases—the Georgetown, San Francisco, and Three Circle phases. The phase names and chronology are based on the sequence established by the Mimbres Foundation for the Mimbres branch of the Mogollon (Anyon et al. 1981; Anyon and LeBlanc 1984; Blake et al. 1986; LeBlanc and Whalen 1980; Nelson and LeBlanc 1986). In this volume, we apply the Mimbres phase nomenclature to all branches of the Upland Mogollon. We hope that our peer researchers will not take offense. We might have used the terms "Mogollon Pithouse I–IV," but these would simply add to the phase-name proliferation problem mentioned earlier. As discussed previously, this nomenclature was chosen for the sake of simplicity and to facilitate broad regional comparisons. In the following discussion we provide the phase-name equivalents for the different branches.

Attributes of the Early Pithouse Period, A.D. 200–600

The Early Pithouse period encompasses several locally defined phases, including the Cumbre phase of the Mimbres branch (Anyon et al. 1981), the Pine Lawn phase of the Reserve branch (Martin and Rinaldo 1947), and the Hilltop phase of the Forestdale branch (Haury 1940). This period is distinguished from the Late Pithouse period by three attributes, the first of which is the near-absence of painted ceramics. Early Pithouse period ceramic assemblages contain coil-and-scrape finished brownwares, some of which have surface texturing such as incising. Red-slipped wares dubbed "Miscellaneous Red" (Anyon and LeBlanc 1984) have been found in some pithouses that were occupied after A.D. 500. The classificatory utility of San Francisco Red Saliz variety, alleged to be an early local (Pine Lawn Valley) red-slipped ware (Martin 1940), was questioned by Shepard (1965). Shepard observed that many sherds of this type are actually highly polished, unslipped plain wares. Subsequent reanalyses by Anyon (Anyon and LeBlanc 1984) support Shepard's reinterpretation of the Saliz variety. True San Francisco Red potsherds are virtually absent from Early Pithouse period contexts. A discussion of the attributes of true San Francisco Red is presented in chapter 10.

The second attribute that distinguishes Early and Late Pithouse period occupations is the association of Early Pithouse villages with high topographic formations, including ridge tops, mesas, and knolls (LeBlanc and Whalen 1980). Regional surveys have shown that, when suitable topographic features are available, most Early Pithouse villages are located on high ridge tops or other places that require considerable effort to reach. Lekson (1992b) objected that the perceived association of Early Pithouse villages with inaccessible locations is spurious because some such villages are *not* located on such landforms, and some later villages *are*. We note, however, that despite a few exceptions, the overwhelming majority of Upland Mogollon Early Pithouse sites are located on high knolls. This pattern holds for the Mimbres area (Anyon et al. 1981; Blake et al. 1986; LeBlanc and Whalen 1980; Stokes 1994), the Blue River area of Arizona (Rice 1975), and the lower San Francisco River area (Accola 1981), and Diehl has observed the same pattern in the vicinity of the Gila Cliff Dwellings National Monument in the Gila Forks area. Danson's (1957:103) survey of the upper Gila Plateau and surrounding area also found early sites "on high mesas or bluffs," and Bluhm (1960:540) noted that in the Pine Lawn Valley area of New Mexico the early villages "were scattered on high mesas or ridges." Wendorf's (1956:23) survey in the nearby Tularosa Valley found that "there was a tendency for [early]

villages to be located in defensive positions, on high, almost inaccessible mesas." Longacre (1962, 1964) found the same pattern for the Vernon–Upper Little Colorado River area of eastern Arizona.

Besides the McAnally and Thompson sites in the Mimbres Valley, examples of such hilltop sites include the Promontory site in the Pine Lawn Valley (Martin et al. 1949), Mogollon Village (Haury 1936a), the Mesa Top (Berman 1978) and Duncan sites (Lightfoot 1984) in southeastern Arizona, and the Bluff site (Haury and Sayles 1947) in eastern Arizona. This list is far from exhaustive, but it is indicative of the pattern. Almost all known Mogollon sites from the Early Pithouse period in this large region are on relatively high locations. In contrast, almost all Late Pithouse period villages are located on the first benches or in other relatively accessible places along rivers and streams.

This use and subsequent abandonment of hilltops is probably one of the most clear-cut and strongest settlement patterns found during the entire prehistory of the Southwest. Lekson's error may be one of applying an absolute measure to a relative phenomenon. It is true that a few Early Pithouse settings are not extremely high or difficult of access. Although some sites in the Mimbres Valley are as much as 275 m above the first terrace, and sites like McAnally, which is 65 m above the terrace, are typical, a few sites are simply located on the most elevated landform around. That is the case for the Mesa Top site, for example. Given the options available in a particular general locality, the Early Pithouse period sites are almost always on the most elevated places that could have been chosen.

The third attribute that separates Early Pithouse period villages from those of the Late Pithouse period is the absence of houses with rectangular floor plans in the former. Early Pithouse villages include some houses that are circular, others that are bean shaped, and quite a few that seem truly amorphous. Most, but not all, early pithouses have long, narrow features that most archaeologists describe as entrance ramps. These features extend outward from one wall of the pithouse and usually face in an easterly direction, but there is considerable variation in the direction of their orientation. They may have served as vents for intramural hearths, storage areas, entryways, or some combination of purposes. A few pithouses at LA 5407 and the SU site, for example, appear to have amorphous antechambers in lieu of ramps or vents.

TABLE 2.4
UPLAND MOGOLLON PITHOUSE PERIOD ATTRIBUTES AND CHRONOLOGY

Occupation Interval	Architectural Form	Topographic Setting	New Ceramic Types Introduced	Occupation Dates
Three Circle phase	Sharp-cornered rectangle or trapezoid, with ramp	1st river terrace, if available	Style I and Style II Black-on-white and Three Circle Red-on-white	A.D. 825/850–1000
San Francisco phase	Rounded rectangle or trapezoid, with ramp	1st river terrace, if available	Mogollon Red-on-brown	A.D. 700–825/850
Georgetown phase	Round or D-shaped, with ramp	1st river terrace, if available	San Francisco Red	A.D. 550–700
Early Pithouse period	Round or amorphous, with ramp or vestibule	Hill- or ridge-top, if available	Plainwares, Mogollon Early Red	A.D. 200–550

Attributes of the Late Pithouse Period, A.D. 600–1000

Table 2.4 provides a summary of the horizon markers that we use to distinguish different temporal intervals in the Upland Mogollon occupational sequence. Emil Haury subdivided what is here called the Late Pithouse period into three phases. Initially, Mimbres Foundation researchers (Anyon et al. 1981) applied these divisions to the Mimbres Valley sites, based on the dates that were available at the time. These phases included the Georgetown (A.D. 600–700), San Francisco (A.D. 700–825/850), and Three Circle phases (A.D. 825/850–1000). Each is marked by the introduction of a new variety of painted ceramics. The presence of true San Francisco Red and the absence of other painted wares are defining attributes of Georgetown phase occupations. San Francisco phase occupations are marked at the earliest by the presence of Mogollon Red-on-brown ceramics. The Three Circle phase is defined by the addition of Three Circle Red-on-white and, soon thereafter, Boldface Black-on-white (also known as Three Circle Black-on-white, Mangas Black-on-white, or Style I Black-on-white; Anyon and LeBlanc 1984; Mills 1984). Style II Black-on-white (which is also called Transitional Black-on-white; Shaffer and Taylor 1986) was manufactured

during the late Three Circle phase and overlaps into the Classic Mimbres period. The end of the Three Circle phase of the Late Pithouse period is marked by the construction of masonry surface structures and the manufacture of Mimbres Classic Black-on-white (Style III Black-on-white) ceramics.

Changes in pithouse shape also roughly correspond to temporally distinct phases. Georgetown phase pithouses are usually ovals, although some are subrectangular (rectangular with rounded corners). San Francisco phase structures are usually subrectangular, and Three Circle phase pithouses are compulsively rectangular or slightly trapezoidal, with sharp corners and neat, straight ramps. Previous researchers (Anyon and LeBlanc 1980; Anyon 1983) noted that changes in the shape of large communal structures lag behind changes in domestic architecture, so the above trends apply to domestic structures only.

A Revised Chronology for the San Francisco and Three Circle Phases

Although Mimbres Foundation researchers (Anyon et al. 1981) initially placed the inception of the Three Circle phase at A.D. 750, Gilman (personal communication, 1993) recently suggested that the advent of the Three Circle phase is more properly placed after A.D.

800. Based on the available tree-ring and radiocarbon dates, we place the start of the Three Circle phase around A.D. 825 through 850.

The attributes that we use to define occupation phases in the Upland Mogollon region are summarized in table 2.4. In this study, the Georgetown phase encompasses the Cottonwood phase of the Forestdale branch, the "early subdivision" of the Circle Prairie phase of the Point of Pines branch (Wheat 1954), and the Georgetown phase of the Mimbres, Reserve, and upper Gila branches. The San Francisco phase encompasses the "late subdivision" of the Circle Prairie phase of the Point of Pines branch; the San Francisco phase of the Mimbres, upper Gila, and Reserve branches; and the Forestdale phase of the Forestdale branch. Finally, the Three Circle phase encompasses the Three Circle phase of the Mimbres, Middle and Upper Gila, and Reserve branches; the Corduroy phase of the Forestdale branch; and the Nantack phase of the Point of Pines branch (Breternitz 1959).

CONCLUSION

In this chapter we defined an area called the Upland Mogollon region of the greater American Southwest. The studies in this volume concentrate on changes in resource acquisition throughout the study area. All of the branches included in the Upland Mogollon region have access to the same suite of resources, so the analytical framework used here is appropriate for the subject of our research. We have also discussed possible objections to our use of a broadly comparative scheme. We find that the documented ceramic and architectural variation among different Upland branches is not sufficient to warrant the exclusion of any of the sites in this study. Instead, based on broadly observable changes in architecture and ceramics, we find that there exists a simple four-part temporal division of the Mogollon Pithouse periods that works well for all branches subsumed within the Upland Mogollon region.

3 Competing Models of Upland Mogollon Pithouse Period Life-Styles

Michael W. Diehl

What does it mean to say that a site is an "Upland Mogollon Early Pithouse village?" The historical answer provided in chapter 2 focused on various descriptive details in the architecture, ceramics, environments, and topographic localities favored by Upland Mogollon people. In effect, we described the prehistoric villagers by a commonly held constellation of traits with a coherent and discrete existence in space and time. We observed that these traits differed from traits manifested during other intervals of time, and that they are convenient for marking four sequential intervals: the Early Pithouse period (A.D. 200–550), Georgetown phase (A.D. 550–700), San Francisco phase (A.D. 700–825/850), and Three Circle phase (A.D. 825/850–1000). This description (the trait lists of architecture, topography, pottery styles, and their changes through time), while helpful for carving up time and space, is not our real goal.

Subsequent chapters in this volume provide various systemic answers to the overarching question posed above. Analyses in those chapters assess changes in the nature of Mogollon Pithouse period diets, resource structure, and land use. All share the common purpose of assessing, to the extent that the preponderance of available data allows, the foods that people ate (and their relative contributions to diets), how subsistence activities were organized, and how architecture, artifacts, and food debris may be used in making such assessments. These analyses make state-

ments about the relative importance of, for example, maize or seasonal migrations in the subsistence strategies of Early Pithouse period (A.D. 200–550) villagers, as compared with subsequent occupants (descendants of Early Pithouse villagers) who lived in the same area. The analyses are based on independent assessments of different kinds of data: architecture (chap. 4), plant remains (chap. 5), ground stone tools (chap. 6), pottery (chap. 7), osteofaunal remains (chap. 8), and chipped stone tools (chap. 9). We feel that the results are consistent. All analyses suggest that although agriculture was important to Early Pithouse period villagers (possibly the most important resource in their diets), it became even more important during subsequent occupations. During the Early Pithouse period, wild foods contributed a substantial proportion of calories and other nutrition to the diet. By the Three Circle phase, however, agriculture was extremely important and farming practices were intensive. Furthermore, Early Pithouse period horticulturists probably changed the locations of their households (from one site to another) more frequently than their descendants; during the A.D. 200 through 1000 period, people settled in and made ever more intensive use of locations. By the Three Circle phase, people were quite sedentary—that is, residentially stable.

Our "model" or characterization of relative degrees of mobility and of the importance of agriculture in subsistence is based on methods and theories associated with specific data sets in subsequent chapters. These are substantive findings, yet they are subject to revision as new data become available. It is quite clear that more data are required to refine estimates of, for example, the caloric contribution of maize as compared with other foods to the diet; one must accept that our account is a "working model" that competes with other working models that have been offered by other scholars. Yet we feel that our model is superior to other models because the method and theory are well articulated and the scope of our efforts is more complete than prior efforts by ourselves and other researchers.

Our description of Early Pithouse period lifestyles, and our account of changes that ensued, is not the first, nor will it be the last. To understand fully our purpose in the analyses in this book, it is important to know what other archaeologists have said about life during the Pithouse periods. This chapter reviews previous work and places our findings in the larger scholarly environment of competing ideas, theories, models, and descriptions. We close this chapter with a discussion of the relationship between Mogollon archaeological research and some interesting anthropological questions. Those questions relate changes in subsistence economies with changes in social organization. Mogollon archaeological research can be used to help provide answers to such broadly interesting questions.

MODELS THAT DESCRIBE WHAT HAPPENED BETWEEN A.D. 200 AND 1000

Before 1980 most archaeologists assumed that Upland Mogollon pithouses were the residential locations where "sedentary" populations lived and worked within a few kilometers of their houses all year round for many successive years. The appearance of substantial houses (in contrast with older and rather insubstantial Archaic period house depressions) was thought to be indicative of a major reduction in the amount of human migration mandated by the subsistence-oriented "seasonal round" (Haury 1985:360, 1936a:92; Lehner 1948:76; Martin 1940:35; Wendorf 1953:74; Wheat 1955, 1954; Woodbury and Zubrow 1979). According to conventional wisdom, the Archaic people who preceded the pithouse villagers were mobile foragers, or possibly foragers who invested modest effort in growing cultigens. In contrast, the occupants of pithouses were assumed to be sedentary farmers. Recent research in the Tucson Basin of south-

ern Arizona casts doubt on this characterization of late Archaic (a.k.a. "Early Agricultural period") people dwelling in the low deserts, although a detailed picture of subsistence and settlement in that area has yet to develop (Diehl 1997). For the Upland Mogollon region, there is very little direct information available about the subsistence practices during the first millennium B.C.

Based on the nonsystematic recovery of small quantities of charred maize, most proponents of the received model assumed that most pithouse villagers provisioned themselves primarily by growing crops, augmenting these with gathered and hunted food. Evidence marshaled in support of this contention included the occasionally observed presence of maize in hearths and on pithouse floors, nonsystematically collected osteofaunal remains and bone tools, and ubiquitous manos and metates. A few villages, such as the Promontory and Bluff sites, seemed enigmatic owing to the apparent absence of any telltale household refuse at all (Haury 1985:290; Martin 1943:131). LeBlanc (LeBlanc 1983; LeBlanc and Whalen 1980) remains a proponent of the view that pithouse villagers were classically sedentary agriculturists. Wills (1996a) envisions a residentially sedentary, agriculture-oriented subsistence economy in the Reserve branch during the Early Pithouse period, augmented by logistical use of outlying regions.

Many other researchers now view pithouse villages as the residential sites of people who were highly "logistically organized" (in the sense used by Binford 1980 and Kelly 1992), but who also abandoned their villages for some interval each year. For most of the year, people lived in their villages and sent out special-purpose task groups (sometimes to great distances) to acquire certain resources and bring them back to the villages. It is also thought that there was total (or nearly total) abandonment of villages for brief intervals during the year. Competing models suggest that Mogollon pithouse dwellers were either (1) largely sedentary with seasonal abandonments of major villages in the spring and early summer, (2) variously engaged in low- to high-frequency moves in different regions at different times, or (3) wholly mobile, occupying winter villages for a few winter months but otherwise quite mobile for the rest of the year.

Based on a cross-cultural study of the use of pithouses worldwide, Gilman (1987) suggested that the occupants of pithouse villages generally engage in biseasonal, bilocational subsistence strategies, with winter occupation of pithouses. Gilman viewed Pithouse period settlement patterns of prehistoric

Mogollon people as less residentially mobile than those of their Archaic ancestors, yet more mobile than their Classic Mimbres period descendants. Gilman was particularly interested in providing an explanation for the "pithouse-to-pueblo transition" in the American Southwest. She suggested that pithouses were replaced by pueblos (surface structures made of stone and wood) because of a fundamental shift in the organization of subsistence. Where pithouse dwellers had been part-time horticulturists with an annual diet composed primarily of gathered wild foods, their pueblo-dwelling descendants relied primarily on the products of their agricultural fields.

Gilman's study is partially consistent with an archaeological case study provided by Hunter-Anderson (1986). She compared artifact assemblages from 23 Upland Mogollon residential villages and caves, whose occupations spanned an interval from roughly 3000 B.C. through A.D. 1300. Using factor analyses, Hunter-Anderson identified groups of sites that may have been associated with winter residential, seasonal hunting support, and early spring planting activities. The two models are consistent to the extent that both view early villages, such as the Reserve area's SU and Turkey Foot Ridge sites, as winter season residences that may have been used in other seasons as well. Hunter-Anderson's and Gilman's interpretations differ, however, in their divergent assessments of the importance of agriculture. Where Gilman envisioned pithouse villagers as foragers who supplemented their diet through agriculture, Hunter-Anderson posited agriculturally dependent part-time foragers (a "density dependent adaptive system"). Diehl (1998) recently reanalyzed artifact distributions from Hunter-Anderson's (and other) sites. In that research it was demonstrated that differences in the composition of artifact assemblages may be a consequence of the sequential occupation or abandonment of sites rather than a product of functional variation.

Other researchers (Minnis 1985a; Shafer and Taylor 1987) suggested that maize, bean, and squash horticulture was a *substantial* component of the diet beginning in the Mimbres region after A.D. 200 and the *primary* component of the diet during and after approximately A.D. 800. Their views about ninth- and tenth-century diets accord well with Hard's (1990) and Lancaster's (1984) studies of Upland Mogollon ground stone. Although they do not directly address the issue of residential mobility, their descriptions are consistent with Gilman's and Hunter-Anderson's studies. Shafer (1995) noted that the pithouse-to-pueblo transition at the NAN Ranch was marked by

successive changes in Late Pithouse period architectural construction (remodeling, greater use of masonry in construction), and suggested that the pithouse-to-pueblo transition in the Mimbres branch was the outcome of a gradual process, rather than a sudden and fundamental shift toward agricultural dependence as Gilman (1987) suggests. Diehl's studies of architecture (Diehl and Gilman 1996; chap. 4, this volume) support Shafer's position.

Some researchers called for a decoupling of the questions of the dietary importance of agriculture and the frequency of residential moves. Rocek (1995) noted that the amount of paleobotanical data from pithouse and pueblo contexts may be expected to differ. Variation in the intensity of site use and the nature of food storage and processing would create different macrobotanical assemblages despite similarities in the dietary importance of crops. For surface pueblo occupations in the eastern Mimbres area, Hegmon et al. (1998) showed that agriculturally focused subsistence strategies are entirely consistent with modest residential mobility.

Lightfoot and Jewett (1986; Jewett and Lightfoot 1986) recognized a wider range of pithouse use, both in the season of use and the duration of occupation. Based largely on the presence and absence of interior hearths, they contended that some pithouse villages were primarily occupied during the summer or warmer months, while other villages that have interior hearths may have been occupied during the winter months. As is discussed in chapter 4, close inspection of excavation notes from Mogollon pithouses shows that many that lacked formal hearth pits may have contained informal "on-floor" hearths. Moreover, cross-cultural research shows that there is no basis for equating the presence of a hearth with a winter occupation, or the absence of a hearth with a summer occupation (Diehl 1990). Jewett and Lightfoot also recognized high spatial and temporal variation in the duration of occupation on the basis of differences along an architectural "diversity index" score of houses at different villages, which was critiqued elsewhere (Diehl 1994). Their research used innovative approaches and was an important contribution to the study of Pithouse period land use; the methodological underpinnings of their analyses, however, have not been supported by cross-cultural studies or subsequent archaeological research.

Wills (1988, 1989, 1991a) and Mauldin (1994) viewed Pithouse period occupations in the Reserve area as spatially and temporally fluctuating. Wills suggested that the large number of intramural floor pits at the SU site indicates that great effort was invested in the construction of storage facilities. Wills associated the architectural construction of the SU pithouses with high dependence on maize as a dietary staple and lengthy pithouse occupations (Wills 1991a, 1992). Based on Mauldin's (1991, 1993) study of published descriptions of the typical manos and metates excavated by Paul Martin in the Pine Lawn Valley in New Mexico, both researchers presently suggest that Late Pithouse period (A.D. 600–1000) villagers in the Reserve area were more residentially mobile and less dependent on agricultural maize than their Early Pithouse period counterparts (Mauldin 1993; Wills 1989:148–149).

The most extreme characterization of Pithouse period subsistence and settlement envisions the occupants of Mimbres Mogollon pithouses and pueblos as extremely mobile foragers who invested scant effort in growing crops. Minnis (1985b) suggested that the earliest Late Archaic horticulturists in the area may have organized subsistence and settlement in a manner similar to the Chiricahua Apaches. His argument accords with Wills's (1985) and Hunter-Anderson's (1986) studies of the use of Archaic period upland caves prior to the common era. Wills, however, distinguished between the Apache model offered by Minnis and a "complex mutualism between cultivation and foraging in which agriculture enhanced foraging efficiency" (Wills and Huckell 1994:33), which may have developed during the Late Archaic period. Wills's mutualistic model implies less residential mobility than was the case with the ethnographically known Apache.

Lekson (1989, 1992a, 1992b) extended the Apache metaphor to include the Pithouse and Pueblo periods, as well as the Archaic. According to Lekson, people migrated between low desert stands of mesquite and cactus fruit and upland stands of acorns and piñon nuts, ignoring their fields and depending little on the crops that they planted. This model does not accord well with most assessments of Pithouse period residential mobility or resource use (Anyon and LeBlanc 1984; Diehl 1994; Hunter-Anderson 1986; Minnis 1985a; Wills 1989, 1991a; chaps. 4 through 8, this volume).

Demographic Trends

There have been two major estimates of demographic change in the Mogollon uplands. The first (Blake et al. 1986) used information from the Mimbres Foundation survey of the Mimbres Valley to estimate changes in the total valley population from the Early Pithouse period through the last Pueblo period occupations. They estimate that a fourfold increase in valley population occurred during the Early through Late Pithouse periods. Their projection is based on the estimated total amount of domestic floor space occupied during each period.

Stephen Lekson compared information from all surveys conducted in the Mogollon region from 1892 through 1989 (Lekson 1992b) against a computer simulation of land-use and mobility strategies that incorporated briefer pithouse use-lives and more frequent opportunities for residential relocation than are used by most models. Lekson found that it is possible to produce the same number of sites with much smaller regional populations and lower population densities—on the order of one-fourth as many people as posited by Blake et al. (1986). Lekson's model, however, does not contradict the *relative* changes in population documented by Blake and others. It also seems unable to explain the well-documented packing of small sites into intermittently flowing secondary drainages that began during the Three Circle phase. If populations were as low as Lekson suggests, would there have been any need to make extensive use of these poorly watered and agriculturally less-productive locations?

More data are needed to accurately assess population sizes during the Pithouse periods. More radiocarbon and tree-ring dates from construction wood and hearths would be particularly helpful. These could be used to provide interval estimates (in years) of pithouse use-lives. At present, archaeologists are free to choose between long and short use-life estimates, because none of the estimates have been substantiated through detailed chronometric analyses of construction elements in pithouses. Interpretations vary. For example, Blake et al. (1986) assumed pithouse use-lives of 75 years. Some interpretations of pithouse use outside of the study area, however, suggest that Basketmaker III Anasazi pithouses may have been used for much briefer intervals, on the order of 10 to 15 years (Ahlstrom 1985; Cameron 1990a; Schlanger 1986). Building on Diehl's (chap. 4, this volume) analysis of architecture, LeBlanc (chap. 11, this volume) observes that although *abandoned* earth structures deteriorate quickly, with maintenance such structures may be used more or less indefinitely.

To refine estimates of pithouse use-lives, we need more chronometric dates. These must include dates from most of the roof beams and posts found in pithouses. If posts are made of cottonwood or juniper rather than piñon, then radiocarbon dates must be obtained from outer rings of wood samples. Where posts are made of pine, dendrochronology should suffice. Archaeomagnetic dates from hearths must also be obtained. A systematic comparison should allow archaeologists to identify when structures were built and remodeled (from studying the wood) and abandoned (since the archaeomagnetic dates from hearths should correspond with the last use of the house).

Further complicating the question is the long-known (for example, Wheat 1955) intersite variation in pithouse floor area and depth during the Early Pithouse period. Indeed, the apparently large average size of pithouses at the SU site (but see chap. 2, this volume) and proportionally high densities of pits have led Wills (1988, 1991b, 1992, 1996a) to suggest that SU may have been used for longer intervals or occupied by relatively more sedentary people than sites in other regions. Although not clearly established, it is possible that not all contemporary houses were occupied for the same length of time. It is interesting that intersite variation in pithouse size is much less pronounced by the Three Circle phase.

Finally, questions regarding the contemporaneity of houses at any given site remain inadequately explored. Can we reasonably assume that all houses in any given village were occupied simultaneously? Can we assume that patterns of village occupation during the Early Pithouse period were similar to those of the Late Pithouse period? These questions were partially addressed by Diehl (1998). Cluster analyses of floor and fill assemblage composition indicated that for any given village, regardless of occupation phase, 20 to 30 percent of the structures have floor assemblages that were similar in composition (have similar frequencies of different kinds of artifacts) and contained usable artifacts that were generally costly to manufacture (such as manos, metates, pestles, mortars, and possibly intact vessels). Diehl associated these assemblages with either unplanned abandonment of the catastrophic "flee the burning house" variety or, more likely, with caching associated with intended continued use. These findings do not preclude simultaneous occupation of all houses, since those with robust floor assemblages may simply have been the last in any village to have been abandoned.

Social Organization

Some of the pioneers of Mogollon archaeology attempted to assess changes in Mogollon social institutions. Wheat suggested that SU pithouses seemed unusually large as compared with contemporary villages in other branches of the Mogollon and that their size might be related to the more frequent occurrence of intramural storage pits at SU, rather than differences in social organization. Martin (1940:132), however, wrote: "I am not certain that all [SU pithouses] were continuously or simultaneously occupied, but I guess that at least eight or ten [of the 16 then excavated] were all occupied at the same time." Martin proposed that the SU site occupants lived together in a village (as opposed to a string of spatially isolated "ranchería"-style settlements) because their social organization "demanded it" or, alternatively, because the SU people shared communal storage facilities.

Bluhm (1960) pursued the threads of Martin's communal cooperation theme when she suggested that the presence of kivas in Mogollon pithouse villages may have marked the advent of more effective social integration mechanisms. Large, possibly communal structures that date to the Early Pithouse period were observed at the Bluff site (Haury and Sayles 1947), Promontory (Martin et al. 1949), SU (Martin 1940, 1943), MN Y:4:6 (Hogg 1977), and Winn Canyon (Fitting 1973). But, since these structures are architecturally similar to smaller "residential" facilities, their function is unclear. Possibly they were simultaneously residences and meeting places, as LeBlanc (LeBlanc and Whalen 1980:139) and Lightfoot and Feinman (1982) suggested. Examples also occur from the first part of the Late Pithouse period, including ones at the Diablo site (Hammack 1966), Harris and Mogollon Village (Haury 1936a), and Galaz Ruin (Anyon and LeBlanc 1984).

Anyon and LeBlanc (1980) suggest that the bean-shaped pithouses of the Early Pithouse period evolved into large communal structures with posts or lobes where the ramp entered the structure. This evolution of shape, combined with the previously mentioned conservatism relating to the shape of communal structures, allows the possibility of similar functions over a very long time. This implies that the extra-large structures on Early Pithouse period sites were not simply the residences of "big men" but had some communal or ceremonial aspect even at that time. This use does not preclude their use as residences.

By A.D. 700 large communal structures were architecturally distinct and included benches and floor trenches and pits that may have been resonating chambers or foot drums. In addition, these structures are typically several times larger than residential structures at the same sites. Shafer and Taylor (1986) identified large communal structures from the Three

Circle phase occupation at the NAN Ranch. Other late communal structures include a large animal or anthropomorphically shaped structure at the Bear Ruin (Haury 1940) and large rectangular structures at Galaz (Anyon and LeBlanc 1984), Cameron Creek (Bradfield 1931), Harris (Haury 1936a), Swarts (Cosgrove and Cosgrove 1932), the Mattocks Ruin, and the Lake Roberts Vista site (Cynthia Bettison, personal communication, 1995). Communitywide ritual institutions may have existed in the Early Pithouse period. Certainly by the Three Circle phase, such institutions were in place and were probably an important mechanism for social interaction.

Perhaps the greatest change since Wheat's (1955) synthesis of Mogollon archaeology has been the proliferation of new ideas regarding the nature of Upland Mogollon Pithouse period social organization. In 1955 most archaeologists viewed pithouse dwellers as living in a consummately egalitarian society. Lightfoot and Feinman (1982) disagreed, portraying large pithouses as dual-purpose kiva-residences that were the domiciles of "big men" who had privileged access to wives, authority, wealth, and power. Their analysis was unfavorably critiqued by Hunter-Anderson and Zan (1984), who felt that potential problems associated with equifinality of settlement size, layout, and artifact distributions weakened the Lightfoot and Feinman study to the point of nonutility. In a more specific critique, Schiffer (Schiffer 1987:294–298) suggested that the observed differences in distributions of exotic goods could be best accounted for as resulting from trash dumping; bigger depressions contained more trash. In a recent analysis, Diehl (1998) showed that trash makes up the floor-context artifact assemblages in roughly 80 percent of excavated pithouses. The unfortunate consequence is that statistically significant assessments of the interhousehold distribution of wealth or other exotic artifacts cannot be obtained unless archaeologists are willing to consider excavating a much larger sample of pithouses on several sites.

As an alternative, the analysis of the distribution of mortuary goods offers greater interpretive potential because statistically significant sample sizes are more easily obtained. Most noteworthy here are the differences between Early Pithouse period mortuary assemblages and later ones (Diehl 1994). Early Pithouse burials usually contain trash, with no accompanying vessels or with a single smashed vessel. Burials that contain *Glycymeris* bracelets, *Olivella* beads, or

turquoise are extremely rare, and in burials that contain any shell, quantities of these items are low. Other variation in the mortuary treatment of Early Pithouse burials is virtually nonexistent, so the social significance of a single individual interred with a few shell beads or a bracelet is not obvious. In all other respects, Early Pithouse period villagers were equals in death; whether or not they were equals in life remains an open question. Later mortuary offerings, however, revealed a pattern that may indicate the presence of individuals who engaged in status competition through entrepreneurial use of exotic goods during the Three Circle phase (Diehl 1994). The distributions do not indicate that access to exotic items was restricted to any particular sex or age grade, nor is there any evidence for the presence of categorical status markers. Gilman observed a similar pattern among Classic Mimbres burials from the Galaz, Mattocks, and NAN Ranch sites (Gilman 1990).

We view Three Circle phase villages as socially flexible, with no obvious differential access to wealth, power, or authority but with self-serving status seekers who operated within, and were tolerated by, the larger social community. Gilman reached essentially the same conclusions for the Classic Mimbres mortuary pattern, envisioning achieved status differences and horizontal distinctions rather than ascribed differences and vertical distinctions. We feel that it is unwise to rely too closely on an analogy to any ethnographically documented group, so we are unable to describe the nature of social interaction during these occupations. Further quantitative research on mortuary distributions should be combined with efforts to assess the nutritional and epidemiological history of individuals through osteological examination or by chemical means.

One final social distinction deserves note. Although most Late Pithouse period burials are situated beneath the floors of rooms, many Three Circle phase sites contain a few cremation burials located in extramural contexts. Creel (1989) examined cremations from the NAN Ranch ruin and observed that they contained proportionally more projectile points, pots, and jewelry than did inhumations. Creel noted that ethnographic literature describes these items as artifacts that are often associated with "unusual circumstances of death," possibly the deaths of witches or other quarrelsome people or deaths involving violence or snakebites.

THE HILLTOP LOCATIONS OF EARLY PITHOUSE VILLAGES: WARFARE VERSUS SOCIAL INTERACTION

Archaeologists have long noted the tendency for Early Pithouse villages to be located on hilltops, knolls, and other places that were difficult to reach. Haury and Sayles (1947) attributed Early Pithouse villagers' preference for hilltop locations to a desire to avoid the effects of cold-air drainage in valley bottoms. Rice (1975) suggested that Early Pithouse villagers were interested in some resource that was available on hilltops. Hogg (1977) offered the suggestion that the locations of Early Pithouse villages were chosen to meet ceremonial requirements. Other explanations could include the desire to use well-drained locations or the need for a position from which one could view the movements of game.

In both our views, Rice's hypothesis seems inadequate because the vegetative and mineral resources available on hilltops vary greatly at the present time and probably varied in the past. We also agree that hypotheses that attribute the locations of Early Pithouse villages to an effort to avoid the effects of cold-air drainage or poorly drained soils may be questioned on the grounds that they fail to account for the movement of Late Pithouse and Classic Mimbres villages to lower river terraces, where the same problems would have been encountered. In our view, a reasonable model would not require that later occupants of the area simply accept the problems that Early Pithouse period occupants sought to avoid. We find some merit in the argument that early pithouses were situated to facilitate hunting. If Early Pithouse villagers were very dependent on game, and if agricultural fields were important for attracting game (in addition to their direct food value), then it might be preferable to locate villages away from agricultural fields in order to avoid frightening animals. We ultimately reject this hypothesis, however, because Early Pithouse period villagers would have had ample opportunities to locate villages away from fields without recourse to the energetically costly solution of residing on high knolls.

Although we agree about many substantive issues surrounding the subsistence practices and social organization of Early Pithouse villagers, the authors of this volume disagree about the interpretive significance of Early Pithouse village locations. As will

be seen below, LeBlanc links hilltops and other difficult places with defense—a consequence of endemic warfare. Without disputing the possibility of endemic, small-scale ambush raiding, Diehl feels that Early Pithouse period population densities and village populations were insufficient to promote the use of massed troop formations, in the absence of which hilltop locations would not have provided any tactical or strategic advantage.

An Argument for Defense

LeBlanc (LeBlanc and Whalen 1980) favors a defensive explanation for the selection of village locations because of the elevated nature of the terrain and because of rock alignments found on the peripheries of some Early Pithouse sites in the Mimbres Valley. In arguing that Early Pithouse village locations were selected for defensive reasons, LeBlanc rejects a priori the requirement for evidence such as injured bodies, burned villages, and the like as proof that actual combat occurred. On the contrary, LeBlanc views such disastrous events as proof of inadequate defensive measures. LeBlanc suggests that the tactical advantage throughout most of human history lay with the quality of defense and that Early Pithouse villages were easily defensible on their hilltop locations. In particular, the attackers would have been using atlatls, which are especially hard to use uphill. In LeBlanc's view these hamlets were so well situated that most people would not have been able to attack them successfully. In these circumstances one would not expect to find widespread or frequent evidence for Early Pithouse villagers who died violently, nor would one expect to find many catastrophically burned houses. It is also probably not a coincidence that these locations were abandoned just about the time the bow and arrow reached this part of the Southwest (LeBlanc 1997). The advent of the bow and arrow presumably decreased the advantage conferred by hilltop locations.

The strongest evidence that the pithouse village locations were chosen for defense comes from elsewhere in the Southwest. LeBlanc (1997, 1998, 1999:126–127) has shown that at roughly this time there were sites in elevated locations in the Anasazi area, and some had palisades. There is evidence of massacres, and specialized weapons usable only for warfare, scalping, and the taking of trophy heads are found. On the northern edge of the Mogollon area, sites such as Pia Mesa (Varien 1990), Flattop (Wendorf

1953), and Sivu'uvi (Burton 1991)—and slightly later, Cerro Colorado (Bullard 1962)—all have evidence of extensive burning of structures. Moreover, in the Hay Hollow Valley, the Hay Hollow site, which dates just prior to the Early Pithouse period, was not defensively located (Martin 1967). It was, however, burned, and the subsequent sites that are temporally equivalent to the Early Pithouse period, such as the Tumbleweed site (Martin et al. 1962), were located on elevated terrain—as if in response to the devastation at the Hay Hollow site. Finally, it is suspected that archaeologists have underestimated the importance of warfare in small-scale, prehistoric communities. As Keeley (1996) demonstrated, lethal warfare is common among people with population densities and social organizations that are broadly equivalent to those of the Early Pithouse period. When viewed in this larger context, there is ample evidence for warfare in the Southwest during times of initial agriculture, defensive sites were common, and the Early Pithouse site locations fit the overall pattern.

An Argument against Defense and for Population Dynamics

In Diehl's view, the case for warfare as an explanation for the locations of Early Pithouse villages is not strong. It is true that a case may be made for both individual and organized violence in many places in the Southwest, and it may even be true that low-level endemic violence prevailed during the Early Pithouse period. The link, however, between endemic, low-intensity, small-scale warfare (the existence of which, although not proven, is not disputed) and hilltop locations has not been adequately demonstrated. In Diehl's view, in a context of endemic skirmish raiding and ambush tactics, hilltop locations would not have provided any defensive advantage. An alternative model considers the low population densities of the Upland Mogollon region and posits that villages were strategically located to promote intervillage social interaction. The argument against hilltops as defensive locations is considered first. The case may be productively distilled to several observations, each of which is discussed below in detail.

Upland Mogollon pithouse villages are not themselves fortifications, nor are they generally fortified. Although there are linear cobble features on a few sites, there are no standing walls or even substantial rubble mounds that indicate the presence of a high barrier that reduced the target aspect of defenders.

Regardless of the case that may be made for the Four Corners region, hundreds of kilometers distant, there is no evidence of the presence of palisades in the Upland Mogollon region. Any defensive advantage to hilltop locations must, therefore, be explained by recourse to the elevated nature of the terrain.

In general, elevations confer two defensive benefits. The first is the ability for a defender to use the crest of the hill-slope as a visual barrier to people at lower elevations. The target aspect of an object on a hill may be reduced substantially when viewed from a lower elevation. Unfortunately, however, this defensive characteristic is only very useful at long ranges, or for persons who shoot while prone (such as those using a crossbow or a rifle). At close range the target aspect increases, and persons firing bows or throwing spears must reveal all of their body. Given the very short ranges of prehistoric Southwestern arms, defenders probably gained little comfort from reduced target aspect.

The second defensive property of elevations is that defenders' missile weapon ranges are extended and attackers' ranges are reduced. Gravity works for the defense and against the attacker. However, this advantage is only significant if the defenders are able to cover all avenues of approach to the hilltop and are able to concentrate *massed fire* on these approaches; as is discussed below, most villages had so few occupants that massed fire was not an available tactic. Prehistoric Southwesterners' atlatls, and to a lesser degree their bows and arrows, were manifestly inaccurate, low-velocity weapons with very short lethal ranges (Keeley 1996:50). It is likely that attackers could sidestep or otherwise dodge defensively fired arrows (other than those fired at point-blank range), since, absent massed fire, a person being fired upon might be able to visually track all projectiles fired at him. Indeed, LeBlanc (1999) recognizes a category of artifact called "fending sticks" that were used to parry the slow-moving atlatl-propelled darts used in the region.

The massed firepower and dense formations required to make terrain a dominant factor in combat probably did not exist. If all of the pithouses at the McAnally site were concurrently occupied by extended families with three adult males, the hilltop would have been defended by 36 men. The larger Thompson site would have been formidably defended by 165 men. Given two men per household, however, and 20 to 30 percent contemporaneous house occupation (both reasonable assumptions), the roughly 140-m perimeter of the hillcrest of the McAnally site would have been defended by 5 to 8 men, and Thompson by 22 to 36 men. These numbers are simply inadequate to defend the perimeters of either hilltop under any set of circumstances using prehistoric Southwestern weaponry.

Defense is also an inadequate explanation because it is inconsistent with extant data. The hypothesis fails to account for the subsequent shift to river terraces during the Late Pithouse period. If combat was sufficiently intense to promote the use of hilltops during the Early Pithouse period, then why was it insufficiently intense to promote continued use of these locations during more recent times? To address this obvious question, LeBlanc suggested that the introduction of the bow obviated the defensive advantage of hilltops; that claim seems inconsistent with the myriad of historically documented battles in which massed groups of archers on elevated terrain wreaked havoc on assaulting forces, as at Agincourt or Crécy.

A Demographic Alternative

Demographic evidence may be used to generate an alternative, "social" hypothesis. According to some estimates, the Mimbres Valley during the Early Pithouse period could have supported much higher populations (Hastorf 1980; Lekson 1992b), unless people were primarily dependent on hunting (Blake et al. 1986), and all researchers seem to agree that the Early Pithouse population of the Mimbres Valley was "low." Given the low population density, there may have been a great deal of demographic pressure to receive guests hospitably. Social ties would have provided opportunities for exchange of products, ideas, information about the distribution of resources, and, most importantly, genes. Early Pithouse villages may have been located in order to increase their visibility to people traveling up and down the various river valleys. Their high visibility would have made them obvious magnets for travelers, especially if village locations shifted from time to time, from one hilltop to another. These locations would also have afforded a good view, to their occupants, of the movements of potential trading and marriage partners (or their relatives, anyhow) and game throughout the region.

This "social hypothesis" predicts that, since it was energetically costly to reside on the tops of high hills, residences would have been constructed at lower elevations as populations increased. As LeBlanc has noted (LeBlanc and Whalen 1980), these locations are energetically costly to maintain as residences. Upon

the alleviation of social pressure for maintaining these sites, villages would have been relocated to river terraces to provide easier access to agricultural fields and water. If this hypothesis is correct, one might expect to find a close temporal correspondence between the movement to river terrace locations and increases in local population densities, or increased evidence of social interaction between the occupants of different drainages, "branches," or regions of the Southwest.

ECONOMIC TRANSITIONS FROM THE ARCHAIC TO THE EARLY PITHOUSE PERIOD

As noted earlier, long-standing models of Archaic versus Pithouse period land use envision Archaic people as residentially mobile foragers with low dependence on agriculture and Pithouse period people as relatively sedentary farmers. Apart from the studies that question the characterization of pithouse villagers as either sedentary or agricultural, there are also new studies that suggest that Archaic foragers were not very different from pithouse villagers. Long-standing models of Archaic period subsistence in the Upland Mogollon (for summaries, see Cordell 1997; LeBlanc 1982; LeBlanc and Whalen 1980; Minnis 1980) may have to be scrapped in favor of more complex models.

Based on recent research in the Tucson Basin, researchers have argued for the existence of a pan-Southwestern brownware cultural pattern that has many characteristics of Upland Mogollon Early Pithouse period sites (Huckell 1988; Huckell et al. 1987; Whittelsey 1995). Among the new developments are the suggestions that during the Late Archaic period occupants of the Sonoran desert environments of southern Arizona were residentially sedentary and that agriculture was well established (Ciolek-Torello 1995; Deaver and Ciolek-Torello 1995:532). However, this characterization of Late Archaic Tucson Basin horticulturists as sedentary farmers has been challenged on the basis of differences between Cienega phase flotation samples and Hohokam ones (Diehl 1997).

Gilman (1995) suggested that, at least for the San Simon branch, the Late Archaic and "pit structure" (pithouse) periods were more similar to each other, in terms of their subsistence economies, than either was to the preceding Middle Archaic or subsequent Pueblo periods. Her views accord well with those of Wills (1996a), who viewed the Archaic to Pithouse transition in the Reserve area as somewhat more seamless than prior studies have suggested. Both scholars appear to view the pithouse occupations in their respective research areas as intensifications of economies based on foraging and agriculture, rather than as radical transitions from foraging to food production.

CONCLUDING THOUGHTS: MOGOLLON PITHOUSE VILLAGE ARCHAEOLOGY AND THE "BIG PICTURE"

It is important to study the worldwide manifestations of the transition from wild food use to crop cultivation for several reasons. Data from Mogollon pithouse villages can be used to investigate the cultural and economic processes that provide the context for the emergence (or suppression) of social inequality. Many archaeologists have expressed a desire to understand the processes that surround the formation and maintenance of complicated, multitiered vertical (and horizontal) power, authority, prestige, wealth, and nutrition hierarchies, as well as the social and economic consequences of these hierarchies (Brumfiel and Earle 1987; Carneiro 1981; Earle 1987; Gregg 1991; Hayden and Gargett 1990; Peebles and Kus 1977; F. Plog 1989). Given the propensity for human societies to coalesce along ethnic and class divisions into deadly combative, self-interested groups, the problem of the origins and perpetuation of social inequality is an important subject of research for all social scientists (Diehl 2000).

In archaeology, Mogollon villages provide an open field for new excavations and analytical efforts. Studies of pithouse villages offer the potential for the improvement of anthropological models of the processes of village formation, social aggregation, the generation of socially integrative institutions, the relationship between social status competition and subsistence economy, and the behavioral ecology of small horticultural and agricultural human societies.

Numerous ethnographic case studies show that individual behaviors consistent with the desire for social status self-aggrandizement are present among "egalitarian" human groups and nonhuman primate bands (Berkovitch 1991; Bernstein 1980; Boehm 1993; Cashdan 1980; Dwyer and Minnegal 1993; Harpending and Rogers 1990; Hawkes 1991; Lyons et al. 1994). Even in most egalitarian societies, individuals vie for enhanced social prestige. Likewise, status competition and social institutions interact in the development of local power hierarchies even in mod-

ern nation-states (Gatewood 1984; Palmer 1991). If self-aggrandizing behavior is endemic to the human species, why did 140,000 years (Cann et al. 1987) of *Homo sapiens* prehistory pass without the development of obvious social stratification?

A number of factors may have provided the proper chemistry for the crystallization of more permanent vertical hierarchies among groups in which, initially, individual autonomy was great (Cashdan 1980; Diehl 1994; Gardner 1991; Hayden 1990). These factors could include a coupling of interpersonal rivalry with an easing of the suppression of self-aggrandizing behavior, subtle demographic changes, and the manipulation of kinship ties. Studies of social change among seemingly egalitarian groups may have the advantage of being close to the social, ecological, and demographic contexts that surround *emergent* social differences. For example, Keeley's (1988) cross-cultural comparison of ethnographically known groups showed that sedentism, food storage, and high population densities seem to be the three most important necessary conditions for the development of non-egalitarian social regimes. Others have argued that the conditions in which inequality develop involve a more complex set of parameters that may include the ability to convert surplus food into other fitness-enhancing, bankable items such as physical wealth or social obligations (see Kelly 1995:293–331). Evidence of trade (the movement of Pacific coastal marine shell, turquoise, obsidian, ceramic vessels, and cotton) occurs with increasing frequency during the Pithouse periods, and all of these phenomena developed in the Upland Mogollon region during the Pithouse periods.

In exploring the relationship between social organization and economic strategies, one can study the suite of social and environmental changes that occurred in the transitions from dependence on primarily wild resources to low-intensity horticulture, and later to high-intensity agriculture. Mogollon pithouse villages provide a very important data set on the secondary transition from hunting and gathering to agriculture, and on the intensification of agriculture from one of the more thoroughly archaeologically studied parts of the world. Most researchers agree that in the Southwest, the Archaic period was a time of high human residential mobility, low agricultural dependence, low population densities, and relatively egalitarian social orders in which human beings lived in small dispersed groups (Blake et al. 1986; Cordell 1984; Minnis 1985a; Wills 1985). In contrast, the Classic Mimbres period occupation of the Mimbres Valley was a time of population aggregation, larger populations, and intensified maize agriculture (Anyon and LeBlanc 1984; Blake et al. 1986; Cordell 1984; Gilman 1987; Herrington 1979; LeBlanc and Whalen 1980; Mauldin 1991). If the early pithouse data set could be brought up to the level of information that we have for later periods, much more useful comparisons could be made.

Finally, data from Upland Mogollon pithouse villages can be used to study in the most general sense the past success of different uses of the land in order to evaluate present or anticipated options for land use. Minnis (1985a) documented environmental changes wrought in the Mimbres Valley by the Classic Mimbres occupants of that region. As a case study, that research provided one example of social change as a response to food stress, and it may provide models or insights for governing the complex relationship between social structure and poverty in the twentieth century. Data from Mogollon pithouse villages may also be used to study the complexity of resource use within specific areas. Comparisons of Mimbres area Pithouse period, Classic Mimbres, Apache, early historic, and late twentieth-century economic uses might

lead to the development of powerful insights for promoting a sustainable economy. The development of a sustainable economy would be unusual in this region, which has experienced a series of boom-to-bust cycles of economic use and occupation from A.D. 1150 through the present day.

Among social scientists, anthropologists presently have a clear lead in developing and testing theories of the maintenance of social inequality. Among anthropologists, archaeologists hold the privileged position of access to the prehistoric contexts in which social inequality first developed. It is no exaggeration to suggest that the continued existence of the species *Homo sapiens* may rest upon the development of insights about the origins and maintenance of social inequality and the social and environmental effects that such inequality produces. Clearly, archaeological studies of foragers and early farmers, like those of the Upland Mogollon region, will be essential for understanding the origins of social inequality and other critical issues about our ability to develop sustainable economies and social organizations.

4 Mogollon Pithouse Architecture and Changes in Residential Mobility

Michael W. Diehl

Two of the pithouses at the McAnally site were sufficiently excavated to provide architectural details, and these are described completely in chapter 10. Ten other house depressions were observed on the surface of the site. When the architectural details of the McAnally pithouses are combined with data from other Early Pithouse period sites and other subsequently occupied Upland Mogollon pithouse sites, they may be used to assess whether or not there were diachronic changes in the intensity of land use.

McAnally pithouses also may be used to test whether or not SU site pithouses are unique relative to pithouses from other Mogollon branches. So far we have briefly discussed the suggestion that SU site pithouses are larger than, and therefore functionally different from, the houses at Early Pithouse period sites in other branches. One of the many compelling observations that we use to justify our treatment of the Upland Mogollon area as a single interpretive entity includes the debunking of the special status that has been accorded to SU. In this case, one can provide a test of the validity of the claim that SU pithouses are generally larger than those on other sites. We have chosen to address this culture-historical question in the present chapter because it requires a level of descriptive detail about McAnally pithouses that seemed inconsistent with the summary character of chapter 2. Since this chapter deals explicitly with architecture, it is the appropriate venue for a more complete consideration of the surface areas of pithouses at the McAnally site.

ARE SU SITE PITHOUSES STATISTICALLY LARGER THAN McANALLY SITE PITHOUSES?

Wheat (1955) claimed that SU site pithouses are larger, on average, than the structures on other sites. At the time, SU was one of very few excavated Early Pithouse villages and the only extensively excavated *early* village in the Upland Mogollon region. Wheat's conclusion was reasonable, given that the only points for comparison were the four and one-half excavated houses at the Promontory site (Martin et al. 1949) and those at the Bluff site (Haury 1985). Although the average sizes of structures certainly vary between sites, houses in some early Mogollon villages are comparable to those at SU. Specifically, we can show that the surface areas of McAnally houses are statistically indistinguishable from SU houses. With an average adjusted floor area of 26.9 m^2 (standard deviation = 9.6), McAnally pithouses are not significantly different from those at the SU site, which have a mean of 31.4 m^2 (standard deviation = 11.6; kivas excluded). The preceding calculation included the following SU pithouses: B, C, E, F, G, H, I, J, L, M, N, O, P, Q, R, S, T, and U.

TABLE 4.1
SURFACE AREAS OF McANALLY PITHOUSES

Pithouse	Length (m)	Width (m)	Estimated Surface Area (m^2)	Adjusted Surface Area (m^2)
1	5.9	4.3	20.4	20.4
2	5.5	4.4	19.2	19.2
3	7.5	7.3	43.0	30.1
4	6.0	4.3	20.1	20.1
5	11.2	7.3	73.6	36.8
6	8.4	7.0	46.6	32.6
7	7.4	5.7	33.7	27.0
8	9.3	7.3	54.1	24.7^a
9	10.2	8.9	71.6	35.8
10	9.0	6.2	50.2	30.1
11	6.7	6.5	34.2	24.0^a
12	5.8	5.4	24.6	22.1

^{a} Actual area.

Table 4.1 presents detailed information about the McAnally pithouses, including the Unit number (house number), the dimensions of the *unexcavated* house pit, the surface area of the *unexcavated* pit, and the adjusted (projected) surface area of the actual pithouse. The adjusted surface areas were used to calculate the mean floor area of McAnally pithouses. The unexcavated surface pits are much larger and have a mean area of 40.9 m^2 (standard deviation = 19.1).

The use of an adjusted surface area recognizes that, in general, the surface areas of unexcavated house pits are larger than the excavated floors of houses. This is a consequence of a natural process of pit in-filling through aeolian and alluvial erosion of the ground surface around the margins of house pits. Furthermore, it ought to be true within any given site that larger surface pits correspond with larger pithouses; the relationship, however, is possibly not linear. We suspect that larger surface pits have a lower correspondence with their actual pithouse floors than smaller surface pits. Accordingly, we require a mechanism to increase the accuracy of our estimates of the underlying floor areas. The adjusted surface areas were determined by the formula $A = O \times (1-x)$; where A is the adjusted surface area, O is the observed surface area of the unexcavated pit, and x varies from zero to 0.5. The value of x is set to zero for houses with unexcavated surface areas that are within one-quarter standard deviation (based on the site mean) of the smallest observed house pit. For all subsequent half standard deviations, x increases by 0.1, up to a limit of 0.5.

The formula is probably inaccurate since it requires refinements that may only be achieved through excavation. The accuracy of the formula is not the principal issue, however, since our formula is designed to bias our estimates generally at or below the actual surface areas of McAnally pithouses. In other words, our formula exaggerates any differences between houses at the SU and McAnally sites. Despite the deliberate bias, the observed difference of mean surface areas between the two sites is not statistically significant ($p = 0.27$). SU houses are not significantly larger than McAnally houses. There is no other Early Pithouse site that appears to have structures that are, on average, larger than those at SU, so at this point, there is no evidence that houses are appreciably larger in one area of the Upland Mogollon than another.

THE USE OF ARCHITECTURAL DETAILS TO ASSESS THE INTENSITY OF SITE OCCUPATIONS

The two fully excavated McAnally pithouses are typical residential structures of the Mogollon Early Pithouse period. Both are elliptical, have obvious ramps oriented in an easterly direction, and are moderately large. By themselves, the architectural data from these pithouses add little to the study of prehistoric lifeways. When used in combination with descriptive details from other sites, however, analysis of architectural data can provide insights about the amount of time that people spent living at a given site.

Comparisons among Early Pithouse period, Georgetown, San Francisco, and Three Circle phase houses are used to assess whether or not there were diachronic changes in the relative amounts of residential mobility. Data on architectural attributes were obtained from a sample of 175 pithouses from the following sites: Bear (AZ P:16:1 [ASM]; Haury 1940), Bluff (AZ P:16:20 [ASM]; Haury and Sayles 1947), Crooked Ridge Village (AZ W:10:15 [ASM]; Wheat 1954), Diablo Village (LA 6538), Duncan (AZ CC:8:12 [ASM]; Lightfoot 1984), Galaz (LA 635; Anyon and LeBlanc 1984), Harris Village (LA 1867; Haury 1936a), Lee Village (LA 5779; Bussey 1975), McAnally (LA 12110; this volume), Mogollon Village (LA 11568; Haury 1936a), Promontory (LA 9713; Martin et al. 1949), SU (LA 64931; Martin 1940, 1943; Martin and Rinaldo 1947), Turkey Foot Ridge (LA 9709; Martin et al. 1949), and Winn Canyon (Fitting 1973).

The purpose of this research is to assess the nature of prehistoric subsistence strategies by studying changes in architectural construction. This study is important because it provides support for one of several competing characterizations of Upland Mogollon Pithouse period subsistence and settlement strategies that we reviewed in chapter 3. The analyses reported here indicate that from A.D. 200 through 1000, Mogollon villagers became increasingly sedentary. Furthermore, the pace at which people settled in to their villages and their horticultural lifestyle was relatively steady. The often–discussed pithouse-to-pueblo transition, which occurred locally around A.D. 1000, may not have been a consequence of a sudden and fundamental reorganization of land or resource use, but rather the outcome of a prolonged, gradual process. In evaluating the nature of Pithouse period subsistence and settlement strategies, we use theories about subsistence and settlement strategies (also called mobility strategies) (Binford 1980; Kelly 1983, 1992), technological design (Bleed 1986; M. Nelson 1991), and architectural design (McGuire and Schiffer 1983).

The Concept of Mobility

This research is designed to assess the residential mobility of prehistoric groups. A "residential move" is a move in which most members of a group relocate their households to a new territory. The number of times that a domestic group changes location in any given year is a frequently used measure of the amount of residential mobility (Binford 1980, 1990; Diehl 1992;

Kelly 1983, 1992). Strategies that involve high residential mobility entail frequent changes in the location of the domestic group (families or groups of families) in order to exploit sequentially resources that are available within a local foraging area. In contrast, strategies that involve low residential mobility entail the use of few residential locations in any given year. Instead, special-purpose task groups engage in "logistical" forays in order to obtain more distant resources and return with them to the residential base. Groups who engage in low residential mobility maintain their access to distant or spatiotemporally heterogeneous resources through frequent use of logistical forays. Residential and logistical mobility are not mutually exclusive. Groups that employ frequent residential moves, for example on an interval of every three weeks, may engage in daily logistical forays between residential moves. Detailed discussions of the concepts of "residential" and "logistical" mobility may be found in Binford (1980), Kelly (1992), and M. Nelson (1991).

The analyses in this study address residential mobility on two temporal scales: (1) the durations of annual occupation of houses, and (2) the number of years that houses are reoccupied. The two scales are closely related, because design solutions that render structures habitable for longer intervals within one year are the same solutions that promote long-term (multiple-year) reliability of structures. There is a need for more accurate means of distinguishing between the frequency of residential moves within one year and the duration of use (or reuse) on a multiple-year scale of analysis. This research offers partial solutions for distinguishing between the two.

A Theory of Architectural Construction

In this research, attributes of the design and construction of prehistoric dwellings are used to make inferences about the amounts of time structures were occupied. The amount of occupation of individual structures is related to the frequency of residential moves. Where villages are continually occupied for an entire year, residential mobility reaches its theoretical minimum of zero residential moves. Conversely, an archaeological landscape filled solely with ephemeral structures that were each used for only a few weeks constitutes evidence for high residential mobility. Using attributes of architectural design and construction, this study asks whether or not Late Pithouse period occupants of the Mogollon region used their houses for longer durations than their Early Pithouse period ancestors. This research assesses changes in residential mobility on two scales: (1) an annual scale, in which the approximate number of months out of each year spent at a site is determined, and (2) a superannual scale, in which the long-term use of the site is assessed.

Our study relies heavily on a theory that was advanced by McGuire and Schiffer (1983). They suggested that the amount of time and labor invested in construction should be conditioned by the anticipated use of a structure. When residents anticipate brief periods of use they should build low-cost structures. When builders anticipate lengthy periods of use they should invest more energy in construction. The choice between building low-cost and high-cost structures reflects differences in the long-term cost of maintaining structures. In comparison with ephemeral structures, dwellings that are very reliable cost more for initial construction, but reliable structures cost less to maintain than ephemeral structures. In contrast, the maintenance of a low-initial-cost, low-reliability structure often entails a substantial overhaul of the structure if it is occupied for longer-than-anticipated intervals. Furthermore, even very brief abandonments of ephemeral structures may necessitate the refabrication of the structure upon the return of occupants.

Several cross-cultural studies support the use of the theoretical framework advanced by McGuire and Schiffer. In a study of residential mobility and materials used in residential architecture, Diehl (1992) found that the number of days that a residence is occupied strongly conditions the kinds of materials used in its construction. Residences occupied fewer than 121 days per year tend to be constructed of nondurable, low-cost materials such as brush. Residences occupied between 121 and 240 days are most often made of wood and earth. Structures occupied for longer than 240 days per year are made of durable materials such as extensively prepared wood (true planks, substantial posts), adobe, or stone, usually in some combination.

Kent (1991) examined site structure and construction materials used by Basarwa and Bantu speakers at 30 camps in southern Africa and found that anticipated mobility was the best predictor of architectural investment. Occupants who anticipated long stays preferred mudbrick construction over woven-grass or stick construction. They also built larger-diameter huts than did those who anticipated brief occupations. Finally, people who anticipated lengthy occupations constructed substantial storage facilities, while those who anticipated brief occupations did not. Kent also found that the amount of internal compartmentalization was strongly conditioned by the anticipated occupation of a dwelling. In structures with long use-lives, activity areas tend to be discretely bounded and separated.

Binford (1990) conducted a cross-cultural study of hunter-gatherers that examined the relationship between mobility and housing. Binford demonstrated that sedentary and semisedentary groups often use different materials for roof construction than they use for walls. This is probably a consequence of the use of rigid frames for supporting the more durable structures used by sedentary groups. Moreover, nomadic and seminomadic groups tend to use grass construction materials, whereas sedentary and semisedentary groups tend to use wood. Where plentiful, grass is a comparatively inexpensive resource by comparison with wood, since grass is more easily cut.

Gilman's (1987) cross-cultural study provided results that are consistent with the other research just described. Taken together, these studies (Binford 1990; Diehl 1992; Gilman 1987; Kent 1991) suggest that the amount of effort that people invest in architectural construction strongly associates with the anticipated use-life of that structure. They also indicate that attributes of architectural construction may be used as indices of the occupation duration of structures.

Technological Design Attributes: Reliability and Maintainability

Construction and maintenance costs are related to concepts used by some engineers—reliability and maintainability. Much has been written about reliability and maintainability in the arena of chipped stone analyses (Bleed 1986; M. Nelson 1991). Reliability is defined by some engineers as the amount of time that an object may be used without failure (Ostrofsky 1977). Maintainability is the ease with which an unusable device is restored to service. Both reliability and maintainability are enhanced by the use of durable materials, standardized construction elements, and redundant parts. Independent elements of architectural construction may be assigned indices that rank them in order of their reliability or maintainability.

Residentially sedentary people construct tools and structures that have design attributes (redundancy, parallel components, overdesigned parts) with high initial costs. The energetic payoff comes in the form of long intervals without failure and brief intervals during which tools or structures are in maintenance. In contrast, highly mobile people do not invest in reliable designs, since energy invested in building structures whose reliability greatly exceeds their anticipated use-intervals is energy wasted. Similarly, maintainability is not an important quality in structures that are used for brief intervals, then abandoned.

ATTRIBUTES OF PREHISTORIC ARCHITECTURAL CONSTRUCTION

We examined diachronic variation in five attributes of pithouse construction: (1) the formality of hearth construction, (2) the presence or absence of interior plaster, (3) the materials used in wall construction, (4) the density of vertical support posts per square meter of floor space, and (5) evidence of remodeling. Of these five attributes, the first four may be indices of the intended intervals of structure occupation on an annual scale or a superannual scale. The last attribute (evidence of remodeling) is treated as an index of the actual long-term use of structures. Prior researchers suggested that the kind of deterioration that mandates remodeling occurs after 10 to 15 years of use (Ahlstrom 1985:89; Cameron 1990a; Schlanger 1986).

Hearth Construction

We use the formality of hearth preparation as one of several indices of change in the occupation of structures. All hearths require frequent maintenance to remove accumulated ash deposits. Hearths excavated into the floors of rooms confine ash deposits, making them easy to gather and remove. More rigid hearths, such as those with slab reinforcements, may be easier to clean and empty than simple pits. The formality of hearth construction, therefore, may be a consequence of the intensity of hearth use; investment in more formal designs decreases the maintenance costs of hearths.

We have assessed relative differences in the cost of manufacturing the heat source by ranking the amount of effort invested in hearth construction. Houses that lack subfloor hearths are treated as having the least formal heat source since they cost nothing to manufacture apart from costs of obtaining the wood used for fuel. These on-floor hearths must have been the most expensive to maintain; in the absence of sub-floor pits, ash and charcoal from these features would have dissipated easily across intramural living surfaces. *Contra* Lightfoot and Jewett (1986), we assume that all pithouses had an internal heat source since traces of on-floor hearths have been observed at sev-

eral sites and since Gilman's (1987) research indicated that pithouses were probably occupied during the cold winter months. On-floor hearths leave no visible depression in the floor surface, but reddened areas on the floors of pithouses at the Flattop, SU, Promontory, and Crooked Ridge Village sites have been attributed to such uses (Anyon 1980:170; Martin 1979; Wendorf 1953:34; Wheat 1954:71, 1955).

The cost of hearth construction increases with the addition of new design elements. Simple basin-type hearths cost more, since they require the builder to dig a pit. Wheat (1954) noted that basin-shaped hearths facilitate cleaning by confining the ashes and charcoal from a hearth within a well-defined area. The addition of a deflector slab or an adobe collar increases the cost another increment, since it requires yet another step in the manufacture of the hearth. These features may reflect attempts to prevent drafts from scattering ash and charcoal from hearths onto other parts of the living surface. Slab-lined hearths are the most formal and are ranked as the most energetically expensive to construct because they require more steps to manufacture than any other kind of hearth. By virtue of their hardness and rigidity they are also probably the easiest to maintain.

Presence of Floor or Wall Plaster

We assume that the use of plaster on the walls and floors of structures represents an additional expenditure of effort in the construction of dwellings beyond that required by simple unplastered foundations. The additional effort required entails the movement of earth (perhaps sifted in order to remove unwanted impurities) and water, the mixing of the two, and the application of the compound to the inside of the structure.

The use of plaster increases the long-term reliability of pithouses. Cameron (1991) noted that the use of plaster on the exterior surfaces of pueblos substantially reduces the deterioration of walls and roofs. When applied to interior walls, plaster reinforces wall faces and prevents elements of the wall from intruding on the living space, and plaster protects wall timbers from insect cohabitants. In the absence of plaster, and as structures were occupied for longer intervals, the walls and roof of a structure were more rapidly fatigued from rot and insect predation. Increased use of wall plaster over time is indicated by higher proportions of pithouses with wall plaster and pithouses with multiple plaster layers

We cannot make the case that the use of floor

plaster increases structural integrity since it is not clear how floor plaster might prevent elements of the walls and roof from falling on the occupants. However, the use of floor plaster does increase the cost of house construction. It also serves a valuable purpose by facilitating the maintenance of the structure; small items of food or other objects are less likely to become embedded in the ground surface. A plastered floor would be somewhat easier to clean— possibly a desirable effect when occupants use structures for longer intervals.

Wall Construction Materials

Materials used in wall construction reflect differences in the amount of annual residential mobility (Binford 1990; Diehl 1992). Generally speaking, structures made out of durable materials are both more reliable and more maintainable than structures made out of ephemeral materials. This study ranked pithouses according to the nature of their construction. Simple pits rated a score of 1. The house cost index was incremented by one point for the use of stone in less than half (of the circumference) of a structure's walls, and by two points for the use of stone in more than half of a structure's walls. The phrase "the use of stone" means that several tiers of masonry, several courses in width, were used for some segment of the wall. The occurrence of an occasional rock or two does not constitute a significant increase in the energy invested in pithouse construction. There is no danger that the formal dichotomy (more than half versus less than half) imposes an arbitrary division between otherwise similar structures. In the data used in this research, houses that had less than half of their circumference made of masonry used masonry in short, discrete patches. Those with more than half usually had masonry lining the entire foundation of the house.

Descriptions of pithouses at Cameron Creek Village (Bradfield 1931), a multicomponent site that had a long history of use, indicate that small patches of masonry may have been used situationally in wall construction when the pit for a new pithouse intruded upon the pit from a prior occupation. Occupants of pithouses excavated into previously disturbed soil may have used masonry patches in their construction to hold back loose earth. Detailed studies of the construction sequence of prehistoric buildings at the NAN Ranch also show that masonry occurs in pithouses that were excavated into loose, previously disturbed soil (Shafer 1995) and in major remodeling episodes (Shafer and Taylor 1986).

Density of Posts

The density of interior load-bearing posts (posts with a diameter of 10 cm or greater) per square meter of floor space may also be used as an index for the cost of pithouse construction, and it is a good indirect measure of the residential mobility of the people who built the structure. The use of standardized parts and redundancy of components are well-established strategies for increasing the reliability of any tool, from chipped stone tools to military aircraft. We contend that longer intended occupations resulted in an increase in the number of posts used to support the roof. The use of extra posts (redundancy) reduced maintenance costs by enabling the occupants to remove and replace weak roof supports without risking a structural collapse. Furthermore, posts used in such a structure would have deteriorated more slowly than would otherwise have been the case, since the use of extra posts reduced the load on all posts.

The density of posts per square meter of floor area is an appropriate index of the amount of effort invested in post construction. An earlier study (Diehl and Gilman 1996) used raw frequencies of posts per pithouse as an index of architectural investment. That study was flawed because it did not account for covariation between the number of posts in a house and house size. Preliminary analyses of the pithouse data used in this research confirmed that the number of posts used in a dwelling is related to the surface area of the floor. Use of the post-density measure eliminates variation that is attributable to house size rather than to the use of redundant designs.

Evidence of Remodeling

Finally, this study uses the number of episodes of floor, hearth, and wall remodeling to assess differences in the relative lengths of occupation. This research assumes that remodeling is an activity that occurs as a consequence of deterioration or use-wear. Accordingly, evidence of remodeling is treated as an index of relative lengths of periodic or, alternatively, continuous occupation. In other words, the amount of remodeling is used to assess changes in the long-term occupations of structures.

In this research, each house starts with a basic score of 0, which is increased by 1 for each floor-plaster layer observed by the archaeologist. This method assumes that a new floor-plaster layer represents an episode of reoccupation or a replastering required because of constant occupation. The presence of one

TABLE 4.2
FREQUENCIES OF DIFFERENT HEARTH TYPES IN MOGOLLON PITHOUSES, BY OCCUPATION INTERVAL

Occupation Interval	"On-Floor" or Informal Hearth	Simple Basin	Plastered or Collared	Slab Lined
Early Pithouse period	24 (9.9)	25 (29.4)	1 (5.0)	1 (6.7)
Georgetown phase	5 (6.4)	19 (19.1)	1 (3.2)	8 (4.3)
San Francisco phase	1 (4.9)	16 (14.4)	7 (2.4)	1 (3.3)
Three Circle phase	4 (12.8)	41 (38.1)	8 (6.4)	13 (8.7)

Notes: Chi-square = 55.9; $p < 0.00$. $N = 175$ (12 missing data). Expected frequency in parentheses.

or several plastered-over floor pits or postholes also counts as one episode of reconstruction. Similarly, evidence of hearth remodeling is treated as a remodeling episode. Since observed replastering in hearths, postholes, and floors may all be consequences of the same remodeling episode, the occurrence of all categories together only counts as one episode of remodeling. The only way to exceed a score of 1 is to have at least two floor-plaster layers.

A COMPARISON OF THE INTENSITY OF SITE OCCUPATION FROM A.D. 200 TO 1000

In the following analyses, five indices of the effort invested in pithouse construction are used to assess changes in the intensity of pithouse occupation. The analyses rely on two statistical tests—Pearson's chi-square statistic with Yates's correction, and the Spjotvoll-Stoline analysis of variance of means test for samples with unequal sample sizes. Four of the five indices show that efforts invested in house construction increased during the first millennium A.D.

Hearth Construction

Table 4.2 describes the distribution and associated chi-square values for hearth construction types by occupation phase. These data show that the amount of energy invested in formal preparation of interior hearths increased through time. In this research, energy invested in hearth design and initial construction is treated as a measure, on the annual scale, of the intended occupation duration of a structure. Since the observed increases in the preparation of hearths—and the inferred decreases in maintenance costs—are consistent with longer anticipated uses, investment in

hearth construction is primarily an index of the amount of time within a typical year that the occupants intended to use structures.

Table 4.2 shows that the number of pithouses with informal or "on-floor" hearths was disproportionately high during the Early Pithouse period and low during subsequent occupation phases. In contrast, the number of houses with costly, more formal hearths (with collars, plastered surfaces, or slab linings) was initially disproportionately low, but subsequently increased.

By inspection, it is clear that the greatest change in hearth preparation occurred when the proportion of houses that lack formal hearths decreased from 44 percent in the Early Pithouse period to 15 percent in the Georgetown phase. The proportion of more costly hearths increased during the Georgetown phase and remained constant thereafter. In general, the trend is from informal hearths to formal hearths, with slowly increasing reliance on lined or collared features later in the sequence.

Intramural Plaster

Table 4.3 shows that the proportion of pithouses with evidence of floor or wall plaster increased from the Early Pithouse period through the Three Circle phase. The strongest increase in the use of wall and floor plaster occurred from the San Francisco phase through the Three Circle phase. The chi-square test of this distribution is statistically significant ($p = 0.00$). Broken down into a sequence of one-tailed Z-tests of the proportion of pithouses with plaster, all pairwise phase comparisons are significant at the $p = 0.05$ level, except for the comparison between the Early Pithouse period and the Georgetown phase ($10 > p > 0.05$). These tests show that effort expended in floor and wall plastering gradually increased over the 800-year interval encompassed by this study, and that the period of greatest

TABLE 4.3
PRESENCE OR ABSENCE OF PLASTER IN MOGOLLON PITHOUSES, BY OCCUPATION INTERVAL

Occupation Interval	Plaster Absent	Plaster Present	N	% of N with Plaster
Early Pithouse period	36 (20.9)	14 (29.1)	50	28
Georgetown phase	21 (15.9)	17 (22.1)	38	45
San Francisco phase	12 (11.3)	15 (15.7)	27	56
Three Circle phase	9 (30.0)	63 (42.4)	72	88

Notes: Chi-square = 47.1, $p < 0.00$. $N = 187$. Expected frequency in parentheses.

change occurred from the San Francisco phase through the Three Circle phase.

Wall Construction

The analysis of wall construction materials shows that most Mogollon pithouse builders used the same basic wall construction materials throughout the Pithouse periods (table 4.4). Most houses (93%) were simply pits that were dug into the prevailing local soil matrix, without the use of masonry, and this proportion did not change significantly through time (chi-square = 10.3, $p = 0.11$). According to the method and theory used in this analysis, the lack of variation in wall construction techniques indicates that there were no diachronic changes in the annual or long-term use of villages.

Subsequent research may show that Three Circle phase pithouse dwellers made more frequent use of masonry than their predecessors. Shafer (1995:28) observed late Three Circle phase pithouses with masonry-lined walls at the NAN Ranch. Inspection of the unpublished Cameron Creek village pithouse

architectural plans (LA 190) shows that many of the rectangular pithouses with long entrance ramps incorporated segments of masonry in their walls. Similar instances can be observed in low frequencies at the Harris Village (Haury 1936a) and the Lee Village (LA 5779). These masonry segments occur where new pithouses were excavated into the soft, middeny deposits of older structures. The pattern suggests that as sites were reused, people had to increase their efforts in order to produce reliable houses.

Posthole Densities

The density of posts (number of posts per m^2 of floor space) used in houses is a measure of both the initial investment in architectural construction and the episodes of remodeling that are a consequence of long-term use. The post density (D) for each pithouse is given by the formula $D = N/A$, where N is the number of posts in a house, and A is the floor area. Table 4.5 shows that Three Circle phase houses have more than twice as many posts per square meter as Early Pithouse period structures, and the difference is statis-

TABLE 4.4
WALL CONSTRUCTION MATERIALS IN UPLAND MOGOLLON PITHOUSES, BY OCCUPATION INTERVAL

Occupation Interval	Simple Pits (no masonry)	Pits with Less than 50% Masonry[a]	Pits with More than 50% Masonry[a]	Total Pits
Early Pithouse period	33	1	1	35
Georgetown phase	30	2	3	35
San Francisco phase	28	0	1	29
Three Circle phase	68	5	0	73

[a] Percentage of the circumference of the pit that used masonry in the pit wall.

Note: No significant difference was found between time intervals in the use of masonry in pits. $N = 172$ (15 missing data).

TABLE 4.5
SPJOTVOLL-STOLINE ANALYSIS OF VARIANCE OF MEAN VALUE OF POST DENSITY, BY OCCUPATION INTERVAL

Occupation Interval	Mean Density (posts/m^2)	Early Pithouse Period	Georgetown Phase	San Francisco Phase
Early Pithouse period	0.19			
Georgetown phase	0.32	$p = 0.24$		
San Francisco phase	0.43	$p = 0.03$	$p = 0.66$	
Three Circle phase	0.52	$p = 0.00$	$p = 0.06$	$p = 0.76$

tically significant using a Spjotvoll-Stoline analysis of variance of means test ($p < 0.1$ for all comparisons between the Three Circle phase and other phases). Moreover, it is noteworthy that although earlier between-phase comparisons are not significant, the relative amounts of effort invested in construction and remodeling of houses increased through time and the likelihood of significant differences increases as well.

The increase in the density of posts used in structures indicates that the average duration of house occupation increased through time. This increase took the form either of longer episodes of continuous occupation within one year or longer episodes of reoccupation on a multiple-year scale of analysis. The low significance of differences (p) of mean post densities in temporally adjacent phases indicates that the trend was a gradual process, rather than a sudden fundamental shift in the nature of land use.

House Remodeling and Repair

This research uses evidence of structure remodeling as an index of the long-term use of a structure on a scale of many years. Table 4.6 shows that, for all occupation phases, most pithouses lacked evidence for remodeling. The proportion of remodeled houses, however,

increased from an inconsequential amount during the San Francisco phase and earlier phases to 26 percent in the Three Circle phase. This pattern indicates that the use of houses increased from a comparatively short number of years of continuous use or of annual reoccupation during and before the San Francisco phase to longer use-intervals during the Three Circle phase.

Discussion

Four of the five architectural indices used in this study suggest that throughout the Mogollon Pithouse periods, the effort invested in the construction and maintenance of dwellings increased. The changes summarized in table 4.7 indicate that the occupation duration of buildings increased. Three Circle phase houses were occupied for longer intervals, or, alternatively, the total number of years in which the structure was occupied was longer than the occupations of Early Pithouse period and Georgetown phase structures.

Apart from two studies (Binford 1990; Diehl 1992) that establish broad temporal limits for occupation, there are few established guidelines that allow us to interpret differences in construction in terms of the number of days a structure was occupied in any given

TABLE 4.6
PRESENCE OR ABSENCE OF REMODELING IN UPLAND MOGOLLON PITHOUSES, BY OCCUPATION INTERVAL

Occupation Interval	Remodeling Absent	Remodeling Present	% Remodeled
Early Pithouse period	50 (45.9)	1 (5.1)	2
Georgetown phase	34 (32.4)	2 (3.6)	6
San Francisco phase	23 (22.5)	2 (2.5)	8
Three Circle phase	46 (52.2)	12 (5.8)	21

Note: Chi-square = 11.9; $p = 0.007$. $N = 170$ (17 missing data).

TABLE 4.7
SUMMARY OF CHANGES IN ARCHITECTURAL INDICES OF OCCUPATION DURATION/RESIDENTIAL MOBILITY, BY OCCUPATION INTERVAL

Occupation Interval	Dominant Wall Type	% with Formal Hearth	% with Plaster	Mean Post Density (posts/m^2)	% with Remodeling
Early Pithouse period	Pit	53	28	0.19	2
Georgetown phase	Pit	85	45	0.32	6
San Francisco phase	Pit	96	56	0.43	8
Three Circle phase	Pit	94	87	0.52	21

year, or the number of years a structure was reoccupied. It is not possible to calibrate precisely the relative changes documented in this study with absolute differences in the use-lives of dwellings. Future research in which the excavation of houses systematically includes the documentation of evidence for remodeling may allow us to isolate the covariances among indices of different scales of occupation.

The theoretical discussion upon which these analyses were based provides some interpretive yardsticks against which the McAnally pithouses may be compared. Gilman's (1987) cross-cultural study strongly suggests that, as pithouses, Units 8 and 11 were occupied at least during the winter months. Diehl's (1992) research suggests that tangible evidence of substantial investment—that is, construction using earth and prepared wood—is consistent with infrequent episodes of household migration. McAnally's occupants probably did not move more than once or twice per year. Other avenues of investigation that draw upon design theory suggest that redundancy in construction such as the close occurrence of two posts (A and B) in Unit 11 either represents an effort to increase the longevity of pithouses during their initial construction or is a consequence of actual long-term use that required some remodeling. Nevertheless, the presence of only thin, single layers of floor plaster indicates that the occupation of McAnally pithouses was briefer and less intense than the occupation of, for example, Pueblo period structures at other sites that have multiple, thick layers of floor plaster.

Despite the danger inherent in generalizing from too few data points, we offer the following preliminary interpretation. The McAnally site was occupied by semisedentary people who returned annually to the same basic winter residence. We suspect, but are at this point unable to verify, that the duration of occupation for McAnally pithouses was substantial, encompassing

most of the year (at least 240 days). Given the preliminary nature of the Thompson excavations, we may speculate that houses there were similar in size and construction and were used in similar ways.

Early Pithouse period sites such as Thompson and McAnally provide the baseline against which later structures may be compared. Based on the analyses in this chapter, we further propose that more recent San Francisco and Three Circle phase sites were occupied more intensively: They were occupied for longer intervals during the year or were repeatedly occupied over a longer span of years. We suspect that Three Circle phase houses were occupied for at least ten months annually. Additionally, Three Circle phase pithouses had longer effective use-lives than their Early Pithouse period counterparts.

SUMMARY

In this chapter we examined changes in the wall construction material, formality of hearth construction, mean number of posts per square meter of floor space, use of floor and wall plaster, and evidence of remodeling found in structures. Diachronic changes in these attributes were used to infer changes in the anticipated and actual occupation durations of Mogollon villages. These analyses indicated that from the Early Pithouse period (A.D. 200–600) through the Three Circle phase (A.D. 825/850–1000), residential mobility decreased gradually and the total use-life of structures increased. Pithouses were likely occupied for longer intervals per year. Occupations on the order of 10 to 12 months occurred during the Three Circle phase, as compared to 8 to 10 months during the Early Pithouse period. Also, Three Circle phase pithouses may have been continuously used for greater numbers of years than their Early Pithouse period counterparts.

5 Paleobotanical Remains

Michael W. Diehl and Paul E. Minnis

The analysis of prehistoric plant remains provides a means of identifying the different kinds of plants used by prehistoric people and understanding changes in their use. Obviously, these analyses are important for understanding prehistoric diets, yet many of the plant remains that archaeologists find had uses that were totally unrelated to diet. Wood was used for fuel, architecture, and tools, for example; fibers were used for manufacturing clothing and tools; and still other plant remains had uses that remain hidden from archaeologists. Other kinds of plant remains, such as pollen, provide evidence of the changes in the immediate environment around the site.

Interpretive caution must be used because the archaeological visibility of different kinds of plants and plant tissues is conditioned by the ways in which the plants were utilized and by the physical and chemical properties of the plants themselves. For example, maize tissue is dense, and maize cobs were often used as a source of fuel. As a consequence, charred pieces of maize are often found in or near hearths. Charring changes the chemical nature of organic tissues, rendering them relatively impervious to forces of biodecomposition (Miksicek 1987). In contrast, beans are usually prepared for consumption by boiling. This process renders them soft, and the likelihood that beans will be accidentally charred does not seem to be very great. As a consequence, the proportion of bean tissue versus maize tissue recovered from archaeological deposits may not accurately reflect the relative dietary importance of the two plants (Miksicek 1987; Pearsall 1989). Spatial and temporal differences in the organization of subsistence tasks are, accordingly, assessed by examining changes in the distributions of each species individually. Table 5.1 provides a list of common and taxonomic names of plants to which this chapter refers.

EXCAVATION AND PROCESSING METHODS

The excavators of the McAnally and Thompson sites collected 5-liter macrobotanical samples from every excavated feature (ash concentrations, hearths, pits, postholes, and the like), as well as nonsystematically selected samples from other depositional contexts. Although a large number of samples were collected, flotation and preliminary sorting revealed that only five samples contained charred seeds and three contained charred wood. Paul Minnis of the University of Oklahoma examined the plant remains and identified the plant taxa, using a variable 10x–20x binocular microscope and an extensive comparative collection of indigenous Southwestern woods and seeds. The recovered taxa and the provenience distributions of the different seed species are described in table 5.2. In this and subsequent tables, "U-L-L/#" refers to the

TABLE 5.1
LATIN TAXONOMIC AND COMMON NAMES OF PLANTS FOUND IN McANALLY AND THOMPSON SITE SAMPLES

Alphabetized by Common Name	Latin Name	Alphabetized by Latin Name	Common Name
Ash	*Fraxinus* sp.	*Acer negundo*	Box elder
Aster/Sunflower family	Compositae	*Amaranthus* sp.	Pigweed
Box elder	*Acer negundo*	*Ambrosia* sp.	Ragweed
Buckwheat	*Eriogonum* sp.	*Argemone platyceras*	Thistle poppy
Cattails	*Typha* sp.	*Artemesia* sp.	Sage
Common reed	*Phragmites* sp.	*Atriplex* sp.	Saltbush
Cottonwood	*Populus* sp.	*Caryx* sp.	Sedge
Duckweed	*Lemna* sp.	*Chenopodium* sp.	Goosefoot
Emory oak	*Quercus emorii*	Compositae	Aster/Sunflower family
Globe mallow	*Spheralcea* sp.	*Ephedra* sp.	Mormon tea/Joint fir
Goosefoot	*Chenopodium* sp.	*Eriogonum* sp.	Buckwheat
Grass family	Gramineae	*Fraxinus* sp.	Ash
Juniper	*Juniperus* sp.	Gramineae	Grass family
Knotweed	*Polygonum* sp.	*Helianthus* sp.	Sunflower
Maize	*Zea mays*	*Juniperus* sp.	Juniper
Mormon tea/Joint fir	*Ephedra* sp.	*Juglans* sp.	Walnut
Oak	*Quercus* sp.	*Lemna* sp.	Duckweed
Pigweed	*Amaranthus* sp.	*Opuntia* sp.	Prickly pear
Pine	*Pinus* sp.	*Phragmites* sp.	Common reed
Piñon pine	*Pinus edulis*	*Pinus edulis*	Piñon pine
Prickly pear	*Opuntia* sp.	*Pinus* sp.	Pine
Purslane	*Portulaca* sp.	*Polygonum* sp.	Knotweed
Ragweed	*Ambrosia* sp.	*Populus* sp.	Cottonwood
Rose family	Rosaceae	*Portulaca* sp.	Purslane
Sage	*Artemesia* sp.	*Quercus emorii*	Emory oak
Saltbush	*Atriplex* sp.	*Quercus* sp.	Oak
Sedge	*Caryx* sp.	Rosaceae	Rose family
Sunflower	*Helianthus* sp.	*Salix* sp.	Willow
Thistle poppy	*Argemone platyceras*	*Spheralcea* sp.	Globe mallow
Walnut	*Juglans* sp.	*Typha* sp.	Cattails
Willow	*Salix* sp.	*Zea mays*	Maize

TABLE 5.2
FREQUENCIES OF CHARRED SEEDS FROM
THE McANALLY AND THOMPSON SITES

Site	Unit (U-L-L)	*Zea mays*	*Chenopodium/ Amaranthus* sp.	*Portulaca* sp.	*Juniperus* sp.	Unknown
McAnally	8-6-11/1	0	0	0	0	2
	11-3-6/8	6	3	0	0	0
Thompson	1-3-4/8	0	0	1	0	0
	2-2-2/2	0	1	1	0	0
	2-2-2/6	0	9	6	0	0

excavation unit (pithouse), level, locus, and specimen number associated with the sample. The recording system that was used while excavating the McAnally and Thompson sites is discussed in detail in chapter 10.

SEEDS AND DIET

Inspection of table 5.2 reveals little about the breadth or intensity of the use of different plant resources that were available to the occupants of the McAnally and Thompson sites. Nevertheless, a few facts are apparent. Agricultural plants, especially maize, were a component of the diet. Although beans and squash were not present in the plant assemblages from these sites, their use cannot be discounted, since both are less durable than maize. A recent synopsis of radiocarbon dates from agricultural plants in Southwestern rockshelters demonstrates that maize and squash were introduced into the Southwest around 4,500 radiocarbon years ago, with beans being introduced perhaps slightly more recently (Mabry 1998:83–87). Furthermore, in the few Early Pithouse sites where preservation was exceptionally good, as at LA 5407, bean and squash seeds and other tissues have been recovered in great quantity.

In addition to agricultural products, a variety of wild plants that were available in the immediate vicinity of these sites were probably used by their occupants. Table 5.3 (below) lists the plants that have been identified in Upland Mogollon Early Pithouse period villages. Especially noteworthy is the frequent presence of piñon nuts at the LA 5407 and SU sites. High in protein and fats (Lanner 1981:101), piñon nuts would have been a welcome supplement to a diet based on agriculture. Like agricultural

plants, piñon nuts would have been easy to harvest in large quantities, when available, and could have been stored for use throughout the winter. Hastorf (1980) suggested that Pithouse period resource use may have placed greater emphasis on piñon than on maize because of the nutritional value and the occasional occurrence of bumper crops of piñon. We disagree with her suggestion, as we discuss below.

Piñon and Maize

A comparison of the growth characteristics, yields, and availability of piñon nuts and maize provides a framework for understanding problems associated with the use of these two plants. From the vantage point of a villager who could choose to invest energy in farming or in nut gathering, piñon nuts were less predictable, less reliable, cost more to obtain and process, and provided lower yields than maize. Occasionally (every five years or so) a good piñon crop was available. For these reasons it seems likely that even for Early Pithouse period villagers, maize was the more important dietary staple. As with most things that have been said about pithouse occupations, our hypothesis requires further testing, but the basis for the idea may be discussed here.

Although the problems associated with farming in the Southwest are complex, it is safe to state that maize would have produced at least a modest crop in most years. Humans can monitor fields and promote the growth of crops through irrigation, hand watering, hoeing, and the removal of crop-damaging pests. Since the growing season in the vicinity of the McAnally and Thompson sites typically lasts from 180 to 220 days, prehistoric villagers would have been able to respond to variations in the timing and availability of rainfall from year to year by maintaining several plots that were planted at staggered intervals (Minnis 1985a). Furthermore, the location of maize plants in floodplains and arroyo outwashes would have ensured access to water, since the Rio Mimbres flows even in years of mild to modest drought.

In contrast, piñon nut groves would have produced comparable yields much less frequently. The growth of pine nuts requires two successive years of average rainfall. Consequently, as noted by Krugman and Jenkinson (1974), piñon pines typically produce a large yield about every five years, depending on the local climate. Nut collection is extremely labor intensive, requiring the collection and processing of 100 pounds of seed cones for every 2 pounds of *potentially* edible nuts (Krugman and Jenkinson 1974:622). Since these pines grow along hill flanks rather than in drainage bottoms, the water catchment effects of local topography are less effective at ameliorating drought conditions in low-rainfall years.

For piñon pines, low rainfall in the second year of growth leads to a high rate of spontaneous seed abortion. Two pounds of harvested seeds might yield almost two pounds of edible nuts in a good year, but in poor years the yields are lower because many of the harvested seeds contain aborted, inedible nuts. A mechanism is available to plant scientists to separate aborted seeds from viable (and edible) ones through flotation, but that mechanism was probably energetically expensive to prehistoric people who lacked the conveniences of modern plumbing. Flotation in water, ethanol, or kerosene can be used to separate the seedless, aborted hulls from the viable ones (Krugman and Jenkinson 1974). Obviously, for prehistoric people the only available flotation medium was water; to use flotation to extract aborted seeds, people had to either transport very large quantities of the unshelled seeds to large sources of water or transport large quantities of water to the sources of seeds. An alternative was to pay the usual energetic costs of parching and milling all nut hulls at the source and accept much lower energetic returns. Either way, a considerable amount of labor (monitoring costs, travel, harvesting, transport of seeds or water, and processing) would have been invested in return for low caloric yields. In years with low piñon yields, prehistoric people probably avoided use of this resource, since the alternative entailed costly efforts at harvesting and processing a crop composed primarily of aborted, inedible shells. During good years, intrinsic piñon yields were reduced through resource competition by rodents, squirrels, birds, and possibly other humans.

Maize was a superior resource when compared with piñon nuts. The transportation costs associated with traveling to fields and returning with the harvested crops were minimal. There were no search costs. Harvesting was straightforward, and problems of recognizing inedible or aborted maize cobs were minimal because inedible tissue was identified at a glance. Maize did not require two years to produce, so it was less susceptible to the vicissitudes of weather. Furthermore, the average two-year yield of a prehistoric agricultural field was probably much greater than the average two-year yield of piñon stands. Finally, the location of maize was controllable, while the location of productive piñon stands was beyond the control of humans.

A small measure of amelioration of the effects of unpredictable yields and competition by other animals could be achieved by monitoring the development of distant piñon stands. When it occasionally happened that a good harvest was expected and realized, people probably moved away from their villages to gather rather abundant nut yields. On a long-term basis, however, we suspect that maize was probably the more important crop. Maize and other agricultural products were, as compared with virtually all of the other major food plants, more reliable, more predictable, and more easily controlled and manipulated. Prehistoric horticulturists could routinely expect to meet a large portion of their annual consumption needs from their own gardens. Probably the subsistence economy of Early Pithouse villagers centered on horticulture with substantial contributions from other resources when they became available.

It must be recognized that the preceding discussion is largely theoretical and limited by the general dearth of flotation samples from Upland Mogollon sites. As a preliminary hypothesis, the statement that "maize was more important than piñon nuts or any other wild plant resource" requires further testing through the systematic study of flotation samples. If this assessment is incorrect, then one would expect to find larger quantities of piñon nuts than maize kernels in archaeological deposits, and a prevalence of tools associated with nut processing rather than those associated with maize processing. Since both maize and piñon produce dense, inedible by-products (cupules for maize, nut shells for piñon), both have high potential recovery rates and their occurrence in archaeological deposits should closely correspond to the frequency of their use.

Archaeologically, the tools used for processing

piñon are macroscopically indistinguishable from the tools used for other large-seeded resources, including maize. Processing required, minimally, vessels (pottery or baskets) in which the nuts and their shells could be parched to render the shells brittle, mortars and pestles or manos and metates to fracture the shells and release the edible seeds, and vessels again for winnowing the inedible shell fragments from the seeds.

Other Seeds

Of the other seeds recovered from the McAnally and Thompson samples, we know that portulaca and goosefoot produce edible (but small) starchy seeds, and that the leaves were used by some Native American groups as potherbs (Minnis 1985a, 1985b). These two plants grow particularly well in disturbed soil—the kind of environment produced by clearing fields for agriculture (Parker 1990). As such, these plants probably flourished in association with horticultural plants. In all likelihood, the occupants of the McAnally and Thompson sites took advantage of local bounties of these plants when and where they became available.

Juniper seeds were also found in one McAnally site sample. Since these seeds are large and are enclosed in a larger fruit, they are unlikely to have been introduced into archaeological sites by accident. Their presence in the McAnally sample is likely a consequence of the consumption of berries, or possibly of the introduction of boughs into some household context.

INTERSITE DISTRIBUTIONS OF SEEDS AT MOGOLLON EARLY PITHOUSE VILLAGES

Owing to inadequate sample sizes, it is difficult to assess the importance of the different plants to the prehistoric occupants of the McAnally and Thompson sites. By examining the distributions of plant taxa from other pithouse villages we may address uses of plants by Mogollon Early Pithouse period villagers in general. The ubiquities (proportional frequency of samples in which the taxon was observed) of different plants from different archaeological sites are listed in table 5.3. To determine the ubiquity of a taxon, the number of samples that contained at least one charred seed of that species is divided by the total number of

analyzed samples that contained at least one charred seed of any species. Ubiquity is a crude measure of the spatial pervasiveness of contexts in which a plant was used. As such, it can be used to compare differences in the importance of a single species at different sites or different points in time. Note that this use of ubiquity assumes that people at different sites, but who seem to be members of the same culture, would have used any given species in a similar fashion at all sites.

Although the frequencies are not statistically conclusive, they suggest that Mogollon Early Pithouse villagers pursued two seed-gathering strategies. One strategy (call it "Strategy 1") focused on agricultural plants (maize, beans, and squash) and on plants that thrive in disturbed soils and produce starchy seeds (amaranth, goosefoot, purslane). These are all plants that grew well in and around agricultural plots and would have been easily monitored and harvested at the appropriate time. The other strategy ("Strategy 2") targeted climax vegetation that produced large, edible fruits or seeds, such as piñon nuts and juniper berries. Since Early Pithouse villagers were largely unable to affect the availability of tree seeds, Strategy 2 may have required the formation of special-purpose task groups that moved to the locations of productive tree stands.

Of the less ubiquitous plants, sunflower (*Helianthus* sp.) is a disturbance plant that could have been acquired under Strategy 1. Walnut (*Juglans* sp.) is a riparian tree that would have provided an extremely valuable resource if available in sufficient quantities. The availability of walnuts is difficult to assess. The species in question would have been *J. microcarpa* and *J. major*, but walnut productivity is not well documented (Brinkman 1974).

DIACHRONIC CHANGES IN THE USE OF MAIZE

Despite the relatively small number of samples upon which diachronic comparisons can be made, analyses of charred macroplant remains suggest that the occupants of Mogollon Early Pithouse period villages may have consumed less maize than occupants of Late Pithouse (Three Circle phase) villages. Table 5.4 describes differences in the ubiquity of charred maize from different kinds of depositional contexts from Mogollon Pithouse period sites. When considering samples from all contexts, however, there is no significant difference in the ubiquity of maize between the

TABLE 5.3
UBIQUITIES OF PLANT SEEDS AT VARIOUS
UPLAND MOGOLLON EARLY PITHOUSE VILLAGES

			Site			
Plant	LA 5407	SU Site	Promontory	Duncan	McAnally	Thompson
Cucurbita sp.	12%	0	50%	0	0	0
Phaseolus sp.	15%	0	0	0	0	0
Zea mays	73%	100%	100%	71%	50%	0
Chenopodium/ *Amaranthus* sp.	61%	14%	0	43%	50%	100%
Compositae	19%	7%	0	0	0	0
Gramineae	12%	7%	0	43%	0	
Pinus edulis	23%	14%	0	0	0	0
Juniperus sp.	8%	64%	50%	0	50%	0
Unknown	12%	14%	50%	14%	50%	0
Helianthus annuus	15%	0	0	0	0	0
Sporobolus sp.	4%	0	0	0	0	0
Portulaca sp.	4%	14%	0	0	0	100%
Juglans sp.	0	29%	0	0	0	0
Opuntia sp.	0	7%	0	0	0	0
Number of samples per site	26	14	2	7	2	2

Sources: LA 5407 (identification by M. Diehl; MollieToll, personal communication, 1993); SU (identification by M. Diehl; McBride 1989); Promontory (identification by M. Diehl); Duncan (Lightfoot 1984); McAnally and Thompson (Paul Minnis, personal communication, 1993).

TABLE 5.4
UBIQUITIES OF MAIZE FROM UPLAND MOGOLLON PITHOUSE INTERVALS

Occupation Interval	All Contexts	All Intramural Contexts	Floor Features Only
Early Pithouse period	77% ($N = 53$)	75% ($N = 44$)	66% ($N = 27$)
San Francisco phase	75% ($N = 8$)	66% ($N = 6$)	$N = 0$
Three Circle phase	69% ($N = 16$)	69% ($N = 16$)	100% ($N = 8$)

N = number of sampled features for that context and occupation interval.

Early and Late Pithouse time frames. There are differences when just floor features are compared, and maize is more common in the later floor features. For reasons that are detailed below, we prefer the data from floor features for diachronic comparisons of maize use. The diachronic trends in the recovery of plants from floor features are consistent with studies of ground stone tools (chap. 6) that suggest that the per capita consumption of maize increased steadily after A.D. 650. They also contradict suggestions by

Mauldin (1991) and Gilman (1987) that during the Pithouse periods, the importance of maize in the diets of Mogollon villagers remained stable and low.

Flotation samples from floor features are the most reliable source of information on maize consumption at Mogollon villages because the only flotation samples that can be meaningfully compared between sites come from intramural floor features. Therefore, although table 5.4 describes the ubiquities of maize from three levels of detail, all contexts include flotation samples that were recovered from extramural features, trash deposits in pithouse depressions, and intramural floor features. Intramural contexts include samples that were recovered from pithouse depressions and from floor features. Floor features only include samples that were recovered from the floor features in pithouses. We prefer the ubiquities derived from floor feature contexts.

Our preference for intramural floor features as appropriate sampling loci is attributable to several factors. First, floor features usually contain ash, charred remains, and floor detritus that are attributable to the last occupants of a house, barring post-occupational disturbance by animals. Schiffer (1987:97) noted that standards of maintenance may relax when the occupants of a house anticipate its imminent abandonment. Accordingly, floor features may provide an excellent sample of the plants used in a house, because the sample may be less affected by potentially irksome activities such as floor sweeping and hearth cleaning. In contrast, extramural features and pithouse fill are likely to contain debris from different occupation episodes. Such debris may include surface trash blown into extramural contexts from earlier and later occupations, trash dumped into pithouse depressions by subsequent occupants of the site, and trash produced by earlier occupants that became bound up in the walls when the house was constructed.

Second, since floor features are sheltered by a containing structure, they are less susceptible to contamination from economically unimportant plants than external features. Minnis (1981) noted that the natural seed rain in an area may introduce large quantities of seeds to archaeological contexts. Some of these are carried by wind or on clothing into intramural contexts, and some of these will in turn be brushed into fires or charred if the pithouse is burned after abandonment. The Minnis study does not directly address differences in the rate of seeds introduced to intramural as opposed to extramural contexts. But it is noteworthy that in a region where seed rain deposits millions of seeds per acre of land, only a few dozen were found in the intramural contexts that Minnis examined. We assume that the frequencies of naturally occurring charred seeds in floor features are lower than those in extramural features because of the additional shelter provided by the walls and roof.

Finally, most floor features are well dated. The temporal assignment of most pithouses is generally accurate to the scale of the occupation phase, based on the seriation of floor assemblages, house floor plans, and available radiocarbon and tree-ring dates from roof-beam fragments. In contrast, extramural contexts and intramural fill contexts are poor loci for diachronic comparisons because they either contain few potsherds or they contain mixed trash from different occupations of sites. Absolute dates from extramural contexts are rare, since few of them have been sampled for dendrochronological or radiocarbon specimens. Radiocarbon dates from recent excavations at Mogollon Village and the SU site indicate that extramural features at a site may substantially predate or postdate the pithouse occupation of the site (Duncan et al. 1991; Gilman et al. 1991; Wills 1991a).

CHARRED WOOD

Table 5.5 describes the frequencies of different wood taxa from McAnally and Thompson site flotation and radiocarbon samples. The archaeological presence of different wood species used by prehistoric people is primarily a consequence of the use of wood in fires (Miksicek 1987) and in architectural construction. Specimens of construction wood are often found in pithouses because Mogollon houses were often burned.

Inspection shows that juniper and piñon pine were the two most frequently used sources of architectural lumber and fuel at the McAnally and Thompson sites. The prevalence of juniper and piñon is consistent with the pattern of wood use at other Mogollon pithouse villages. Table 5.6 illustrates the distributions and ubiquities of the most prominent wood taxa by site and depositional context from several Early Pithouse period sites. Although samples of wood charcoal described in table 5.6 are not numerous, they constitute all of the identified wood charcoal samples from intramural contexts in Upland Mogollon Early Pithouse period villages. We suggest that these data are sufficient for the formulation of several hypotheses that may be evaluated in future research.

First, Mogollon Early Pithouse villagers used woods that were available within a few kilometers of each village. This hypothesis is based on the observation that, except for reeds, all of the wood taxa listed in table 5.6 are at present locally obtainable within 1 km of the sites in which they appear. If we assume that people avoided traveling far for wood that could be obtained nearby, then it follows that the pattern of

TABLE 5.5
FREQUENCIES OF CHARRED WOOD TAXA FROM THE McANALLY AND THOMPSON SITES, BY UNIT AND SAMPLE TYPE

	McAnally									Thompson
Wood Taxa	8-3-4* Flotation†	8-6-11/1* Flotation†	11-2-7* Flotation†	8-4-7/1* C-14†	8-5-2/2* C-14†	11-1-2/2* C-14†	11-3-7* C-14†	11-3-8* C-14†	11-4-5* C-14†	1-3-4* C-14†
Rosaceae	0	4	3	0	0	0	0	0	0	1
Fraxinus sp.	0	0	0	0	0	0	0	1	0	1
Populus/Salix sp.	0	0	2	0	0	0	0	2	0	4
Celtis sp.	0	0	0	0	0	0	0	0	0	2
Juniperus sp.	0	10	1	0	0	0	8	11	0	1
Monocot stem	0	0	0	0	0	0	0	1	0	0
Quercus sp.	0	9	0	0	0	0	1	0	0	3
Pinus edulis	5	1	11	5	5	5	8	0	5	0
Unknown	0	3	3	0	0	0	3	5	0	0

* Unit (U-L-L).
† Type of sample.

TABLE 5.6
UBIQUITIES OF CHARRED WOOD TAXA AT UPLAND MOGOLLON PITHOUSE VILLAGES, BY SITE AND CONTEXT

Site	Context	N	*Populus* or *Salix*	*Pinus edulis*	*Juniperus* sp.	Unknown Dicot	*Phragmites* sp.	*Quercus emoryii* sp.
LA 5407	Posts	20	0	70	50	10	5	0
	Fill	9	88	100	33	22	66	33
	Vessels	2	0	50	100	0	0	0
SU	Fill	3	67	100	100	100	0	67
Promontory	Fill	2	50	100	100	0	0	0
McAnally	Feature	1	0	100	100	100	0	100
	Fill	2	50	100	50	50	0	50
Thompson	Feature	1	100	0	100	100	0	0

Sources: Thompson and McAnally sites: Paul Minnis (personal communication, 1993). All others analyzed by Diehl.
N = number of analyzed contexts.

wood use indicates that most fuel and architectural wood was obtained within a relatively short distance.

Second, during the Early Pithouse period, land use was not sufficiently intense to cause the depletion of local riparian wood resources. In turn, this may suggest that agricultural land clearance was not so widespread as to seriously alter the local forest ecology. Low-intensity agricultural land clearing is consistent with the suggestion that Early Pithouse villagers were not as intensively agricultural as their Late Pithouse and Classic Mimbres period counterparts. Low-intensity land clearing, however, is also consis-

tent with the suggestion that Mimbres Valley populations (and those of other Mogollon localities) were very low (Blake et al. 1986; Lekson 1992b) during the first few centuries A.D. The absence of damage to the riparian wood community is supported by the observation of both riparian and xerophytic plants in most of the Early Pithouse period flotation and architectural wood samples. The results presented here may be compared with Minnis's analyses of Classic Mimbres period (A.D. 1000–1150) samples, which contained low ubiquities of riparian woods. Minnis suggested that the Classic Mimbres occupants of the middle Rio

Mimbres valley harvested riparian woods to near depletion—in effect exhausting the local riparian wood supply (Minnis 1985a:88–90). If we assume that the presence of high-visibility, easily harvested sources of firewood indicates that such woods were still locally available, then it follows that riparian deforestation was not a problem in the Early Pithouse period.

Finally, we suggest that Mogollon Early Pithouse villagers selectively favored juniper and piñon for architectural construction. It is interesting to note that postholes at LA 5407 and McAnally contained primarily juniper and piñon, even though cottonwood was widely available. Cottonwood and willow, although abundant in the area, were not heavily used in construction. Both conifer species contain resins that confer resistance to the depredations of insects and dry rot (Schiffer 1987:165–167), whereas cottonwood and willow have relatively poor decay resistance. Early Pithouse villagers may have been aware of the decay-resistant properties of juniper and piñon and may have preferred these species for construction materials for this reason.

POLLEN

Pollen samples from the McAnally and Thompson sites were collected and analyzed in order to assess spatiotemporal differences in room function, site function, and subsistence strategies within and between sites. Although the raw pollen counts have not heretofore been published, a detailed discussion of those analyses has been previously available (Anyon and LeBlanc 1984:201–213). Raw pollen scores for different depositional contexts at the McAnally and Thompson sites are listed in table 5.7. The utility of recording pollen aggregates, a very valuable and useful procedure, was unknown when these samples were counted in the 1970s. A brief discussion follows that recapitulates the results of the earlier study.

Most of the pollen samples from the McAnally and Thompson sites were collected from the floor surfaces of pithouses by scraping away a thin layer of the floor surface (to eliminate modern contaminants) and removing a 1- to 2-cm-thick chunk of floor. The ash-pit sample was collected by removing the sample from the bottom of the pit in a similar fashion. One sample (McAnally 11-5F-5/15) was recovered by washing pollen from the partially cleaned surface of a metate that had been sealed in a bag immediately upon exca-

vation (Halbirt 1985). Another sample from the same unit was taken from soil on top of a metate, but it was not an actual pollen wash. The extraction of the pollen from soil samples followed procedures described by Mehringer (1967) for alkaline soils.

Mimbres Foundation analyses compared pollen samples from the Thompson and McAnally sites against samples recovered from 11 other Mimbres Valley archaeological sites (Anyon and LeBlanc 1984). Occupation of the 13 Mimbres Valley sites spanned the Early Pithouse period (A.D. 200–550) through the Cliff phase (late fourteenth century). Mimbres Foundation analysts focused on changes in the ratio of *pinus* to *juniperus* (P-J ratio), the ratio of *Chenopodium/Amaranthus* (goosefoot and amaranth) to Gramineae (grass family) (CA-G ratio), and the ratio of high-spine to low-spine Compositae (H-L ratio). Spatial and temporal variation in the P-J ratio may provide evidence of changes in the local abundance of rain (Anyon and LeBlanc 1984:206; Euler et al. 1979). Changes in the CA-G and H-L ratios may be used to measure the amount of disturbance in the vicinity of archaeological sites (Anyon and LeBlanc 1984:206; Euler et al. 1979; Fish 1984).

Factor analyses of different ratios from Mimbres Valley sites indicated that local plant communities were affected by the populations of nearby villages. The results revealed relatively high rates of disturbance around Late Pithouse period and Mimbres Classic period villages and low disturbances—and, by inference, lower populations—at Early Pithouse villages and Cliff phase villages (Anyon and LeBlanc 1984:206). More data are needed in order to assess the statistical significance of the temporal differences in the proportional frequencies of different pollen types. At present, pollen spectra from Mimbres Valley sites show that Mogollon Early Pithouse period villages may have been occupied less intensively than later Mogollon sites. Here, "less intensively" is taken to mean either that early villages were occupied by fewer people or that they were occupied for less time on the average (or both) than later villages. As a cautionary note, it should be added that the interpretation of pollen ratios from Early Pithouse period contexts is complicated because early sites are usually found in elevated locations that are quite removed from the locations of later sites. When this factor is combined with the low number of samples from Early Pithouse period contexts, the results presented here must be viewed as preliminary findings.

TABLE 5.7
POLLEN COUNTS FROM McANALLY AND THOMPSON SITE SAMPLES, BY UNIT AND CONTEXT

	McAnally							Thompson		
Pollen Type	8-4-7/1* Floor†	8-6-10/2* Ash pit†	8-4-3/2* Floor†	11-5-5/19a* Floor†	11-5-5/15v Metate†	11-2-6/12* Metate†	11-5-5/19b* Floor†	1-3-4/5* Floor†	2-2-2/7* Floor†	2-2-2/5* Floor†
Arboreal pollen										
Pinus sp.	1	5	2	5	9	4		4	2	
Juniperus sp.	4	67	7	6	15	29	6	3	5	
Populus sp.				2	2		4			6
Quercus sp.	2			1	2		1			3
Salix sp.								1		
Acer sp.									2	
Unknown	1									
Chenopodium/ Amaranthus sp.	182	13	169	135	110	75	91	337	199	260
Compositae (Low spine)	20	12	16	22	37	17	31	10	13	23
Compositae (High spine)	4	5	3	3	8	2	4	4	12	9
Gramineae	25	100	55	31	31	86	58	30	41	33
Artemisia sp.				2		0	4	3	1	2
Ambrosia sp.	2									
Lemna sp.	1		1					1	1	
Cleome sp.	1				1	0				
Rubiaceae								1		
Tidestromis sp.								8	1	
Non-arboreal pollen										
Unknown								2	1	3
Liliaceae		0				0				
Euphorbia sp.									1	
Flouquieriaceae										1
Borhavia sp.										1
Zea mays	1	3	2	1			3		1	
Opuntia sp.	1	0						1		
Polygonae	1									
Typha sp.				1			1			
Leguminosae								4	2	3
Ephedra sp.									2	7
Cercex sp.							2			
TOTAL	245	205	255	204	215	220	204	408	282	351

* Unit (U-L-L).

† Context.

Note: Analyses performed by Richard Halbirt and Charles Miksicek.

CONCLUSION

Interpretations based on the analyses of charred seeds, wood, and pollen from the McAnally site and other pithouse villages are tenuous because of the small number of paleoethnobotanical samples available for study. Interpretations of diet and land use offered in this chapter should be viewed not as conclusive results, but rather as well-informed hypotheses, based both on the *best* of the presently available array of data and on considerations of the costs and benefits associated with the use of different resources. These working hypotheses should be the subject of future study. The hypotheses are listed below, and the data that support them are enclosed in parentheses.

1. Agricultural domesticates, including maize, beans, and squash, were present and moderately important in the diets of Mogollon Early Pithouse villagers (charred seeds).
2. During the Early Pithouse period, starchy and oily wild plants, including pigweed (*Amaranth*), goosefoot, and piñon were also important (charred seeds).
3. The dietary importance of agricultural domesticates increased continually during the Late Pithouse period (charred maize tissue).

4. Increased consumption of agricultural plants during the Late Pithouse period occurred at the expense of starchy wild plants such as pigweed and goosefoot.
5. Maize was used more intensively than piñon nuts during all Mogollon Pithouse period occupations (predicted from the known properties of maize and piñon).
6. Most of the wild plants, especially the wood, used by Mogollon pithouse villagers could have been obtained from within a few kilometers of residential sites (charred wood).
7. Mogollon Early Pithouse period villagers' subsistence strategies did not significantly deplete the wood resources available in the local riparian communities (charred wood).
8. Mogollon Early Pithouse villagers preferred to use decay-resistant, resinous woods such as juniper and pine for architectural construction (charred wood).
9. Mogollon Early Pithouse villages were occupied less intensively than Late Pithouse villages (pollen).

6 Ground Stone Analyses

Michael W. Diehl

Twenty-three ground stone tools or tool fragments were recovered from the McAnally and Thompson sites, most of them from the former. Specimens included whole manos and metates and fragments of the same, slabs, and a pipe "blank." Detailed descriptions of these tools are provided in table 6.1. Researchers who have reason to study the excavation notes from these sites will note that more artifacts are listed on the excavation forms. Specimens listed on the excavation forms that do not appear in the table were discarded because, after they were cleaned, close inspection resulted in their reclassification as rocks that were unaffected by human use.

This chapter compares the McAnally and Thompson samples with a more comprehensive study of manos and metates from the Upland Mogollon region. The purpose is to determine whether or not there were relative changes in the consumption of maize from the Early Pithouse period through the Three Circle phase. In making the assessment, this study evaluates models of Pithouse period land use by combining data from ground stone analyses and macrobotanical analysis. The results described here suggest that the first millennium A.D. saw a shift away from the foraging and horticultural land-use pattern that prevailed during the Early Pithouse period (A.D. 200–600) and Georgetown phase (A.D. 600–700) to a sedentary land-use pattern in which agriculture was

extremely important during the Three Circle phase (A.D. 825/850–1000). The transition may have started during the San Francisco phase (A.D. 700–825/850) and, as is discussed below, may be attributable to two events: the introduction of a more productive variety of maize during the late Georgetown phase and a possible fourfold increase in population in some areas of the Upland Mogollon region during the Pithouse periods.

NEW PLANTS AND HIGHER POPULATIONS: CATALYSTS FOR CHANGE?

This chapter documents a change in ground stone morphology that has been interpreted as evidence for an increase in maize consumption. According to the analyses reported below, the changes in ground stone morphology are statistically significant when Early Pithouse period and Georgetown phase tools are contrasted with those of the Three Circle phase. Furthermore, while the differences between San Francisco phase ground stone tools and those of prior and subsequent occupations are not statistically significant, the San Francisco phase manos fit neatly into a linear trend.

Two triggers of change have been identified. One

TABLE 6.1
GROUND STONE ARTIFACTS FROM THE McANALLY AND THOMPSON SITES

Site	Unit (U-L-L)	Description
McAnally	3-1-1/1	Metate fragment, possible trough type, basalt. Side and end moderately pecked. No obvious striations on the grinding surface. Thickness: 12 cm. Depth of trough: 3.5 cm. Length and width unknown.
	8-1-4/2	Metate fragment, indeterminate type, sandstone. Two concave grinding surfaces, pecked and ground. No obvious use-wear striations. Thickness 10.2 cm. Depth of basin or trough: obverse: 5.5 cm, reverse: 2.5 cm.
	8-3-3/2	Metate fragment, trough or full-trough type, vesicular basalt. One grinding surface. The bottom of the trough is basin shaped in cross section. Thickness: 20.7 cm. Length: unknown. Width: 30.3 cm. Depth of trough: 6.6 cm. Width of trough walls not specified.
	8-4-3/1	Mano, elliptical, unifacial, sandstone. Grinding surface convex lengthwise and in cross section. Length: 17.6 cm. Width: 13.9 cm. Thickness: 3.2 cm. Multiple linear striations in all directions. Grinding surface area: 95 cm^2.
	8-4-4/1	Mano fragment, basalt. One grinding surface, surface slightly convex lengthwise and in cross section, no obvious use-wear striations, pecked on ends. Length: 10.4–13 cm. Width: 5.2 cm at widest extent.
	8-4-7/2	Mano, rectangular, unifacial, vesicular basalt. Possible use-wear striations on the grinding surface, parallel to the short axis. Convex lengthwise and in cross section. Length: 19.0 cm. Width: 14.3 cm. Thickness: 6.8 cm. Grinding surface area: 244 cm^2.
	8-4-7/3	Mano, irregular oval, unifacial, basalt. Possible linear use-wear striations in multiple directions. Length: 20.9 cm. Width: 14.7 cm. Thickness: 4.6 cm. Grinding surface area: 246 cm^2.
	11-1-7/2	Mano, oval, unifacial, rhyolite. Convex lengthwise and in cross section. Possible use-wear striations parallel to the short axis. Length: 17.0 cm. Width: 13.3 cm. Thickness: 4.4 cm. Grinding surface area: 193 cm^2.
	11-2-6/12	Metate, trough type, sandstone. Length: 40.0 cm. Width: 21.6 cm. Thickness: 9.0 cm. Trough length: 25.7 cm. Width: 16.0 cm.
	11-2-6/13	Mano, rhyolite, bifacial, oval-shaped. Both surfaces convex lengthwise and in cross section. Striations in multiple directions on obverse, not evident on reverse. Both surfaces and sides pecked. Length: 14.4 cm. Width: 11.2 cm. Thickness: 5.8 cm. Grinding surface on obverse approximates the dimensions of the mano. Grinding surface on reverse is approximately 10.4 cm x 7.2 cm. Weight: 42 oz.
	11-2-7/9	Possible mano, bifacial, irregular, sandstone. Obverse grinding surface is slightly convex lengthwise and in cross section. Reverse grinding surface is flat. Both surfaces have linear use-wear striations running parallel to the long axis of the mano. Length: 22.2 cm. Width: 10.4 cm. Thickness: 3.2 cm. Weight: 48 oz.
	11-3-6/8	Mano, circular, unifacial, rhyolite. Grinding surface convex lengthwise and in cross section, except where heavily re-pecked near the center. No use-wear striations apparent on the grinding surface. Length: 11 cm. Width: 10.5 cm. Thickness: 7.7 cm. Weight: 55.5 oz.
	11-3-6/9	Mano, rectangular, unifacial, vesicular basalt. Convex lengthwise and in cross section. Possible use-wear striations parallel to the short axis. Length: 21.0 cm. Width: 13.3 cm. Thickness: 5.0 cm. Grinding surface area: 279 cm^2.
	11-3-6/11	Mano, rectangular, sandstone. Flat on both surfaces. No obvious use-wear striations. Length: 20.5 cm. Width: 11.9 cm. Thickness: 3.6 cm.

Continued on next page

TABLE 6.1 — *Continued*

Site	Unit (U-L-L)	Description
McAnally, *cont.*	11-3-6/12	Mano fragment, unifacial, vesicular basalt. Dimensions unknown.
	11-3-8/11	Mano, circular, unifacial, rhyolite. Length: 8.9 cm. Width: 7.5 cm. Thickness: 6.8 cm. Red mineral stain on grinding surface. Surface area: 61 cm^2.
	11-3-8/12	Metate, trough type, basalt. Length: 25.9 cm. Width: 20.4 cm. Thickness: 9.4 cm. Trough length: 25.7 cm. Width: 18.0 cm.
	11-5-1	Slab fragment, sandstone, ground on one face, fire-blackened. Thickness: 5.5 cm. Length: 16 cm. Width: unknown.
	11-5-5-15	Metate fragment, trough or through-trough type, vesicular basalt. Dimensions unknown.
	11-5-5/18	Slab, sandstone, half-lunate shaped, ground and pecked on both faces. Fire-blackened. Length: 33.0 cm. Width: 17.5 cm. Thickness: 3.1–4.0 cm.
	Unit 11 backdirt	Possible pipe blank, tubular, vesicular basalt, cylindrical. No bore.
Thompson	1-1-2/1	Stone disk (circular), material unknown. Obverse flat, reverse exfoliating. No apparent use-wear striations. Length: 9.4 cm. Width: 8.6 cm. Thickness: 1.3 cm.
	1-3-4/16	Mano, elliptical, bifacial, rhyolite. Convex lengthwise and in cross section. Possible use-wear striations along both axes. Length: 23.2 cm. Width: 18.4 cm. Grinding surface area: 362 cm^2.

possible catalyst for changes in ground stone morphology is the purported introduction of a new variety of maize (improved *maiz de ocho*) around A.D. 500–700 (Cutler 1952; Galinat 1988; Upham et al. 1987; Upham et al. 1988). Studies of maize morphology indicate that the new maize was a large-kernelled flour variety that replaced a smaller, flint-kernelled variety that had been introduced during the Archaic period. Persons interested in the occurrence of new varieties of maize in the Southwest should refer to Karen Adams's (1993) comprehensive overview.

We may speculate that as a larger-cobbed, bigger-kernelled, soft-kernelled variety, the new maize produced greater yields per plant than the older maize. It may also have been easier to grind. Both attributes may have made the new maize a more attractive plant to Mogollon pithouse villagers than the Archaic variety. Increased use of the plant may have occurred as its advantages became appreciated, and increased use may have led to increased per capita consumption of maize.

Population growth may have been a second catalyst for increased dependence on maize. Two demographic studies of Mimbres and Upper Gila population densities have documented a fourfold increase

in population between A.D. 650 and 1000. The analyses were based on comprehensive regional surface surveys (Blake et al. 1986; Lekson 1992b). Using observations about the frequency of sites from different occupation phases and frequencies of pithouses on different sites, these studies found that changes in the overall number of pithouses in the region are consistent with a fourfold increase in population and an annual population growth rate of 0.3 percent.

In addition to these lines of evidence, it appears that Three Circle and Classic Mimbres phase people made increasing use of less productive side drainages, where water flowed more intermittently (Minnis 1985a:58–60). This usage may be interpreted as a response to resource stress. Population increases would have placed more stress on the productivity of wild animals and would have increased competition for wild game and plants. Under such circumstances, the replacement of increasingly rare wild resources with cultivated maize is a logical expectation. In general, higher yields may be expected from maize than from wild plant resources, and in the face of increasing competition for wild foods, maize would have provided a less risky, more reliable food supply.

THE METHODOLOGY OF THE GROUND STONE ANALYSIS

This study uses changes in the morphology of prehistoric manos and metates (implements used to grind maize) in order to observe changes in the intensity of the consumption of maize in the Mogollon region. The analyses combine methods developed by Hard (1990), Lancaster (1983, 1984), and Mauldin (1991) for the study of manos. Related techniques for the analysis of metates are developed and used herein. Previous attempts to derive inferences regarding agricultural dependence from the morphology of grinding tools are discussed below.

Previous Research

During the 1930s, Southwestern archaeologists used nonquantitative observations about the morphology of manos and metates to reconstruct prehistoric subsistence practices. For example, Paul Martin (Martin 1943:177; Martin and Rinaldo 1947) suggested that the variety and frequency of different types of ground stone artifacts could be used to evaluate a prehistoric group's relative dependence on wild rather than domesticated foods. Mauldin (1991) noted that the same general idea was advanced as early 1933 by Bartlett (1933). Until the 1980s, however, archaeologists lacked well-developed theories to link mano morphology with agricultural dependence.

In the last two decades, several archaeologists used changes in the morphology of prehistoric grinding stones to infer changes in the intensity of agricultural production. Lancaster (1983, 1984) measured the lengths and widths of ground stone artifacts from Mimbres Valley sites and found that manos clustered into two categories (Type I and Type II) based on attributes of size and use-wear. The smaller Type I manos were most often used with a rotary grinding motion. They may represent a generalized grinding tool that was used to process many different substances. Type II manos were most often used in a linear motion (with striations running parallel to the short axis) and probably were used to grind corn (Lancaster 1984:251).

Cross-cultural comparative studies show that large manos are more efficient than smaller manos and that mean mano size is strongly associated with the dietary importance of agricultural crops. In a comparison of ethnographically known Southwestern groups, Hard found a strong and statistically significant correlation between the length of manos and the relative dependence on agriculture (Hard 1990:140). Mauldin (1991) studied maize grinding in a contemporary Bolivian village and found that local maize grinders could prepare more grain in a fixed amount of time with manos that had large surface areas than they could with smaller manos. In addition, large manos were used to mill grain, while small stones were used to process chile and salt.

Experimental research by Adams (J. Adams 1988, 1993) also shows that mano and metate morphology may be used to draw inferences about the efficiency of prehistoric grinding tools. Adams found that the use of two hands on a large mano in a trough metate allows grinders to mill more grain per unit of time than is possible with small manos and a basin metate. The use of large, flat metates with high-walled mealing bins is even more efficient than trough metates, because flat metates avoid some of the problems associated with the fit between the mano and trough metate pair. In short, larger manos (and associated metates) are more efficient than smaller manos, and flat-bottomed (trough and slab type) metates are more efficient than basin-bottomed metates for grinding corn.

Hard (1990) and Mauldin (1991) both examined prehistoric manos from the Upland Mogollon region, but they arrived at contradictory conclusions regarding the dependence on agriculture of prehistoric pithouse dwellers. Although Hard found "substantial dependence on agriculture in the Mimbres . . . area by A.D. 700" (Hard 1990:147), Mauldin (1991) found no evidence for a unidirectional change in mano size. Instead, Mauldin inferred "a pattern of fluctuating levels of agricultural dependence, with essentially the same level of agriculture in the diet at A.D. 400 and A.D. 1000" (Mauldin 1991:68). Both studies relied primarily on published descriptions from Paul Martin's excavations of villages in the Reserve branch.

Dietary Change, Time Stress, and Technological Change

Why should mano size be affected by agricultural dependence? Figure 6.1 illustrates a model, initially proposed by Hard (1990), that links changes in grinding-tool morphology with changes in agricultural production. Increases in maize production and consumption required greater amounts of time invested in grinding maize. Torrence (1983:12) suggested that, in general, where the total amount of time available for a

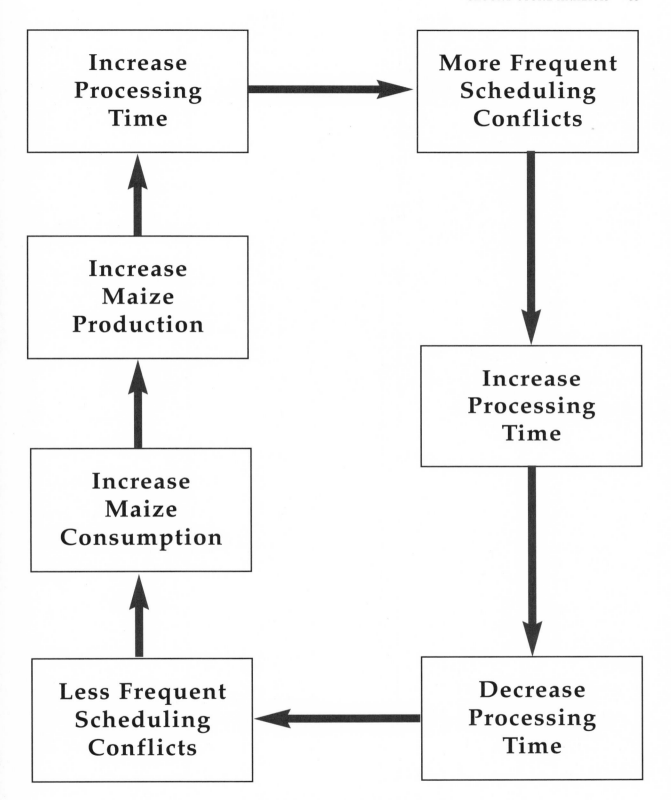

FIGURE 6.1. *The relationship between time stress, grinding tool size, and efficiency.*

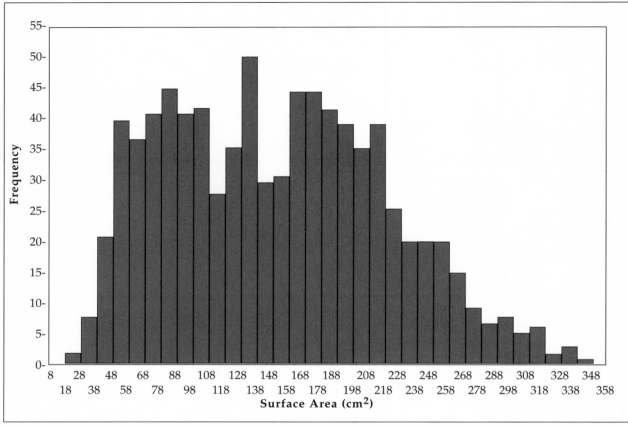

FIGURE 6.2. *Histogram of surface areas of manos from Upland Mogollon pithouse villages.*

specific task is limited, selective pressure should result in the development of tools that increase the speed at which activities are carried out. Therefore, as the per capita consumption of maize increased, the time required to prepare it would increase to the point where it conflicted with other tasks. Accordingly, prehistoric maize grinders would have welcomed any technological response that increased grinding efficiency and reduced the amount of time required to prepare food. Since the use of larger manos would have reduced the amount of time required to process each unit of maize, the use of these tools would have alleviated scheduling conflicts brought about by increased maize consumption.

Approaches Used in This Study

Although the present study builds on prior analyses of Mogollon grinding tools, it differs from Hard's (1990) and Mauldin's (1991) studies in several details. Prior studies have relied heavily on Paul Martin's descriptions of manos from the Reserve area (Martin

1943; Martin and Rinaldo 1947), but the "typical" and "average" dimensional data reported by Martin are judgmental estimates and not statistical means. In contrast, the present analyses are based primarily on direct examination of manos and metates in extant collections and archived drawings and descriptions of individual artifacts. More importantly, this study uses data from 14 sites rather than just the 4 Reserve area sites. Our sample of Pithouse period manos is considerably larger than the samples used by other researchers and represents a wider geographic area.

Finally, this study uses a finer-grained temporal scale. Hard and Mauldin both grouped manos into Early Pithouse and Late Pithouse temporal categories. In contrast, here each mano is assigned to a specific occupation phase: Early Pithouse period (A.D. 200–550), Georgetown phase (A.D. 550–700), San Francisco phase (A.D. 700–825/850), and Three Circle phase (A.D. 825/850–1000). In most cases, the phase assigned to each house by the excavator was the phase assigned to manos from that house. The phase assignments were, however, double-checked by examining

TABLE 6.2
MANOS FROM MOGOLLON PITHOUSE PERIOD SITES USED IN THIS RESEARCH

Site	Number of Manos	Location	Source of Data
SU	278	Reserve branch	Field Museum of Natural History
Turkey Foot Ridge	188	Reserve branch	Field Museum of Natural History
Promontory	33	Reserve branch	Field Museum of Natural History
Harris Village	14	Mimbres branch	Arizona State Museum
McAnally	12	Mimbres branch	Maxwell Museum of Anthropology, University of New Mexico
Galaz Ruin	48	Mimbres branch	Anyon and LeBlanc (1984)
Diablo Village	58	Upper Gila branch	Laboratory of Anthropology, Museum of New Mexico
Lee Village	40	Upper Gila branch	Laboratory of Anthropology, Museum of New Mexico
Winn Canyon	17	Upper Gila branch	Fitting (1973)
Duncan	47	Middle Gila River branch	Arizona State University, Department of Anthropology
Bear Ruin	39	Forestdale branch	Arizona State Museum
Bluff	29	Forestdale branch	Arizona State Museum
Crooked Ridge Village	165	Point of Pines branch	Arizona State Museum
Flattop	38	Petrified Forest branch	Museum of Northern Arizona

Note: Unless otherwise specified, the source of data is a collection.

excavation notes. Manos from SU site houses W, X, and Y were assigned to the Three Circle phase because the prevalence of Style I black-on-white ceramics in near-floor contexts indicated that these houses may have been filled with Three Circle phase trash.

MANO ANALYSES

Manos used in the following analyses were drawn from a population of 1,007 Mogollon Pithouse period manos from 14 sites. A histogram of the surface areas of these manos is presented in figure 6.2. The sites were excavated over six decades of research in the Mogollon area. Most of the data were obtained by physical inspection of the artifacts or from "stone list cards" that were created in lieu of retaining the actual tools. These cards provided measurements of the tool dimensions and shape, and often included measurements of the grinding surface areas and the wear patterns on the surfaces. Information on Winn Canyon manos was obtained from a publication (Fitting 1973). Sites that contributed to the ground stone analyses are listed in table 6.2. These sites were chosen because the

depositional contexts were well described, many of the manos were available for study, and most are housed in major museums where multiple collections were available for study.

Problems of Sample Bias

Three potential sources of sample bias were identified that could have affected this research. These are (1) sample bias caused by the insufficient recovery of samples from a broad range of excavation contexts, (2) sample bias caused by the inclusion of manos that were not primarily used to grind maize, and (3) sample bias caused by regional variation in the size of available raw materials. In the following discussion each of these potential sources of bias is assessed and addressed.

Potential Recovery Bias

Studies of changes in the morphology of prehistoric tools may be affected by biases caused by the recovery of manos from an insufficiently broad range of depositional contexts. In the case of grinding stones, Schlanger (1991) cautioned that the exclusive use of manos and metates from floor contexts may bias the results of studies of prehistoric grinding-tool morphology. Schlanger studied the discard patterns of whole and broken manos and trough metates. At sites with long occupations, fill assemblages accounted for larger proportions of all artifact classes than they did at short-occupation sites. According to Schlanger, the observed differences may be attributed to the effects of scavenging of floor assemblages and the dumping of expended tools into the fill of abandoned houses. The selection of manos from only one context might lead, for example, to the overrepresentation of manos that were excessively ground down because of scavenging and reuse. In effect, where scavenging and reuse were prevalent, the frequencies of small manos (which might be interpreted as one-hand manos) would be artificially inflated. A study of changes in mano size would therefore run the risk of analytical bias.

Fortunately, potential analytical biases from this source may be eliminated by the use of data from multiple depositional contexts. Close inspection of Schlanger's data indicates that, when the ground stone assemblages from different sites are compared in their entirety and when the sample includes ground stones from both floor contexts and fill contexts, the ratio of one-hand to two-hand manos in short-occupation sites is 0.25, while the ratio from longer-occupation sites is 0.27. The ratios do not differ significantly (chi-square = 1.16, $df = 1$, $p = 0.28$). Since intrasite variation in manos from intramural and extramural contexts probably does exist, this study eliminates the potential effects of sampling bias by using only manos that were recovered from both pithouse floor and fill assemblages.

Potential Bias Caused by Differences in Mano Use

The use of attributes of mano morphology to identify differences in the efficiency of maize processing may require that we be able to distinguish between manos associated with general-purpose use and others associated specifically with maize grinding. To ensure that this research tracked changes in the morphology of manos associated with maize grinding, I examined changes in the morphology and evidence of use-wear (following Lancaster 1983, 1984) and eliminated manos that were likely used for more general tasks. Large manos from the Galaz Ruin and other Mimbres sites exhibited linear striations, observable under low

magnification, caused by use-wear. According to experimental and ethnographic studies described earlier (J. Adams 1988, 1993; Hard 1990), the differences in the wear patterns observed on large and small manos may be attributed to differences in their use.

Under 10x magnification, striations associated with use-wear could be observed on 208 of the manos in this study. Of these, 137 had surface areas greater than 128 cm^2. In turn, 84 percent (115) of these had linear striations that ran parallel to their short axes. Seventeen other large manos had linear striations that ran both parallel to and perpendicular to their short axes. I attribute the presence of bidirectional linear wear to the expedient use, for other grinding purposes, of manos that were designed primarily for grinding maize. Ultimately, only five of the large manos bore evidence of curvilinear wear. It is my opinion, therefore, that at least 96 percent of the large manos in this study were used to grind maize.

Potential Bias Caused by Spatial Variation in Raw Material Size

Stone (1994) noted that geographical variation in raw material availability may affect ground stone size. If variation in site locations placed some sites closer to larger materials, then changes in the sizes of ground stones might simply track variation in the availability of larger raw materials. For geographic variation to affect the size of raw materials one would have to assume that there exists spatial variation in the size of locally available raw materials. This assumption is probably wrong since the geological localities of most of the sites used in this study, except Flattop, are regionally quite similar, and since the raw materials were likely obtained from secondary contexts—that is, riverbeds.

The proposition that geographic variation in raw materials affected tool size may, nevertheless, be tested by comparing the sizes of manos from different sites. Assume that people either selected the largest raw materials for large manos to process maize or they selected randomly from the local population of available raw materials. Under these conditions, intersite variation in the size of available raw materials should cause corresponding variation in the mean sizes of manos from sites that were occupied at roughly the same time. To test the proposition, one may compare a large number of manos from contemporary sites in different locations (generally on different drainages) in the Upland Mogollon region. If the size of local

TABLE 6.3
MEAN GRINDING SURFACE AREAS OF MANOS FROM EARLY PITHOUSE PERIOD UPLAND MOGOLLON SITES

Site	N	Mean Area (cm^2)	Standard Error
SU	130	191	5.7
Promontory	16	172	11.9
McAnally	9	225	16.2
Thompson	1	353	—
Bluff	15	159	8.1
Duncan	14	160	7.7
Flattop	36	172	3.9

Note: No significant differences of means.

resources affected the sizes of finished ground stone tools, then there should be significant differences in the sizes of manos from different sites. The sizes of manos from a sample of sites in different areas are given in table 6.3. A Spjotvoll-Stoline analysis of variance of means test indicated that there were no significant differences in the mean sizes of manos from sites in different locations. There is no evidence to suggest that spatial variation in raw material availability contributed to the diachronic changes in mano size that are documented in this study.

Statistically Significant Diachronic Variation in Mean Mano Areas

Figure 6.3 and table 6.4 present the results of the diachronic analysis of mano surface areas, using the 493 manos that were associated with maize grinding. The results presented here indicate that the mean surface areas of maize-processing manos significantly increased from the Early Pithouse period through the Three Circle phase. During this interval, mano areas increased by approximately 30 cm^2. This

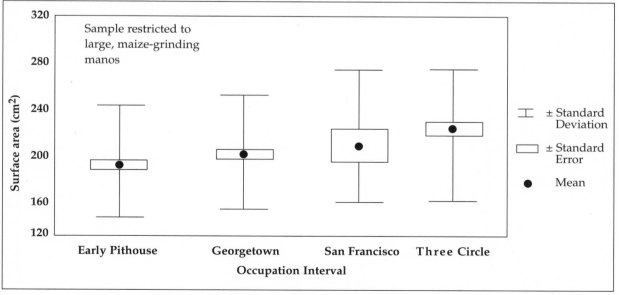

FIGURE 6.3. *Surface areas of large, maize-grinding manos from Upland Mogollon pithouse villages, by occupation interval.*

TABLE 6.4
SPJOTVOLL-STOLINE ANALYSIS OF VARIANCE OF MEAN SURFACE AREAS FOR PITHOUSE PERIOD MAIZE-GRINDING MANOS, BY OCCUPATION INTERVAL

Occupation Interval	N	Grinding Surface Area (cm^2)	Early Pithouse Period	Georgetown Phase	San Francisco Phase
Early Pithouse period	179	185.3			
Georgetown phase	124	194.2	$p = 0.60$		
San Francisco phase	40	211.6	$p = 0.16$	$p = 0.51$	
Three Circle phase	150	224.1	$p = 0.00$	$p = 0.00$	$p = 0.75$

change represents a relative increase of approximately 21 percent. As mean surface areas from Early Pithouse period and Georgetown phase manos do not differ, it is likely that the period of most rapid increase began sometime after or near the end of the Georgetown phase (A.D. 700).

SUMMARY AND CONCLUSION

The analyses in this study suggest that Upland Mogollon subsistence strategies began to shift from a foraging and horticultural mode to a classically sedentary agricultural mode around A.D. 650 or 700. The research reported here suggests that by A.D. 850 (the Three Circle phase), Upland Mogollon pithouse dwellers were heavily invested in agriculture. This research shows that changes in mano size and shape were probably motivated by selective pressure caused by increased consumption of maize. Macrobotanical analysis described in chapter 5 provided independent, qualitative support for the trends observed in the mano morphology data. As noted earlier, results of the macrobotanical research are equivocal, owing to the low number of high-quality flotation samples available for analysis. Further recovery and analyses of Pithouse period macrobotanical samples are required.

The essential assumption that time stress was induced by increased consumption of maize may be challenged because time stress may be caused by increased effort devoted to any of a number of hypothetically occurring activities. These activities may in turn have encroached on time that was normally devoted to maize processing. In other words, even if the amount of maize consumption remained constant,

increased investment in other activities might cause scheduling conflicts with maize grinding that may have been solved by increasing the efficiency of grinding tools.

At present there is no conclusive evidence of intensification of other kinds of activities. There are, however, other notable changes that may be important. These include increased evidence of trade during the Three Circle phase (Diehl 1994; Minnis 1985a:60), the possible shift to nuclear family (as opposed to extended family) co-residential groups during the Three Circle phase (Diehl 1994), and greater extremes in the quantity of mortuary goods interred with the deceased (Diehl 1994; Gilman 1990). These are potential candidates for activities that may have conflicted with maize processing, yet at present there is no logical chain of inference that connects these events with changes in ground stone morphology.

This research has identified two catalysts for change that would have provided the impetus for increased consumption of maize. First, agricultural intensification may be related to population increases. Based on the surface estimates of the number of rooms per site, researchers (Blake et al. 1986; Lekson 1992b) posited a 400 percent population increase in the Mimbres and Gila valleys from the Early Pithouse period through the Late Pithouse period. Under these circumstances, increased consumption of maize is a logical response. Second, the introduction of a new variety of *maiz de ocho* around A.D. 500–700 roughly coincided with the onset of the technological changes documented in this chapter. Advantages inherent in the new plant may have provided an irresistible attraction to early horticulturists that promoted increased dependence on cultivated plants.

7 A Functional Analysis of Early Pithouse Period Ceramics

John W. Arthur

The study of technological attributes of Southwestern ceramics may allow researchers to assess changes in the production and use of ceramics as these relate to changes in subsistence. Recent analyses of the technological attributes of ceramics have proven useful in understanding the problems associated with the use of ceramic vessels for different tasks such as cooking, storage, and carrying. Solutions to these problems may be achieved by selecting appropriate tempers, vessel shapes, and surface treatments (see Braun 1980, 1983, 1987; Bronitsky and Hamer 1986; Kobayashi 1994). Although functional studies of Southwestern ceramics are not uncommon (i.e., Bray 1982; Heidke and Elson 1988; Jones 1989; Lerner 1984; Mills 1984, 1989; Nelson and LeBlanc 1986; S. Plog 1980; Schiffer 1988; Whittlesey 1974), there have been only two previous functional studies of Early Pithouse period sites in the Upland Mogollon region (Anyon and LeBlanc 1984:165–171; Lightfoot 1984:62–69).

This study of the form, use-alteration, temper, and surface treatment of ceramic rims and partially reconstructable vessels, in conjunction with technological and ethnographic studies, provides a framework for understanding the function of the ceramic vessels at the McAnally and Thompson sites. Results suggest that occupants of the McAnally site used jars primarily for cooking, bowls for serving, and tecomates (seed jars) for storage. These data cannot be used to assess directly the importance of cultigens as opposed to wild starchy seeds, but the prevailing use of jars for cooking indicates that ceramics played an important role in the transition to food production in the Upland Mogollon region (Arthur 1994).

The analyses reported in this chapter are based on attributes of 181 rim sherds and 13 partially reconstructable vessels from the McAnally site, and 12 rim sherds and 1 reconstructable vessel from the Thompson site. The McAnally specimens include 6 rim sherds from Pithouse 1, 5 rim sherds from Pithouse 3, 65 rim sherds from Pithouse 8, and 105 rim sherds and 13 partially reconstructable vessels from the floor of Pithouse 11. Most of the McAnally rim sherds (71.3%) are of the Alma Plain type (for a formal type definition, see Haury 1936a), with the remainder falling in the general Mogollon Early Red category discussed in chapter 10.

RELATIONSHIPS BETWEEN ATTRIBUTES OF CERAMIC DESIGN AND USE

Analyses used in this study compare associations of attributes of pottery design (vessel form, temper, and surface treatment) and use-alteration (sooting, spalling, and pedestalled temper). Use of these attributes is justified by ethnographic analogy and experimental studies of the performance of attributes of ceramic design under different conditions of use. Evidence of use and the relationships between design and performance attributes are discussed below.

Vessel Form

Ethnographic evidence demonstrates that ceramic form changes with the intended use of the vessel. A vessel's primary use is indicated by the attributes of volume, orifice diameter, and wall thickness (Beals et al. 1945; Braun 1980; Lerner 1984; Mills 1985; S. Plog 1977; P. Rice 1987; Turner and Lofgren 1966).

The volumes of three McAnally vessels—F, H, and L—were determined by drawing the vessel profiles and dividing the containers into a number of stacked cylinders that, together, approximated the shape and size of each vessel, following the technique used by Anyon and LeBlanc (1984:166). The volume of a fourth vessel, vessel B (which was not available for direct examination), was calculated from measurements of the rim diameter, maximum body diameter, and a regression formula provided by B. Nelson (1985:312).

The rim diameter of a vessel may be related to its use. Braun's (1980, 1983) ethnographic study of Yuman, Piman, and Puebloan uses of ceramic vessels indicated that vessel uses condition their orifice forms and diameters. Jars with small orifice diameters (up to 15 cm) were typically used for transporting liquids. Vessels with medium-sized orifices (16–30 cm) were most often used for short-term storage, cooling, or cooking for small groups. Vessels with large orifices (greater than 30 cm) were used as temporary food storage and to prepare food for large groups. Following P. Rice (1987), in this study the term "jars" refers to vessels with necks, "bowls" are neckless vessels with unrestricted orifices, and "tecomates" are neckless vessels with restricted orifices.

The thickness of a vessel's wall affects its thermal conductivity, flexural strength, and resistance to thermal shock, and it may be related to the cooking requirements of specific kinds of food (Braun 1983, 1987). Boiling starchy seeds such as maize to a hominy may increase palatability and digestibility, but the effort requires longer cooking at higher temperatures than is required for other foods (Braun 1983:116). Longer cooking times and higher temperatures cause stresses that may be alleviated by altering the properties of the vessel wall. A vessel's ability to withstand rapid temperature changes (its resistance to "thermal shock") increases as the wall thickness decreases (Braun 1983:119; Lawrence 1972:174–183; Rado

1968:198–199; Sinopoli 1991:230) and may affect the use-life of vessels (B. Nelson 1991). Furthermore, the thermal conductivity increases as wall thickness decreases, allowing contents of cooking pots to achieve higher temperatures. Finally, although the ability of a vessel to withstand mechanical stress generally decreases with wall thickness, a vessel's resilience also depends on the curvature of the vessel wall. Vessels with smaller curvature radii are more resistant to mechanical stress than vessels with large radii (Braun 1983). Using a dial caliper, I measured the wall thickness (in mm) of the McAnally and Thompson ceramics as near as possible to the margin of the vessel orifice. Whenever possible, measurements were taken 1 cm below the lip of the rim.

Use-Alteration

Alterations to the surfaces of ceramic vessels occur as a consequence of vessel use and may allow researchers to distinguish between different uses (P. Rice 1987). For this research, I examined thermal spalling, pedestalled temper, and the presence and appearance of carbonization on vessel walls in order to infer vessel use. Diagnostic indicators of different kinds of vessel use are discussed below.

Recent research suggests that the presence of carbon deposits on vessel walls is a clear indication of cooking (Halley 1983; Skibo 1992). Soot deposits and fire clouds on the exterior of the vessel may reveal whether a vessel was used for boiling, frying, or simply warming. The presence of soot running from the base to the point of greatest vessel diameter signifies that the vessel was placed in the fire (Hally 1983; Skibo 1992) and may have been used for boiling, frying, or simmering (P. Rice 1987). In contrast, vessels suspended over a fire exhibit soot deposits on the base and sides of the vessel (Hally 1983; P. Rice 1987; Skibo 1992). This pattern may be associated with activities that require less intense heat, such as warming or serving. The texture of soot may also provide clues to the nature of vessel use. When vessels that contain liquids are subjected to high temperatures, a glossy soot without an oxidized patch is produced (Skibo 1992). The absence of moisture in cooking vessels produces a dull soot (Skibo 1992). In this study, the presence and location of soot were used to assess vessel use.

Thermal spalling occurs when water in the wall of a vessel vaporizes and, in escaping, spalls off a small portion of the interior surface. This most typically occurs when a vessel that contains liquid is heated, although the conditions that promote spalling are complex. According to Skibo (1992:134), the conditions for thermal spalling include "moisture in the vessel wall, heat, the interior surface must have a permeability lower than the interior of the vessel wall, and immediately next to the low-permeability surface, there must be less moisture than in the vessel wall interior." Thermal spalling causes circular erosion that ranges in diameter from 1 to 3 mm on the surface of a vessel (Skibo 1992:134). The presence or absence of thermal spalling was recorded for each rim sherd examined in this study.

The term "pedestalled temper" refers to the erosion of ceramic material around individual temper particles (Skibo 1992:116). Pedestalled temper occurs on vessel exteriors as a consequence of abrasion against the hearth or its contents, and on interiors when contents are stirred (Skibo 1992). Using a 10x binocular microscope, I recorded the presence of thermal spalling on the bases of the restorable vessels, and pedestalled temper on the interiors of vessel walls.

Temper

The size, shape, and density of temper may affect a vessel's mechanical strength. Specifically, properties of temper affect the porosity of a vessel. In a study of Southwestern ceramics, S. Plog (1980:87–88) concluded that vessels with coarse-grained temper are more resistant to thermal shock than those with fine-grained tempers. P. Rice (1987:105) explained that resistance to thermal shock increases with porosity, and coarse-tempered ceramics are more porous than fine-tempered ceramics. Mills (1984) studied vessels from the Anderson site and suggested that cooking vessels can be distinguished from other vessels by the presence, in the former, of coarse temper texture and by the absence of a painted decoration or slip.

The thermal properties of the temper may also affect a vessel's performance (P. Rice 1987:229, 365). Thus, some researchers have observed that fine-tempered vessels can perform better than coarse-tempered ones (Braun 1983; Bronitsky and Hamer 1986). For this study, rim sherds were assigned to a category that was determined by the range of temper size. I used the following increments: very coarse sand (2.0–1.0 mm), coarse sand (1.0–0.5 mm), medium sand 0.5–0.25 mm), fine sand (0.25–0.125 mm), very fine sand (0.125–0.062 mm), and silt (less than 0.062 mm).

The angularity of temper particles determines the amount of temper surface area, in turn affecting vessel porosity. As noted earlier, the porosity of a ves-

sel affects its resistance to thermal shock. I observed temper shape using a 10x binocular microscope, assigning tempers to the following categories: angular, subangular, subrounded, and rounded.

The proportion of temper to paste in a vessel also influences porosity, thereby affecting the vessel's resistance to thermal shock. For instance, high amounts of coarse temper increase vessel porosity (Mills 1984; S. Plog 1980). I quantified the amount of temper present in each potsherd in two ways. The first measure records the number of temper particles within a 4-mm-square cross section of each potsherd. The second measure, which I call the "percent of composition," is the proportion of temper to paste within a 4-mm-square cross section. In assessing the percent of composition, I visually compared the ratio of temper to paste in each sample with a percentage composition chart (USDA 1974).

Surface Treatment

Surface treatments can affect the containment of liquids within vessels. P. Rice (1987:231) noted that liquids boiled in permeable vessels can seep through, causing the vessel to crack. Insofar as polishing, burnishing, and slipping decrease permeability (Schiffer et al. 1994), they can be used to improve the long-term reliability of cooking vessels. Following P. Rice (1987:138), the term "burnished" refers to a surface with a lustrous appearance and narrow parallel linear facets produced by rubbing an object on "leather-hard" or dry clay. "Polished" is used to describe a surface with a uniform luster without the parallel facets found on burnished surfaces. A "slipped" surface is one to which liquid clay has been applied before firing. I examined the interior and exterior surface finish on the McAnally and Thompson site rim sherds and restorable vessels for evidence of polishing, burnishing, red slip, and plain surfaces.

McANALLY SITE CERAMICS

Analyses of the functional attributes of the McAnally site rim sherds are discussed separately for each type (form) of vessel. Of the 181 rim sherds that I examined, jars were the most frequent vessel form ($N = 82$, 45%). Bowls were the second most frequent form ($N = 53$, 30%), and tecomates were the least frequent ($N = 31$, 17%). A small number of rim sherds could not be classified and are not discussed in the analyses that follow ($N = 15$, 8%).

**TABLE 7.1
RIM DIAMETERS
OF McANALLY SITE JARS**

Jar Rim Diameter	Number of Sherds
< 8 cm	1
8–9 cm	10
9–10 cm	16
11–12 cm	14
13–14 cm	3
15–16 cm	2
17–18 cm	1
23–24 cm	1

**TABLE 7.2
RIM DIAMETERS
OF McANALLY SITE BOWLS**

Rim Diameter	Number of Sherds
< 11 cm	3
16–17 cm	3
18–19 cm	4
20–21 cm	6
22–23 cm	3
24–25 cm	2
28–29 cm	1

Jar Volumes, Orifice Diameters, and Vessel Use

Four of the McAnally jars were sufficiently reconstructable to allow volume measurements. In order of size, the volume measurements were: 1.46 liters (vessel F), 2 liters (vessel H), 8.3 liters (vessel B), and 10.4 liters (vessel L). Ethnographic studies provide information that allows one to speculate about the relationship between the sizes of vessels and their intended uses. B. Nelson (1991:169) noted that the highland Maya occupants of San Mateo Ixtatlan used several types of boiling vessels to reduce maize to a state that was deemed palatable. The size range evident in the McAnally vessels could represent vessels associated with different stages of food processing in ways that were consistent with Nelson's observations. However, the Tarahumara normally use a single vessel form for steeping maize (Robert Hard, personal communication, 1994), and the uncritical use of any single ethnographic example therefore seems inappropriate.

Do the McAnally jar volumes represent points on a continuum of vessel size (as in the Tarahumara case) or, alternatively, do they represent examples from several different size categories (as among the highland Maya)? Given the inadequate sample size, it is not possible to determine whether the distribution of Early Pithouse jar volumes is discrete (multiple modes) or continuous. Anyon and LeBlanc (1984:168) combined Early Pithouse, Late Pithouse, and Classic Mimbres vessels from a range of sites and observed three distinct modes. The McAnally site vessels fall into their "small" (6 liters or less) and "medium" (7–14 liters) categories. Following B. Nelson (1980) and Turner and Lofgren (1966), one may suggest that

the McAnally vessels were probably not associated with storing or processing food for large numbers of people.

Forty-eight McAnally jar rims were sufficiently intact to allow me to estimate their diameters (table 7.1). Most range from 8 to 12 cm in diameter. The orifice diameters are small, with a mean of 11.0 cm and a standard deviation (hereafter, "s.d.") of 3.0, in comparison with those from the Duncan site jars (mean 16.2 cm; Lightfoot 1984:64). Given these small diameters, I suggest that containment and heat effectiveness for cooking were concerns in the production of McAnally jars.

Bowl Volumes, Rim Diameters, and Vessel Use

None of the McAnally bowls were sufficiently reconstructable to allow a measurement of their volumes. Seven Early Pithouse period bowls examined by Anyon and LeBlanc (1984:169) had a mean volume of 2.3 liters. Unpainted bowls probably were used for the full range of serving, storing, or preparation tasks that were later separated between the larger painted bowls and smaller unpainted ones (Anyon and LeBlanc 1984:169).

Orifice diameters were obtained from 22 bowl rims (table 7.2). Most range from 16 to 28 cm, but a small number form a separate group at 10 cm. The McAnally bowl rims are slightly smaller, averaging 18.7 cm (s.d. = 4.5), but do not differ significantly from those at the Duncan site (mean = 22.4 cm.; s.d. = 10.1; Lightfoot 1984:68). Based on these data, I am unable to determine whether bowls were constructed for a specific purpose or for a variety of purposes. The presence of a possible bimodal distribution in the McAnally orifice rims may, however, be indicative of the manufacture of two size categories with different intended uses. Overall, the McAnally bowls were probably shallow, with continuous rims, and not well suited for holding liquids. I suggest that they may have been used as parching, drying, or serving vessels (following Braun 1980) and were probably not used for cooking or storing liquids.

Tecomate Volumes, Orifice Diameters, and Vessel Use

None of the tecomates from the McAnally site were reconstructable, and so it was not possible to obtain volume measurements. It was possible, however, to determine the diameter of 13 of the 31 possible tecomate rims (table 7.3). Tecomates are generally interpreted as storage containers for substances other than liquids (Braun 1980:183), and tecomates that have narrow orifice diameters may have been used to store seeds. Most of the McAnally tecomates have medium orifice diameters and may have been used as temporary storage jars (Braun 1980:183).

TABLE 7.3
RIM DIAMETERS
OF McANALLY SITE TECOMATES

Rim Diameter	Number of Sherds
< 9 cm	1
12–13 cm	3
14–15 cm	2
16–17 cm	1
18–19 cm	5
20–21 cm	1

Vessel Wall Thickness for All Forms

There are no significant differences in mean wall thickness among vessel forms. In general, the McAnally ceramic walls are thin (mean = 5.7 mm; s.d. = 1.1). Thin walls in combination with the round bases and slight curves would have increased the thermal conductivity and thermal shock resistance of the McAnally jars (Braun 1983). Although the bowl walls are also thin, these forms are not well suited for cooking.

Use-Alteration of Jars, Bowls, and Tecomates

Of the 13 partially reconstructable jars from McAnally site Unit 11, 11 had evidence of use-alteration in the form of soot, oxidized patches, pedestalled temper, or thermal spalling (table 7.4). These attributes indicate that most of the jars were used for cooking. The presence of glossy soot and thermal spalling on five of the vessels specifically indicates that jars were often used for boiling. Pedestalled temper was found on five of the jars. Oxidized patches were noted on three of the vessels, and thermal spalling on one.

The absence of sooting on McAnally bowl and tecomate rim sherds is interesting in light of the earlier discussion of their morphological attributes. McAnally bowl rims did not have soot deposits and had straight rims rather than everted rims. Cliff phase bowls with everted rims had a higher percentage of soot when compared to bowls with continuous rims (Nelson and LeBlanc 1986). The absence of sooting and everted rims on McAnally bowls shows that early Mimbres bowls were probably not used for cooking or restrictive containment. Likewise, McAnally tecomate rims did not have soot deposits. As noted earlier, the morphology of the rim and the ethnographic data indicate that tecomates functioned as storage containers and not cooking vessels (Braun 1980). On the whole, McAnally jars were frequently used for cooking, while other vessel shapes were exclusively used for storage and serving.

Temper Attributes and Vessel Use for Jars, Bowls, and Tecomates

Overall, the temper analyses revealed that the potters did not differentiate among the three vessel forms in selecting or using temper. The homogeneity of temper attributes among different vessel forms may be a consequence of the inclusions that occurred naturally in the clay deposits. Potters probably quarried clay from similar deposits (or even the same deposit) in the Mimbres River floodplain. To the extent that temper attributes are rather homogeneous among vessel forms, the results described below are consistent with studies of temper from the Late Pithouse period Galaz Ruin ceramics (Anyon and LeBlanc 1984:169) and the Early Pithouse period Duncan site (Lightfoot 1984). Early potters apparently did not select different tempers for cooking and noncooking vessels.

TABLE 7.4
USE-ALTERATION OF PARTIALLY RECONSTRUCTED McANALLY SITE JARS

Vessel	Soot	Soot Luster	Oxidization	Pedestaled Temper	Thermal Spalling
11-2 and 3- 7/1	Present	Dull	Absent	Present	Absent
C	Absent	—	Absent	Present	Absent
D	Present	Dull	Present	Absent	Absent
E	Absent	—	Absent	Present	Absent
11-3-7/10	Present	Dull	Present	Absent	Absent
G	Present	Glossy	Absent	Present	Absent
11-3-8/2	Present	Both	Absent	Present	Absent
I	Present	Both	Absent	Absent	Absent
J	Present	Dull	Absent	Absent	Present
K	Present	Both	Absent	Absent	Absent
11-3-6/5	Present	Dull	Present	Absent	Absent

The temper used in manufacturing McAnally site jars, bowls, and tecomates was consistently angular to subangular and did not vary among vessel forms. As noted earlier, angular temper has a greater surface area, creating an increased porosity of the vessel walls—an attribute that may have been advantageous for vessels used in cooking. These results are consistent with temper studies of rim sherds from the Duncan site, which may also have been from vessels that were used for cooking (Lightfoot 1984). The uniformity of temper shape, however, among the different vessel forms (which were presumably used for different tasks) suggests that the high percentage of angular temper in the McAnally rims may partially be a consequence of local clay composition.

The proportions of vessels with different-sized temper grains did not vary greatly among the different forms. All 31 jar sherds from Pithouse 8 were tempered with very fine sand. In contrast, only 40 percent ($N = 20$) of the jar sherds from Pithouse 11 were tempered with very fine sand. This result is problematic. If vessel form and temper are associated with different uses, then there should be greater variation between forms than between depositional contexts. By way of an explanation, I suggest that differences in the temper sizes in Unit 8 and Unit 11 potsherds may be a consequence of several other factors, including (1) the use of different clay or temper sources by occupants of different houses, (2) interhousehold differences in knowledge or skills associated with manufacturing vessels that are resistant to thermal shock, or (3) interhousehold differences in the need to produce vessels that are resistant to thermal shock.

Finally, I noted earlier that the proportions of temper to paste (measured here in two ways) may affect vessel porosity. Generally, vessels with greater amounts of temper are more porous and more resistant to thermal shock. Inspection of the vessel rims revealed that most vessels contained four to six temper particles per 4-mm^2 cross section, and the proportion of temper to paste varied only slightly among vessel forms. In all vessel forms, the proportion of temper to paste most frequently ranged from 20 to 30 percent, with almost as many in the 11 to 20 percent range. Because the proportion of temper to paste in McAnally vessels did not vary greatly among vessel forms, I find no evidence for differences in vessel use based on proportions of temper in different forms.

Surface Treatment

Of the 66 Alma Plain jars, approximately half of the interior surfaces were polished or burnished, as were half of the exterior surfaces. As I noted earlier, burnishing and polishing would have increased the resistance of vessel walls to the permeation of liquids stored or cooked in the vessels. Resistance to permeation is an attribute that may be advantageous for cooking. Schiffer (1990) and Skibo (1992) demonstrated that vessels with high water permeability are less efficient for heating than impermeable ones and would not bring water to a boil. It should be noted, however, that other ethnographic studies indicate that vessels that are slipped, polished, or burnished would not be used for cooking (Chapman 1977; Fontana et al. 1962; Russell 1908; Stanislawski 1978; Tschopik 1941).

To help determine whether burnishing on McAnally rim sherds was associated with cooking, one can examine the reconstructable jars from Unit 11. Notably, all of the partially reconstructed jars had either soot, burnishing, or polishing on the exterior and interior surfaces. The association of attributes that resist permeation with sooting indicates that the McAnally jars were probably used for cooking.

Of the 23 Alma Plain bowl rim sherds, 10 had polished or burnished interior surfaces, and 11 had polished or burnished exterior surfaces. Of the 30 Mogollon Early Red bowl rims, 26 had interior surface treatments (slip, polish, or burnish) that would have reduced permeability, and all had exterior surface treatments. The surface treatment of the bowls is important since the majority of the bowls probably contained food for serving or eating. Ethnographic studies indicate that decorated pots (slipped, polished, smudged, burnished, and painted) were most commonly used for serving food or for storage, rather than for cooking (Chapman 1977; Fontana et al. 1962; Russell 1908; Stanislawski 1978; Tschopik 1941). Since most bowls have surface treatments that reduced permeability, I suggest that they were used for serving food or for temporarily storing liquids or, more probably (since they are poorly shaped for containing liquids), wet foods.

Of the 29 Alma Plain tecomate rim sherds that I studied, 15 had polished or burnished exterior surfaces and 9 had polished or burnished interiors. None were sooted. Since tecomates are generally associated with storage (as opposed to serving or cooking), and given the low frequency of vessels with treated interiors (that would reduce permeability), I suggest that these vessels were primarily associated with storing dry goods.

THOMPSON SITE CERAMICS

The Thompson site ceramic assemblage was too small to support similar analyses, but some general conclusions may be offered. An examination of eight rim sherds indicates that the Thompson assemblage is not appreciably different from the McAnally assemblage. Different forms included jars (1), bowls (3), and tecomates (4). The temper was angular to subangular. Overall, the proportions of Alma Plain and Mogollon Early Red were similar at the McAnally and Thompson sites. The partially reconstructable Alma Plain vessel from Unit 1 is possibly a jar and has a bur-

nished exterior and a plain interior. This vessel was insufficiently complete to allow me to estimate its volume. The vessel was possibly used for cooking, based on dull soot deposits present on the exterior surface and a carbonized substance—possibly burned food—on the interior surface.

SUMMARY

Analyses of form, use-alteration, temper, and surface treatment of the McAnally vessels indicate that jars may have been used for multiple purposes, including cooking and storage. Given the small orifice diameters, thin walls, soot, temper pedestalling, thermal spalling, angular temper, and permeation-resistant walls, cooking was probably the most frequent use for the jars. The thin walls among the McAnally site jars facilitated rapid heating through increased thermal conductivity and resistance to thermal stress (Braun 1983). The rounded bases permitted air flow to the heat source, thereby allowing it to generate high levels of heat (Hally 1986:280). Analyses of soot, temper pedestalling, and thermal spalling support the conclusion that 11 of the partially reconstructable vessels functioned as cooking vessels. The angular temper found throughout the assemblage may have provided enough porosity and structural strength to increase resistance to thermal shock and improve cooking efficiency.

Bowls have interior surface treatments that allowed them to resist permeation by water, making them suitable for holding liquids. They were, however, generally shallow and would not have served well as long-term containers. Moreover, the continuous rims on the bowls were not particularly suited to retaining or cooking liquids. Most of the bowls were slipped, but none were sooted—as one might expect had they been exposed to a cooking fire. I suggest that the McAnally site bowls were used for serving or temporarily storing wet foods, rather than for cooking.

Tecomates generally lacked evidence of use as cooking vessels, and their interior treatments did not offer special resistance to water permeation. The rim forms and diameters of tecomates indicated that they were probably used as containers for storing dry goods, possibly seeds.

The use of a ceramic assemblage that is suitable for reducing maize to a gelatinous state does not, of itself, indicate the types of the foods that were cooked. Technological attributes that make vessels suitable for boiling maize render them equally suitable for cooking wild starchy seeds such as amaranth or goosefoot. To the extent that other analyses in this volume show that maize was important during the Early Pithouse period, this study of McAnally and Thompson ceramic design attributes and use-wear suggests that ceramics were probably closely associated with the development of food production among the Mimbres people during the Early Pithouse period.

8 Osteofaunal Remains

Animal bones from the McAnally and Thompson sites were recovered in low frequencies, 75 pieces altogether, and the data do not support statistical analysis. The frequencies of different taxa in the McAnally assemblage are presented in table 8.1. In addition to these, one deer antler tool was recovered (fig. 8.1). The six bones from the Thompson site are very fragmentary, and that site is not considered further in this chapter. Judging from comments made by archaeologists at the SU, Promontory, Bluff, and Duncan sites, the dearth of unworked animal bones from Early Pithouse villages is a phenomenon that is not restricted to the Mimbres Valley (i.e., see Haury 1985:290–291; Lightfoot 1984:184; Martin et al. 1949:176; Martin and Rinaldo 1947:358). No bones that were definitely from small animals were recovered from either McAnally or Thompson. As seen in table 8.2, small animal bones dominated the assemblage in Late Pithouse contexts from the nearby Galaz site. Moreover, 90 percent of all the bone recovered from Galaz could not be assigned to a taxonomic family. This is in contrast with sites of later periods where over 25 percent of the bone could be so classified. In summary, the bone assemblage is numerically small, heavily processed, and generally represents large animals.

Comparisons of the frequencies of animal bones are often used as an indicator of the relative importance of animals. When the low frequencies of animal bones from sites such as McAnally and Bluff are considered in light of the dearth of other plant food remains, however, one is led to a paradox. Haury (1985:290–291) suggested that the scarcity of animal bones at Bluff meant that hunting was not important. Yet, using the same reasoning, one must conclude that plants were also not important, since Haury recovered few specimens of charred plants. The paradox, of course, resides in the question, "What did people eat if they did not eat plants or animals?"

Faced with the paradox, one can pursue several alternative hypotheses. One possibility is that people ate very little food in or around their houses. For example, houses could have been special-purpose facilities in which people pursued a few marginal or secretive activities, or where people slept, but where food was not consumed. In other words, these "pit structures" are not residences where the full suite of daily human activities occurred, but rather special-purpose structures in which only a few activities occurred. Based on an analysis of the distributions of different tool types in pithouse fill, Hunter-Anderson (1986) concluded that there was variation in the function of different pithouse sites. Types of sites recognized by Hunter-Anderson included residential sites, field houses, and hunting camps. Reanalysis of the same data and other bodies of data demonstrated that the variation observed by Hunter-Anderson was

TABLE 8.1
OSTEOFAUNAL REMAINS FROM THE McANALLY SITE

Taxon	N	Elements
Deer (*Odocoileus* sp.)	2	Metatarsal, tibia
Dog (*Canis* sp.)	1	Sternum
Artiodactyls	5	Metatarsal (2), humerus(2), radius (1)
Mammals	19	Unidentified
Vertebrates	48	Unidentified

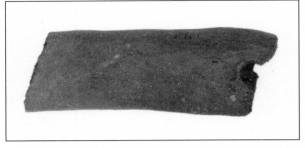

FIGURE 8.1. *Antler tool from the McAnally site, 8-4-4/2.*

probably not related to the nature of the activities at the studied sites; instead, the differences are more reasonably attributed to variation in the intensity of trash dumping, scavenging, and the relative haste with which houses were abandoned (Diehl 1998).

The suggestion that Early Pithouse dwellers did not hunt much becomes less tenable if, guided by a quest for simplicity in explanation, we insist that our interpretive tools (our methods and theories) remain consistent independently of the subject matter. Consider that, in the Southwest, most scholars attribute large Archaic period projectile points that predate the Early Pithouse period to the hunting or processing (either way, *consumption*) of large game. Consider also that similar large projectile points were used by Early Pithouse villagers (see chap. 10, this volume). An argument *against* Early Pithouse period hunting requires that we treat Early Pithouse projectile points as functionally distinct objects from Archaic projectile points. In other words, stone tools from pithouses deserve a special method and theory for interpretation that applies uniquely to the study of Upland Mogollon pithouse villagers. Clearly such an interpretive leap would violate the sensibilities of any scholar concerned with simplicity or consistency in explanations.

The other alternative was also offered by Haury (1985:290): "A dearth of animal bones in the refuse of the [Bluff] site presents a paradoxical situation which, in the final analysis, may be more apparent than real." In the popular rush to see diversity or variation in prehistoric subsistence activities on a fine-grained scale (for example, between Mogollon branches), the reality of the "dearth" of animal bones in pithouse sites has not been adequately considered.

Close inspection of the methods used to obtain animal bones from pithouse villages suggests that in

almost all cases the absence of animal bones may be attributed to one of two causes. Either the data from excavated sites were collected before screens were commonly used to sift excavated deposits, or (in more recent excavations) too few houses were excavated to permit a statistical test of statements about food consumption.

Consider, for example, the SU site. Paul Martin excavated 26 pithouses and numerous features during three seasons of excavation (1939, 1941, and 1946). During those years, few archaeologists screened deposits, and the artifacts that were collected were usually large or otherwise visually distinctive. The reports from all three seasons describe bone awls, pins, needles, and the like—a total of 71 specimens (Martin 1940:70, 1943:224–28; Martin and Rinaldo 1947:350). Thus, despite the fact that SU remains the most thoroughly tested pithouse site, it is the site that has provided (compared with the scale of excavation) the least amount of information.

In light of changes in recovery techniques, it is interesting to note that Wills (1991a: appendices) reported no fewer than 70 field collection numbers associated with bone collected as individual fragments and as bulk samples, even though the volume of earth excavated in the recent tests was a small fraction of the volume excavated by Paul Martin. Although interested scholars await the publication of the recent excavations, we may be certain that SU does not lack faunal remains. Moreover, if it is true that SU faunal remains were systematically overlooked simply as a consequence of the use of different field methods a half-century ago, it seems extremely likely that animal bones will be under-represented at other sites where investigators did not use screens. Unfortunately, inspection shows that most Mogollon pithouse villages fall into that category. Bear, Bluff,

Cameron Creek Village, Crooked Ridge Village, Diablo, Galaz (early excavations by Paul Nesbitt), Harris, Lee, Mogollon Village (Haury's excavations), Promontory, SU (the Field Museum excavations), Turkey Foot Ridge, and Winn Canyon were all excavated without the use of screens. Given only the limited faunal data at our disposal, it is clear that the suspicion voiced by the earliest Mogollon archaeologists that Mogollon Early Pithouse villagers did not make substantial use of animals may be dismissed.

In addition to the aforementioned concerns about recovery techniques, the locations of Early Pithouse sites are also an important factor that is generally ignored. The hilltop locations might be expected to result in less bone reaching the site. If, in the interests of efficiency, large animals were processed before being carried up the hills, then we would expect Early Pithouse villages to have lower frequencies of large animal bones than later villages located on lower terraces, regardless of actual differences in the intensity of large animal use. Moreover, discarded bone is less likely to accumulate on hilltops than on low, flat sites; bone discarded on hilltops would likely have washed or been thrown down the hill, where it is unlikely to be recovered by archaeologists. A number of McAnally and Thompson pithouses were tested in the hope of finding one that had been abandoned and filled with trash. That we were unable to find any significant trash deposits on the Early Pithouse sites, in marked contrast to the later ones, implies that the depositional processes were different. Care must be taken in comparing the abundance of materials recovered.

Thus, despite the amount of excavations undertaken, the nature of the excavation techniques and the site locations have resulted in very small and biased samples of faunal remains. The basis upon which we may judge the use of animals during the Early Pithouse period rests solely upon a few reasonably sized and relatively unbiased samples. These include one and a half pithouses at the McAnally site excavated by the Mimbres Foundation, several atypical pithouses at the Duncan Site in southeastern Arizona (Lightfoot 1984), unpublished data that were recovered from the SU site during the late 1980s, and a scatter of nonsystematically collected samples from other sites that were excavated during the last half-century. Taken together, these constitute an inadequate data base upon which one might attempt statistically meaningful generalizations about the importance of meat in pithouse villagers' diets.

Although the paucity of bone from the Early Pithouse period sites does not appear to be culturally meaningful, the composition of some assemblages has some, albeit limited, interpretive value. The presence of deer, general artiodactyl, and large mammal specimens in the limited array of McAnally osteofaunal elements indicates that large game were exploited, to an unassessed degree, by the occupants of the sites. As is indicated in table 8.2, the species list from the McAnally site is qualitatively consistent with the list of animals recovered at other Early Pithouse period sites. There may be a tendency for the faunal remains at Early Pithouse sites (apart from the Duncan site) to represent large game relatively more frequently than in later periods.

As discussed, the tendency to recover bone from large animals cannot be explained by the locations of Early Pithouse sites. In fact, as discussed earlier, we would expect large animals to be underrepresented in proportion to their actual consumption, since they may have been processed in locations removed from sites. We might, therefore, expect the bone from large animals to be relatively *less* common than on later sites. We suggest that large animals may have been used more intensively during the Early Pithouse period than in later periods. We suspect that the bone that did reach McAnally and Thompson was highly processed, which may account for the low frequencies of recovery.

In the future, researchers of the Mogollon Pithouse period should attempt to resolve at least the following three questions: First, which animals were most important? For example, did Early Pithouse villagers rely primarily on large game, or were small game more important? Second, what were the technological and social means by which animals were obtained? For example, do the ages of small game point to a pattern of cooperative hunting, such as "rabbit driving?" Do the distributions of large animal parts among houses indicate the presence of interhousehold food sharing, or, alternatively, differential uses of (or even access to) high-quality foods? Third, and finally, to what extent were animals processed? Is there evidence, for example, of extensive bone breakage for marrow extraction, or were Early Pithouse villagers solely interested in fleshy tissue? Were particular animals preferred for tool manufacturing? Systematic attempts to resolve these questions will greatly improve archaeological assessments about the nature of resource use among Upland Mogollon pithouse villagers.

TABLE 8.2
FAUNAL REMAINS FROM OTHER UPLAND MOGOLLON PITHOUSE SITES

Site	Occupation Date (A.D.)	Taxon	Count	Proportion of Identified Specimens from Site
Bear Ruin[a]	850–1000	Deer (*Odocoileus hemionis*)	Not specified	About 75%
		"Rabbits"	Not specified	Ranked second
Bluff[b]	200–550	Deer (*Odocoileus hemionis*)	13	65%
		Pronghorn (*Antilocapra americana*)	4	20%
		"Gopher"	2	10%
		"Coyote"	1	5%
Duncan[c]	200–550	"Deer"	1	1%
		"Jackrabbit"	21	30%
		"Cottontail"	17	24%
		Other identified specimens[d]	30	43%
Galaz Ruin[e]	850–1000	Deer (*Odocoileus* spp.)	57	4%
		Antelope (*Antilocapra americana*)	8	< 1%
		Undifferentiated artiodactyls	61	4%
		Jackrabbits (*Lepus* spp.)	295	18%
		Rabbits (*Sylvilagus* sp.)	217	14%
		Other identified spp.	965	60%
Promontory[f]	200–550	Deer (*Odocoileus* spp.)	20	87%
		Turkey (*Meleagris gallopavo*)	3	13%
SU[g]	200–550	"Deer" bone awls	23	32%
		"Dog?" bone awls	1	1%
		"Large mammal" bone awls	32	45%
		Unspecified bone awls	15	21%
Turkey Foot Ridge[h]	850–1000	Deer (*Odocoileus* spp.)	37	54%
		Jackrabbit (*Lepus* sp.)	8	12%
		Rabbit (*Sylvilagus* sp.)	5	7%
		Other identified spp.	19	28%

[a] "Elements of the mule deer outnumbered those of all other animals by a ratio of three to one" (Haury 1985:147).

[b] Haury 1985:291.

[c] Lightfoot 1984:133. Unidentified fragments were dominated by "large mammal" remains, most likely Artiodactyla (Lightfoot 1984:45–46).

[d] Excludes domestic livestock.

[e] Anyon and LeBlanc 1984:216.

[f] Martin et al. 1949:176.

[g] Martin 1940:70; 1943:224–228, Martin and Rinaldo 1947:350.

[h] Martin and Rinaldo 1950:350.

9 Chipped Stone

Steven A. LeBlanc

The excavations on the McAnally and Thompson sites produced only a moderate-sized sample of chipped stone. In addition, the amount recovered from each context was small, greatly limiting the potential for intrasite, as well as intersite, comparisons. McAnally yielded 2,962 specimens—compared with 6,526 specimens from the Late Pithouse period on the Galaz Ruin, 11,197 specimens from good Classic Mimbres period contexts on the Mattocks site, and 1,459 specimens from the nearby Cliff phase Stailey site. (The other Cliff phase sites produced more than 15,000 specimens each.) The Thompson site produced only 795 pieces of chipped stone.

The overall composition of the chipped stone sample is presented in table 9.1. Margaret Nelson recorded these data between 1976 and 1980. The samples were sorted into general classes: flake debitage, unshaped flake tools (utilized flakes), and shaped flake tools. These were then sorted by raw materials and flake stage. Three hundred and fifty-eight utilized flakes from the McAnally site were analyzed individually. Each flake edge was examined through a 10x hand lens, evidence of use was noted, and a series of edge forms was recorded.

The chipped stone sample was recovered by 1/4-inch screening. It is possible that very small pieces of stone were less frequently recovered because they were hidden in the concretelike matrix and because

very small flakes could pass through the 1/4-inch screen. Since the comparative sample was also recovered by 1/4-inch screening, however, the recovery issues do not affect the comparative analysis.

EFFICIENCY, FORAGING, AND FARMING

Lithic data from the McAnally and Thompson sites have been used in interpretations of the changing adaptations of the prehistoric population in the Mimbres Valley. These interpretations are discussed elsewhere (Anyon and LeBlanc 1980; Minnis 1985a; Nelson and LeBlanc 1986) and are only briefly reiterated here. Survey data summarized by Blake et al. (1986) showed that the human population in the valley grew from the Early Pithouse period through the Mimbres Classic, then declined to a low point in the late 1300s, after which the valley was abandoned by sedentary farming people until well into the historic period. In general, the people responded to these changes in population size by changing their use of plant and animal resources, and the lithic tools and assemblage exhibit correlated changes. Although this may seem to be an obvious relationship, it was not found in all artifact classes. The ceramic technologies, for example, did not change in response to either the changing population size or the relative reliance on animal or wild plant resources.

Several attributes of the chipped stone tool assemblage indicate that Early Pithouse period villagers and Cliff phase pueblo dwellers were more reliant on hunting than their Late Pithouse period and Classic Mimbres period counterparts. One encounters a difficulty when interpreting changes in the chipped stone assemblage, however—namely, the potential problems of equifinality. In other words, multiple interpretations are logically consistent with the observed trends. During the Early Pithouse period, high reliance on wild plants and animals could indicate that people had not developed an effective agricultural technology. Alternatively, people at that time may have possessed adequate agricultural technology but lacked the need to invest heavily in agriculture.

An "efficient forager" model (Bettinger 1991) predicts that, in circumstances of high wild food productivity, foraging might be preferred over farming. To meet the conditions of the efficient forager model, one would expect to see two conditions: (1) higher return rates from wild foods than from farming, and (2) selective advantages conferred by the optimization of energy expended for caloric return. One of these two conditions may have been met during the Early Pithouse period, as well as during the Cliff phase. Given the low population densities observed for those periods, one suspects that wild plants and animals were in greater abundance than during other, more populated times. Such an efficiency model for these periods is unlikely, however, given the high annual variation in wild food availability. As was noted earlier in this volume, maize may have offered better energetic return rates than the best wild plant foods—piñon and acorns—because in many years wild nut masts fall substantially short of their long-term average annual yield. Of the resources that were probably available to Early Pithouse period forager-farmers, only large animals might have routinely provided superior energetic return rates, compared with cultigens.

An alternative to the efficient forager model would be a reliance primarily on maize, with resort to wild foods as a backup strategy during those years in which cultivation failed to meet consumption needs. Planting enough domesticates to provide a large portion of the caloric needs each year would, in most years, provide enough food to account for a large proportion of the diet. During years when agricultural productivity was very low (owing, for example, to drought), the population might fall back on wild plants and animals. At such times, these wild resources might be available in great abundance, since they would have been lightly cropped in years when agricultural production was high.

During later periods, the population was so large that fewer wild plants and animals were available on a per capita basis, and the best strategy may have been to overplant each year. During very good years, overplanting yielded sufficient harvests to store for lean years. And, in average-to-bad years, overplanting ensured a modest harvest even if the yield was low. That is, it was rational for the high-density populations to expend relatively more energy on farming because their outlook in poor crop-yield years may have been quite bleak. Wild foods may have been incapable of meeting the energetic demands of high-density populations; they were not sufficiently abundant to provide an adequate backup for everyone in the event of a crop failure.

Among low-density populations, low-intensity farming may have been preferable to a pure foraging strategy. The low-density farming populations would not consume, on an annual basis, as many wild plants and animals as an equal-sized, purely hunter-gatherer population (because of their substantial reliance on cultigens). As a result, their ability to extract wild foods in poor years would have been greater than for the pure hunter-gatherers. Thus, regardless of whether farming would have been more efficient than pure hunting and gathering, its ability to minimize failure may have made it the strategy of choice.

POTENTIAL INTERPRETIVE BIASES

There are a number of variables that can be compared between the Early Pithouse period and later samples. Some exhibit little temporal variation, and the variability of others, such as the amount of debitage in the samples and the frequency of unretouched tools, has no meaningful patterning. Some attributes, however, varied significantly. It must be remembered that interpretation of the Early Pithouse samples may be hampered because of biases in the samples owing to differences in site locations. The Early Pithouse villagers likely engaged in activities away from the hilltop locations of their villages to a greater extent than did subsequent occupants of the area. All other period sites are in broadly similar first-terrace settings, so comparisons between the early hilltop locations and the subsequent first-terrace locations may be biased. In particular, many processing activities would most likely

TABLE 9.1

GENERAL COMPOSITION OF THE CHIPPED STONE SAMPLES FROM THE McANALLY AND THOMPSON SITES

Site	Flake Debitage[a]	Unshaped Flake Tools[b]	Shaped Flake Tools[c]	
			Projectiles	Nonprojectiles
McAnally	2,412	540	14	0
Thompson	547	247	5	1

[a] Flake debitage includes all debris from knapping that shows evidence of concoidal fracture, including angular debris (Crabtree 1972; Geier 1973), but shows no sign of having been used as a tool. Tool use was determined by retouch of the marginal edge or edge damage from utilization as viewed through 10x magnification.

[b] Unshaped flake tools are those with evidence of edge damage from utilization, some of which have marginal retouch (Chapman 1977:378). The latter was distinguished from facial retouch by the extent to which retouch scars extended over the face of the flake. Marginal retouch was arbitrarily defined as retouch scarring extending over less than one-third of the face of the tool.

[c] Shaped tools include any items with retouch extending over more than one-third of the dorsal face. Projectile points were separated from the other shaped tools because they are the only shaped stone tool class in the study area that is represented by more than a few pieces in the collections of most sites excavated by the Mimbres Foundation. Definitions apply to the overall sample, and particular items are not necessarily represented in the Early Pithouse sample. Projectile points include dart and arrow points; they must be small enough to be projected on a shaft (Browne 1940; Fenenga 1953), and most have hafting elements. Other shaped tools include oval bifaces, drills, and unifaces. Some items in this class are quite fragmentary.

have taken place at the foot of the hills in order to reduce the weight of the material that was carried uphill. Activities that occurred away from Early Pithouse villages probably included some animal butchering and plant processing, as well as some lithic manufacturing. While these activities may also have been conducted off-site in later periods or may have taken place in specialized areas some of the time, it is likely that they are more heavily represented in the lithic assemblages of later sites than they are in Early Pithouse period sites. Conversely, some kinds of tool maintenance and production may have been more likely to be carried out on-site during the Early Pithouse period than later, because hilltop locations may have provided good vantage points to look for game. In subsequent periods, men may have moved off-site to watch for game and may have worked on tools while they were waiting. It is not really possible to factor out all these variables, but they do need to be kept in mind while considering these data.

THE McANALLY AND THOMPSON SITE ASSEMBLAGES

The general composition of the samples from the two sites is given in table 9.1. Overall, the samples are dominated by flake debitage, with a large number of unshaped flake tools. Only a small number of formally prepared tools occurred in any of the assemblages from any period in the entire valley. The only Early Pithouse period shaped tools were whole or fragmentary projectile points. The McAnally assemblage contained 81 percent debitage. That proportion is similar to the proportions observed among later sites in the area, which all ranged between 83 and 88 percent. The 18 percent proportion of unshaped flake tools from McAnally was also similar to that from the nearby sites in the area. Shaped tools, however, represented only 0.3 percent of the McAnally sample, whereas they made up 1 percent of the Late Pithouse and Classic Mimbres samples, and about 2 percent of the Cliff phase samples.

The Thompson site assemblage had an even lower frequency of shaped tools (0.1%) but had a very high proportion of unshaped flake tools (31.1%). The lack of comparative material from other periods near the Thompson site makes interpretation of its assemblage difficult. As noted below, the presence of high frequencies of biface thinning flakes in the Early Pithouse period sites suggests that stone projectile point production was as common as in later periods, even though the percentage of these tools was low. It is likely that either the sample size was too small to be reliable, or that the use and discard behaviors differed among the hilltop sites and the later first-terrace sites.

TABLE 9.2
CHIPPED STONE MATERIALS USED
IN THE McANALLY AND THOMPSON SITES

Site	Flake Debitage		Utilized Flakes	
	Coarse	Fine	Coarse	Fine
McAnally	1,888	512	409	139
Thompson	248	284	84	163

Note: Stone materials were grouped as coarse or fine based on the properties of the stone matrix as they influence flake production and use (Goodyear 1989; Hayden 1976; Lischka 1969; Speth 1972). Those that are fairly isotropic were classified as fine; they include all cryptocrystallines, obsidian, and a form of rhyolite that has a fine, glassy matrix. Coarse materials were more crystalline, producing blockier flake forms; these include basalt, andesite, most rhyolite, and quartzite. A few materials (such as dolomite) could not be classified. Descriptions of the stone materials are provided in M. Nelson (1981).

Coarse versus Fine Raw Materials

A basic attribute of the chipped stone assemblage is the raw material from which it was derived. Table 9.2 presents the frequencies of coarse and fine materials for both debitage and utilized flakes. Comparative values for the valley as a whole are given elsewhere (Nelson and LeBlanc 1986: table 8.3). For the valley as a whole we found that during lower population density periods there was a lower proportion of coarse raw materials. The one exception was the McAnally site, with 78 percent coarse materials—higher than the proportion observed in any other site. The proportion for the other low population density period, the Cliff phase, was only 43 percent. Even among sites that were occupied during the high population density Classic Mimbres phase, the proportion of coarse materials was only 58 percent. In contrast, the Thompson site had only 43 percent coarse materials. M. Nelson (1981, 1984, 1986b) argued that the use of coarse raw materials correlated with the processing of plant materials, in contrast to the processing of animals or the production of animal procurement tools. While the proportions of coarse and fine materials may in general be related to the relative efforts invested in plant versus animal processing, some other factor must account for both the very high value at the McAnally site and the low value at the Thompson site.

If only the utilized flakes from these sites are examined, the proportions of coarse materials are quite similar to those just noted. Among the utilized flakes, McAnally again had a high frequency of coarse raw materials (about 71%), whereas the Late Pithouse and Classic period assemblages had frequencies of utilized flakes made from coarse materials that ranged from 53 to 69 percent. The Cliff phase had only 44 percent coarse utilized flakes, and the Thompson site had a remarkably low 34 percent coarse utilized flakes.

An obvious explanation for these ratios—that the Thompson site residents had greater access to fine materials—is hard to test without better comparative material from that area. The scarcity of fine material at the McAnally site may be a result of the paucity of fine raw materials in the immediate vicinity of the site. That suggestion is supported by our off-site lithic material sampling study (M. Nelson 1981). If we assume that raw material procurement was embedded in other activities, particularly longer-distance, logistically organized hunting forays, we might conclude that occupants of the McAnally site engaged in long-distance hunting trips less frequently than the occupants of more recent sites. As mentioned above, however, the site location may be a factor. Fine materials would have had to have been procured elsewhere and then carried up the steep hill to the McAnally site. More effort may have been invested in reducing the fine materials before transporting them, so relatively less fine material debitage would have reached the top of the hill. It is not clear how one can differentiate between these two alternatives.

Production Edge Angle

Like material type, production edge angle is a variable that attempts to measure the durability of working edges. It should relate to the relative use of plants and animals in the same way as do the proportions of coarse and fine materials. Production edge angle data are presented in table 9.3. Comparative data for all periods are presented elsewhere (Nelson and LeBlanc

TABLE 9.3
CHARACTERISTICS OF UTILIZED EDGES ON UNRETOUCHED AND MARGINALLY RETOUCHED FLAKES FROM THE McANALLY SITE

Category	Percentage in Categories	Mean
Maximum production edge angle		
19–40 degrees	20	
41–60 degrees	45	
> 60 degrees	35	
Maximum angle value from each edge		55 ± 15.9
Minimum angle value from each edge		42 ± 13.3
Utilized edges with cortex on edge	16	
Edges with marginal retouch	12	
Edge shapes (in plan view)		
Slightly concave	13	
Straight	25	
Slightly convex	21	
Convex	20	
Uneven	5	
Convex uneven	1	
Pointed	2	
Denticulate convex	1	
Denticulate straight	1	
Notch on convex	1	
Notch on straight	1	
Concave	2	
Projection	2	
Extremely convex	1	
Extremely pointed	1	

Notes: Production edge angle is the angle created by the dorsal and ventral faces of the original, unaltered flake. It represents a characteristic of the initial edge form selected for use, rather than the effect of use damage on that edge form. In measuring edge angle, the values vary considerably because of indentations and ridges along the dorsal face and curvature of the ventral face. The maximum value and minimum value were recorded.

Marginal retouch is differentiated from damage resulting from utilization by the regularity of the microscarring along the edge and the extent to which it invaded the flake face. To distinguish marginal from facial retouch, the former was arbitrarily defined as scarring that did not extend more than one-third of the distance across the flake face.

Plan view edge shapes are illustrated in M. Nelson (1981:214).

1986: tables 8.8 and 8.9). Edge angles were analyzed in two ways. First, the average minimum and maximum edge angles for each flake were determined. Then, since averages from different sites could be similar while masking significant variability, the range of distribution of the maximum edge angles was also considered.

The average minimum edge angle for each site studied for all periods was remarkably consistent, 40 to 43 degrees, while the middle valley site sample varied from 42 to 43 degrees. The average maximum edge angle did have a somewhat greater range. The Late Pithouse and Classic periods each had 60 degree mean

angles, while the Early Pithouse period and Cliff phase averaged 55 degrees and 53 degrees, respectively. The greater use of small edge angles was seen by Nelson (1981) as evidence for less reliance on plant processing.

For analytical purposes, the measurements of maximum production edge angles were divided into three categories: 19 to 41 degrees (narrow), 41 to 60 degrees (medium), and greater than 60 degrees (wide). Both the Early Pithouse and Cliff phase samples had considerably more narrow-angled edges and fewer wide edges than the Late Pithouse and Classic samples. That is, during periods of low population

TABLE 9.4
STAGES OF FLAKE FORMS IN THE DEBITAGE AND UTILIZED FLAKE SAMPLES FROM THE McANALLY AND THOMPSON SITES

Site	Debitage			Utilized Flakes		
	Cortical	Noncortical	Biface Thinning	Cortical	Noncortical	Biface Thinning
McAnally	887	1,497	28	190	348	2
Thompson	95	439	15	63	184	0

Notes: Cortical flakes are any flake forms or angular debris (whole or fragmentary) that have cortex on the dorsal face. This does not include cortex on the platform, which may be present to facilitate some techniques of flake removal. The presence of cortex was used as an indicator of early stage reduction of cores.

Noncortical flakes have no cortex on the dorsal face. This group includes tertiary flakes (Geier 1973) and angular debris from farther into the core than those in the cortical category.

Biface thinning flakes must have lipping where the platform contacts the ventral face. They also have no bulb or a very reduced bulb of percussion. The dorsal face has numerous small flake scars. The platform frequently has flake scars as well.

size there were relatively more narrow-angled edges than during periods when the population was larger. In particular, the McAnally site had 20 percent narrow edges and the Cliff phase sample had 23 percent. In contrast, the Late Pithouse sites had only 12 percent, and the Classic sites had 10 percent narrow-edged flakes. The frequency of the medium angles was remarkably consistent for all periods at 42 to 48 percent. In other words, the change in the mean edge angle was the result of far fewer "wide" edges and far more common "narrow" edges, with the "medium" edges being equally common in all periods. Once again, the Early Pithouse period lithic assemblage looks more like the Cliff phase assemblage than it does the Late Pithouse or Classic period assemblage.

Cortex Reinforcement

The frequency of cortex found on flake debitage did not vary greatly within the middle valley during different periods, although it did vary for utilized flakes. The variation is described in table 9.4 and in Nelson and LeBlanc (1986: table 8.5). The Thompson site produced substantially lower (17.7%) proportions of debitage with cortex than the McAnally site (37%). The difference may be attributable to differences in the availability of raw material types near the sites.

The frequency of cortex reinforcement on tool working edges is another measure of tool design variability. Cortex reinforcement was a solution to edge durability that was similar to use of wide-edge angles

and the use of coarse raw materials. Valleywide distributions are given in Nelson and LeBlanc (1986: table 8.6). In the assemblage from the McAnally site, 15.6 percent of tool working edges showed cortex reinforcement. This is close to the proportion in Cliff phase assemblages (18.7%). These proportions contrast with 24.8 percent and 23.2 percent in the Late Pithouse and Classic period assemblages, respectively. The northern Mimbres Valley samples had even lower frequencies of cortex reinforcement than the middle valley. That is, in samples from sites where we think hunting was relatively more important both in time and space, the frequency of cortex reinforcement was relatively low. With respect to the cortex reinforcement variable, the Early Pithouse period sample looks more like the Cliff phase sample than either of the two looks like the Late Pithouse or Classic Mimbres phase samples.

Biface Thinning Flakes

If one associates the use of bifaces with hunting, then the proportion of biface thinning flakes (which measures the intensity of manufacturing or resharpening projectile points and knives) provides a relative measure of the importance of hunted game to other foods. Biface thinning flakes are rare in all periods, but they are more common in the Early Pithouse period assemblages than in those of any other period. (Table 9.4 gives the number of biface thinning flakes for the Early Pithouse period.) This observation would seem to suggest that hunting occurred more frequently during the Early Pithouse period than during the subsequent Late Pithouse and Classic Mimbres period occupations.

Biface thinning flakes constitute 1.0 percent of the McAnally site and 1.9 percent of the Thompson site samples. During the Late Pithouse period the Galaz Ruin had only 0.5 percent biface thinning flakes, and the Classic Mimbres period at the Mattocks site had 0.1 percent. As biface thinning flakes tend to be small, and small flakes may be underrepresented in the McAnally sample (because of the aforementioned difficulties entailed in screening the concretelike matrix), this percentage is not a function of recovery techniques. The nearby Stailey site, which dates to the low human population density Cliff phase, had 1.0 percent biface thinning flakes. Thus, the proportions from the McAnally site resemble those from the Cliff phase, and both differ from the proportions observed in the Late Pithouse and Classic period assemblages.

Geographic variation in the proportional frequency of biface thinning flakes also supports the contention that their proportions are governed by the intensity of hunting. Sites located in the northern portion of the Mimbres Valley seem to be situated for more intensive hunting, since upland fauna are more frequently found in this area. In the northern valley segment, the frequency of biface thinning flakes was comparatively high for all periods. The Late Pithouse sample had 0.3 percent, the Classic period sample had 1.5 percent, and the Cliff phase had 3.3 percent. Early Pithouse period samples were not available for the northern valley segment; however, the high proportion of Cliff phase biface thinning flakes as compared with earlier ones suggests that the temporal trends in the northern valley segment and middle valley segment were similar.

The 1.9-percent frequency of biface thinning flakes at the Thompson site is intriguing. This frequency is almost twice that seen on the McAnally site. It would suggest that the more open plains near the Thompson site may have been more useful for hunting than might be expected, but the small overall sample and lack of corroborating evidence make further interpretation difficult.

Projectile Points

There were only 11 points or fragments from the Early Pithouse period sites that could be analyzed. Their dimensions are given in table 9.5, and some are pictured in figure 9.1. The size of these points suggests that they were intended for atlatl darts—as is generally accepted for this time range in the southern Southwest. The points were equally divided into stemmed and unstemmed shapes, but no real typological analysis can be done with such a small sample. Impressionistically, the points do not seem more skillfully made or more standardized than the arrow points from later periods, nor do they otherwise represent a more highly specialized tool kit. It is possible that some of these points were knives, but none is so large as to make this an obvious interpretation, and all are treated here as projectile points.

Interestingly, a large number of arrows have been recovered from dry caves in the Gila area within the Mimbres cultural area that seem to date to the Classic Mimbres period (Cosgrove 1947; Hibben 1938). Wooden points dominate these collections, and stone tips are relatively rare. In contrast, in the Southwest as a whole, atlatl darts recovered from caves seem almost always to have stone tips and not wooden tips. Thus, the actual number of projectile points used would seem to be underestimated for the Classic sites in comparison with the Early Pithouse sites, because the wooden points from the later time periods would not have survived.

As noted above, projectile points constitute 0.3 percent and 0.1 percent of the McAnally and Thompson assemblages, respectively, while proportions in assemblages from later sites range from 1 to 2 percent. Thus, the Early Pithouse period sites had one-third as many stone projectile points as the Classic sites, or even fewer. Because the number of stone projectile points underrepresents the number of actual points in the Classic sites, as many were presumably of wood, the discrepancy between periods is even greater. Whether this low frequency of projectile points in the Early Pithouse period represents a difference in curation behaviors, actual differences in projectile point production, differences in the intensity of reuse, or differences in the available hunting technologies is unclear and requires further investigation.

TABLE 9.5

ATTRIBUTES AND DIMENSIONS OF McANALLY AND THOMPSON SITE PROJECTILE POINTS

Site	Provenience	Blade Length	Length	Width	Thickness	Stem Width	Constriction Width	Shoulder Angle	Weight	Material	Notch	Stem	Figure
McAnally	Surface/A	35E	35E	21	7	UN	UN	95, 105	—	C	U	U	
	Surface/B	23	19	23E	6	16E	13	55, 0	16	C	S	UN	
	1-4-1/1	41E	41E	24	6	UN	UN	97, 89	49	Q	U	U	9.1b
	1-3-1/1	UN	UN	UN	3	UN	UN	0, 0	—	J	UN	UN	
	1-3-1/C	23	23	17	6	UN	UN	88, 92	15	C	U	U	
	3-2-2/1	23E	19E	13	4	10	7	68, 111	—	C	C	CE	9.1c
	3-5-3/1	29E	22E	22	5	15	10	74, 70	—	C	C	CE	9.1l
	8-2-7/1	39	33	26	3	15	11	80, 27	27	J	C	CE	9.1i
	8-surface/A	30	24	21E	4	11E	8	86, 62	16	J	C/B	CE	9.1j
	8-surface/B	27	23	13E	3	6	6	84, 0	8	O	C	CP	9.1g
	8-5-1/1	UN	UN	UN	3	UN	UN	0, 0	8	O	UN	UN	9.1f
	8-5-2/0	31E	31E	23	3	UN	UN	100, 95	—	J	U	U	9.1h
	11-4-1/1	UN	UN	UN	3	UN	UN	0, 0	—	C	UN	UN	
	11-3-4/1	34	26	22	7	16	12	0, 0	44	J	C	CE	9.1k
	11-4-5-3	31E	26E	22	4	14	14	92, 78	—	C	C	CE	9.1n
	11-2-1/A	UN	UN	UN	6	17	12	74, 0	—	C	C	CE	9.1m
	11-5-5/11	23	17	19	3	12	9	73, 84	12	C	C	U	9.1o
Thompson	11-3-6/9	34E	34E	18	5	UN	UN	102, 102	—	C	U	U	
	Surface-D2/a	34E	29E	22E	UN	9	9	83, 85	—	C	C	CP	
	Surface-D2/b	39E	34E	27E	UN	7	7	42, 69	—	C	C	CP	
	Surface-Q1/a	36E	36E	16	UN	UN	UN	0, 0	—	C	UN	UN	
	1-2-4/3	46	39	33	UN	10	7	42, 45	—	C	C	CE	9.1a
	1-3-4/3	49	49	28	12	UN	UN	72, 108	162	C	U	U	9.1d
	1-3-4/2	21	21	16	3	UN	UN	90, 122	9	C	U	U	
	1-2-4/1	UN	UN	UN	3	16	UN	0, 0	—	C	UN	CE	
	1-1-2/2	UN	UN	UN	5	UN	UN	0, 0	—	J	UN	UN	
	1-1-1/A	29E	29E	24	5	UN	UN	85, 90	18	C	UN	U	9.1e

Definitions:

Length: Maximal length in mm. A measurement followed by an "E" denotes a measurement estimated due to breakage. "UN" means the point was too fragmentary to even estimate the measurement.

Blade length: From tip to shoulder for stemmed points, or to the base for unstemmed points.

Stem width: Widest portion of the stem; not recorded for unstemmed points.

Constriction width: The minimum distance between side or corner notches; not recorded for unstemmed points.

Shoulder angle: Each angle measured in degrees. The angle was found by projecting from the tip of a shoulder to the longitudinal axis. For stemmed points, this is a measurement of the downward curvature.

Weight: In tenths of a gram. Broken points were weighed only when missing portions would have contributed insignificantly to overall weight.

Material: C = chalcedony; J = jasper; O = obsidian; Q = quartzite.

Notch position: U = unnotched; S = side notched; C = corner notched; B = base notched.

Stem shape: U = unstemmed; CE = corner notched expanding base; CP = corner notched parallel sided; SC = side notched, anvil contracting; SP = side notched, anvil parallel.

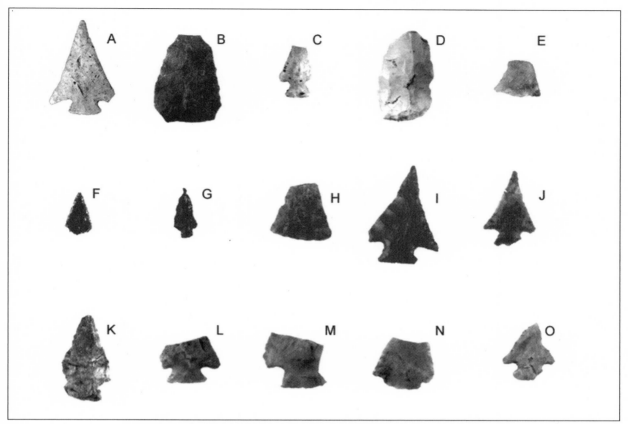

FIGURE 9.1. *Projectile points from the Thompson and McAnally sites.
Provenience information is given in table 9.5.*

CONCLUSIONS

The Early Pithouse lithic samples in this study were broadly similar to those from later periods in the Mimbres Valley. Where they differed, they resembled the samples from the low population density Cliff phase sites rather than those from the Late Pithouse and Classic Mimbres periods, during which population densities were greater. A number of independent variables all show the same directional tendency: When population densities were low, there was a greater tendency to have less durable lithic tools, edges were sharper, and there was less cortex reinforcement on edges. It seems reasonable to attribute these differences in lithics to differences in food processing and tool production. Hunting was more important during periods when population densities were low than it was when population densities were high.

Such an interpretation is not necessary, however, to support the argument that the Early Pithouse samples are more similar to the Cliff phase samples than either of them is to the Late Pithouse and Classic Mimbres samples. Thus, even if the differences are not wholly attributable to variation in the importance of hunting, they are empirically real and require an explanation. Given the temporal separation between the Early Pithouse period and the Cliff phase (some 800 years), it is unlikely that the relationship may be attributed to nontechnical variation or "preferences." We feel that the differences are more likely related to changes in basic subsistence strategies.

10 Miscellaneous Studies on the McAnally and Thompson Sites
Excavated Units and Depositional Contexts, Ceramic Seriation, and Miscellaneous Artifacts

Roger Anyon, Steven A. LeBlanc, and Michael W. Diehl

This chapter provides descriptive summaries of the excavated deposits at the McAnally and Thompson sites. Basic information provided in this chapter includes site plans, descriptions of architectural features, chronometric samples, and analytical descriptions of the depositional contexts from which the excavators obtained artifacts and special samples. In addition, this chapter describes the potsherds found in the McAnally and Thompson sites and places them in the Upland Mogollon pithouse chronology. Finally, artifacts that are not incorporated in the analyses in the preceding chapters are described at the end of the present chapter.

EXCAVATION METHODS

Mimbres Foundation staff excavated the pithouses and test units using the "unit-level-locus" system (LeBlanc 1976b). Units and loci are judgmental, non-randomly selected two-dimensional areas of the site. These can be any size or shape. At pithouse villages, a unit is a pithouse depression or a rectangular test pit located in an extramural area. A locus is a subdivision of a unit, defined sometimes for the excavators' convenience, as when a pithouse is divided into four quadrants. A locus can also be an obvious feature within the unit, such as a posthole, storage pit, hearth, ash lens, artifact concentration, or rodent burrow.

Levels are vertical strata within the unit. These may be an arbitrary constant depth, such as 10 cm, or they may correspond to obvious changes in soil color or consistency. For example, a deep roof-fall deposit may contain three 10-cm levels, and a fourth level of 7 cm that stops immediately before contacting the floor of a room. In this manner, archaeologists retain fine analytical control over deep homogeneous deposits, yet can respond to obvious changes in the stratigraphy that do not neatly correspond with the selected constant. Artifacts or special samples that were point provenienced are assigned an additional number. For example, an artifact designated 1-3-2/4 would be the fourth point-provenienced artifact from Unit 1, level 3, locus 2.

At both sites, all excavated deposits were passed through a 1/4-inch screen, and the chipped stone, ground stone, bone, and ceramics were stored separately. The contents of floor features were saved for macrobotanical analysis, and elements of floor plaster were reserved for palynological studies. Charcoal samples were saved to be submitted for radiocarbon and dendrochronology assays. Unfortunately, no tree-ring dates were obtainable from either the McAnally or the Thompson site.

FIGURE 10.1. *The Rio Mimbres floodplain as viewed from the McAnally site, looking west.*

FIGURE 10.2. *A typical summer flow of the Rio Mimbres near the McAnally site.*

THE McANALLY SITE (LA 12110)

The McAnally site is a Mogollon Early Pithouse period village located on a high knoll on the east side of the Rio Mimbres in the modern town of Mimbres, New Mexico (figs. 10.1, 10.2, and 10.3). Surveyors estimated that the site contained 12 house depressions (fig. 10.4). The initial plan was to excavate in contexts that would allow us to recover artifacts in good association with datable materials. Architectural information was considered desirable but was not the focus of the effort. It was thought that we might encounter burned or trash-filled pithouse depressions or extramural pits. Once we realized how hard the soil was, efforts at shovel scraping to expose extramural pits were abandoned. We did test one small depression we thought might be a pit, but it was a natural feature. Test pits did not reveal well-burned or densely trash-filled pithouses, except to some minor extent in what was subsequently labeled Pithouse 11. Because the site was on the top of a domed hill, the likelihood of locating stratified trash deposits was negligible.

In 1974, initial excavations focused on Pithouse 8. This structure was excavated using a method that LeBlanc had earlier employed with circular buildings in the Near East. By excavating what are essentially opposite wedges of a circular pie, one obtains more than half the available information for half the effort that would be required to excavate the entire structure. At the same time, the surviving balks provide complete profiles across the structure in two right-angle directions. This "pieces of pie" approach is particularly effective in the Southwest, where one has a reasonable chance of predicting the location of ramps and hearths. This was the approach taken with both Units 8 and 11. For Unit 8, the 50-percent sample seemed to be more than enough. We had the ramp, the probable fire area, and a reasonably good sample of recoverable specimens. In Unit 11, which was excavated in 1976, the initial excavations followed the "pieces of pie" approach; the observation of some apparently *in situ* floor deposits and burned material convinced us to excavate the entire house. Test units revealed that Units 1 and 3 were pithouses as well, but they did not appear to contain *in situ* artifacts, and since the soil was very compact they were not further excavated. Unit 13 was initially thought to be the location of an extramural feature, but excavations revealed it to be the depression of a rotten tree stump.

In summary, four pithouses were sampled. One pithouse (Unit 8) was partially excavated, and another (Unit 11) was completely excavated. Small test pits were placed in two other pithouses (Units 1 and 3). Although the excavated sample was small and we encountered no extramural trash middens or pits, we obtained a surprising amount of information for our efforts.

Occupation Dates

Analyses of the ceramics and a limited set of radiocarbon samples indicate that the McAnally site was occupied during the Early Pithouse period (A.D. 200–550). All of the ceramics on the site were undecorated brownwares (Alma Plain), textured brownwares (Alma Scored and a possible early Alma Neck-banded), and a poorly slipped, poorly polished redware. The redware may be a prototypical variant of San Francisco Red (LeBlanc 1976a). Since true San Francisco Red is a diagnostic ceramic of subsequent Georgetown phase structures (A.D. 550–700), it is likely that some of the McAnally pithouses were occupied during the late Early Pithouse period, dating to the first half of the sixth century A.D. Radiocarbon dates from the McAnally site are listed in table 10.1. Inspection reveals that some of the few available radiocarbon dates from McAnally site are consistent with a sixth-century occupation.

TABLE 10.1
RADIOCARBON ASSAYS
FROM THE McANALLY SITE

Sample I.D.	Context	Date
UCLA-2153A	Unit 11	A.D. 548–762[a]
UCLA-1953C	Unit 8	A.D. 180 ± 60[b]
UCLA-1953C	Unit 8	A.D. 580 ± 60
UCLA-1953C	Unit 11	A.D. 545 ± 85[b]

[a] 2-sigma calibrated age (Stuiver and Reimer 1993).
[b] *Source*: LeBlanc and Whalen 1980:513.

FIGURE 10.3. *Aerial view of the McAnally site and the Mattocks Ruin in 1975. The McAnally site is situated on the steep hill in the center of the photo. The Mattocks Ruin is in the foreground to the left of the houses.*

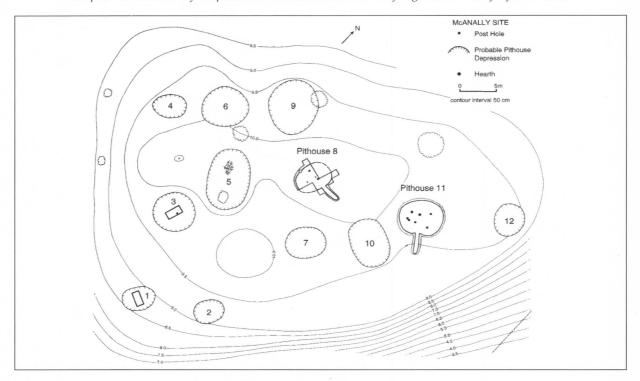

FIGURE 10.4. *Site plan for the McAnally site.*

Excavation Units

The excavated units were classified into analytically similar depositional contexts. These have been assigned letter names for convenience. Category A includes deposits that contain aeolian fill, possible post-occupational midden, and elements of the superstructure (fragments of roof beams, matting, and packed earth used in the roof). Category B is similar to category A but excludes obvious aeolian deposits. Category C contains superstructure material (roof beams and roof earth) exclusively. Category D contains superstructure and deposits on or near floor contact. Category E includes only artifacts in contact with the floor surface. Category F refers to subfloor contexts (the contents of hearths, pits, postholes, and other floor features). Category G refers to units that were excavated as an undifferentiated mass of fill and may include materials found in all other analytical categories.

Unit 1. Unit 1 is a house depression located on the southern extreme of the site, approximately 1.5 vertical meters downslope from the crest of the knoll. One 2-m^2 test unit was placed near the center of the depression. Excavated in six levels down to a floor surface, the unit was not divided into subsequent loci. Table 10.2 describes the deposits found within Unit 1.

Artifacts found within Unit 1 included chipped stone debitage, Alma Plain ceramics, animal bone fragments, a projectile point fragment, and fragments of charred and uncharred wood. The soil was extremely compact, and excavators were forced to rely primarily on picks to excavate the highly calcified ground. Excavators did not observe any evidence of rodent disturbance.

No floor features were identified in the limited excavations within this structure, and architectural data are scanty. No plaster was observed on the floor of the pithouse; rather, the limit of the deposits (the floor) was defined by the presence of cobble-strewn

TABLE 10.2
DEPOSITIONAL CONTEXTS WITHIN THE McANALLY SITE, UNIT 1

Unit (U-L-L)	Datum	Average Depth	Depositional Context	Remarks
1-1-1	F	23 cm	A	Mixed sheet midden and aeolian deposit
1-2-1	F	38 cm	A	Mixed sheet midden and aeolian deposit
1-3-1	F	53 cm	B	Higher concentration of midden with gravel
1-4-1	F	67 cm	B	Higher concentration of midden with gravel
1-5-1	F	75 cm	C	Soft ashy fill with roof fall fragments
1-6-1	F	80 cm	D	Roof fall on floor

Notes: U-L-L = Unit-level-locus.
Average depth is given in centimeters below datum.
Datum F height above site datum = 8.87 m.

TABLE 10.3
DEPOSITIONAL CONTEXTS WITHIN THE McANALLY SITE, UNIT 3

Unit (U-L-L)	Datum	Average Depth	Depositional Context	Remarks
3-1-1	None	—	C	1 x 1 m locus in pithouse roof and wall fall
3-1-2	E	33 cm	C	1 x 1 m locus in pithouse roof and wall fall
3-2-2	E	44 cm	C	1 x 1 m locus in pithouse roof and wall fall
3-3-2	E	60 cm	C	1 x 1 m locus in pithouse roof and wall fall
3-4-2	E	73 cm	C	1 x 1 m locus in pithouse roof and wall fall
3-5-3	E	83 cm	C	1 x 2 m locus in pithouse roof and wall fall
3-6-3	E	94 cm	C	1 x 2 m locus in pithouse roof and wall fall
3-7-4	E	125 cm	—	Posthole

Notes: Approximate depth is given in centimeters below datum.
Datum E height above site datum = 10.12 m.

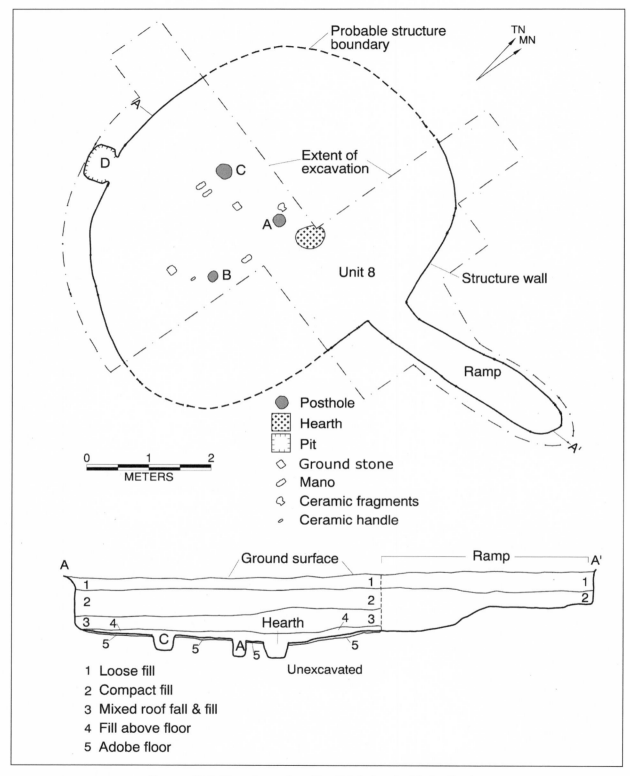

FIGURE 10.5. *Plan view and profile of Unit 8 at the McAnally site.*

sterile red conglomerate beneath the darker ashy fill of the house superstructure. Elements of the superstructure included hard clumps of wall and roof material made of compacted, clay-rich mud.

Unit 3. Unit 3 is a large pithouse depression located on the south part of the site, approximately one-half vertical meter downslope from the crest of the knoll. Two 2-m^2 test units were initially placed near the center of the depression (loci 1 and 2); these were subsequently joined and excavated as locus 3. Excavated in seven levels down to the sterile soil, the unit was divided into four loci altogether. As with Unit 1, excavators did not find a plastered or otherwise well-defined floor surface. Table 10.3 describes the depositional contexts found within Unit 3.

Artifacts found in Unit 3 included predominantly Alma Plain potsherds, a few red-washed potsherds, ground stone fragments, chipped stone debitage, a whole projectile point, and animal bone fragments. No chronometrically datable charcoal or wood fragments were recovered. As with Unit 1, the fill was extremely compact and mandated the use of picks.

In the absence of a plastered floor surface, the limit of excavation in the unit was defined by the presence of cobble-strewn red sterile soil beneath the darker fill. One pebble-lined posthole (locus 4) was excavated. The posthole diameter was approximately 25 cm, and it extended 20 cm into the sterile material beneath the structure. The posthole had vertical sides and a flat, level base. Two chipped stone fragments were found within the posthole fill.

FIGURE 10.6. *McAnally site, Unit 8, excavated to floor.*

Unit 8. The reader is directed to figure 10.5 for a plan view and profile of the excavated loci within Unit 8. Approximately 50 percent of the pithouse was excavated down to the floor surface in 1974 (figs. 10.6 and 10.7). The initial plan was to excavate two opposite wedges of the house depression. Given our expectations concerning the location of the ramp, we hoped to expose the ramp and hearth and define enough postholes to determine the overall shape and construction style. Since we were successful in our effort, the remainder of the house was left unexcavated. The sequence of excavated levels and loci is complicated, and detailed descriptions of the depositional contexts of excavated strata are provided in table 10.4.

FIGURE 10.7. *McAnally site, Unit 8, excavated to floor, with detail of Loci 3, 4, and 7.*

TABLE 10.4
DEPOSITIONAL CONTEXTS WITHIN THE McANALLY SITE, UNIT 8

Unit (U-L-L)	Datum	Depth	Remarks
		Ground Surface, Pithouse Superstructure, and Aeolian Fill (Context A)	
8-1-1	A1	32–37 cm	1 x 3 m trench extending south from center
8-1-2	A1	19–30 cm	1 x 2.7 m trench extending east from center
8-1-3	A2	40–50 cm	1 x 3 m trench extending north from center
8-1-4	A2	69–72 cm	1 x 3 m trench extending west from center
8-1-5	A1	23 cm	0.80 x 0.85 m trench SE to loci 1 and 2
8-1-6	A1	46–61 cm	1 x 1 m trench at ramp and south wall
8-1-7	A2	61–72 cm	Wedge in NW quadrant of pithouse
8-1-8	A1	38–42 cm	Ramp
8-1-9	A1	30–25 cm	1 x 2 m trench connecting locus 3 and locus 6
		Pithouse Superstructure and Aeolian Fill (Analytical Context B)	
8-2-1	A1	51 cm	1 x 3 m trench extending south from center
8-2-2	A1	34 cm	1 x 2.7 m trench extending east from center
8-2-3	A2	93 cm	1 x 3 m trench extending north from center
8-2-4	A2	90 cm	1 x 3 m trench extending west from center
8-2-5	A1	35 cm	0.80 x 0.85 m trench SE to loci 1 and 2
8-2-6	A1	46 cm	1 x 1 m trench at ramp and south wall
8-2-7	A2	90 cm	Wedge in NW quadrant of pithouse
8-2-9	A1	62–65 cm	1 x 2 m trench connecting locus 3 and locus 6
8-3-1	A1	65–68 cm	1 x 3 m trench extending south from center
8-3-5	A1	66 cm	0.80 x 0.85 m trench SE to loci 1 and 2
		Pithouse Superstructure and Compact Soil (Analytical Context C)	
8-2-2	A1	54–72 cm	Ramp
8-3-2	A1	76 cm	1 x 2.7 m trench extending east from center
8-3-3	A2	115 cm	1 x 3 m trench extending north from center
8-3-4	A2	105 cm	1 x 3 m trench extending west from center
8-3-7	A2	105 cm	Wedge in NW quadrant of pithouse
8-3-9	A1	80–85 cm	1 x 2 m trench connecting locus 3 and locus 6
8-4-1	A1	89–94 cm	1 x 2.7 m trench extending south from center
8-4-2	A1	34 cm	1 x 3 m trench extending east from center
8-4-5	A1	90 cm	0.80 x 0.85 m trench SE to loci 1 and 2
		Floor Surface (Analytical Context E)	
8-5-1	A1	102 cm	1 x 3 m trench extending south from center
8-5-2	A1	98 cm	1 x 2.7 m trench extending east from center
8-4-3	A2	93 cm	1 x 3 m trench extending north from center
8-4-4	A2	124 cm	1 x 3 m trench extending west from center
8-5-5	A1	93 cm	0.80 x 0.85 m trench SE to loci 1 and 2
8-4-7	A2	123 cm	Wedge in NW quadrant of pithouse
8-4-9	A1	106 cm	1 x 2 m trench connecting locus 3 and locus 6
		Floor and Floor Features (Analytical Context E)	
—	—	—	2 postholes that were not assigned locus numbers (see table 10.5)
—	—	—	1 hearth pit that was not assigned a locus number (see table 10.5)
8-6-1	A1	105–121 cm	1.05–1.21 m x 3 m trench extending south from center
8-6-10	A2	130 cm	Entire pithouse floor except locus 8-6-1
8-6-11	A2	128 cm	Alcove tangential to NW wall

Notes: Approximate depth is given in centimeters below datum.
Datum A1 height above site datum = 10.00 m. Datum A2 height above site datum = 10.14 m.

TABLE 10.5
ARCHITECTURAL FLOOR FEATURES IN THE McANALLY SITE, UNIT 8

(U-L-L/I.D.) Unit	Plan View	Profile	Plaster	Length	Width	Depth	Remarks
8-6-11	Oval	Flat	Absent	70 cm	60 cm	19 cm	Wall alcove at floor level
Hearth	Oval	Basin	Absent	40 cm	38 cm	25 cm	Ash-filled pit, no deflector
"Pit 1"	Round	U-shaped	Absent	30 cm	Diameter	20 cm	Posthole
"Pit 2"	Round	U-shaped	Absent	25 cm	Diameter	23 cm	Posthole

Note: Depth of feature is depth below floor surface.

Artifacts found within the pithouse included Alma Plain potsherds, chipped stone artifacts, ground stone and ground stone fragments, a projectile point, and animal bone fragments. Special samples that we collected included charred wood for chronometric dating, pollen samples, and flotation samples. As with Units 1 and 3, the fill was extremely compact and mandated the use of picks.

Architecturally, Unit 8 is a typical Early Pithouse period structure. The main chamber is elliptical, and the 6-m-long major axis runs northeast to southwest. The minor axis measured 4.85 m. Excavators estimated the total surface area of the floor to be approximately 24 m^2. The ramp, which extends 3.4 m southward from the chamber, is 0.65 m wide at the chamber wall and at its southern terminus, but narrows to about 0.50 m just outside the wall of the room. The ramp slopes upward approximately 0.62 m along its length (approximately an 18% grade). The main chamber was excavated by its builders into the hilltop to a depth of approximately 0.95 to 1.05 m below the modern ground surface.

Excavators noted the presence of a sporadic, thin floor surface alternatively described as a "hard packed dark brown matrix" and a "thin adobe facing." Probably the floor was finished with a thin layer of adobe or mud plaster before occupation. Two postholes and an ash-filled hearth intruded into the bedrock. There was a small alcove in the north wall at floor level. The diameters and depths of the floor features are described in table 10.5.

Unit 11. Unit 11 is a pithouse located on the north side of site, approximately 0.5 m (vertical distance) below the crest of the knoll. Figure 10.8 provides a plan view and profile of Unit 11, and table 10.6 describes the depositional contexts of the different strata. Mimbres Foundation staff excavated the entire pithouse depression down to the bedrock floor surface in 1976 (fig. 10.9).

Artifacts found within the pithouse included fragmentary and reconstructable Alma Plain jars and bowls, a red-slipped jar, vesicular basalt manos and metates, ground stone fragments, projectile points, chipped stone flakes, worked and unworked potsherds, animal bone fragments, hammerstones, and a bifacially worked sandstone slab. Excavators collected flotation samples, pollen samples, and fragments of charred wood for subsequent analyses. The fill was also very compact, requiring the use of pickaxes to excavate. The matrix was so compact that some objects had to be soaked with water before they could be removed without breaking.

Unit 11 is a bean-shaped pithouse that measured 6.2 m by 5.2 m, with a total surface area in the main chamber of approximately 24 m^2. The ramp extended 2.9 m southeast from the main chamber with a 13 percent upward grade. It was 0.80 m wide at its conjunction with the wall but narrowed to 0.45 m at its southern terminus. A compact surface with intermittent areas of smooth adobelike plaster defined the floor of the room. No hearth or obvious ash pit was found in the room. Posthole G, however, was exceptionally large and shallow and may have been a hearth depression; excavation notes do not describe the contents of the posthole fill. Table 10.7 describes the diameters and depths of the seven postholes found in this room.

Unit 13. Unit 13 was initially thought to be the location of an extramural hearth, but excavation revealed it to be the location of a rotting juniper stump. Excavators removed the fill around the stump until they hit the orange, gravelly bedrock at a depth of 25 cm below the modern ground surface.

McAnally Site Summary

In two seasons of excavation, Mimbres Foundation staff placed three test trenches inside structures and excavated half of one pithouse (Unit 8) and all of

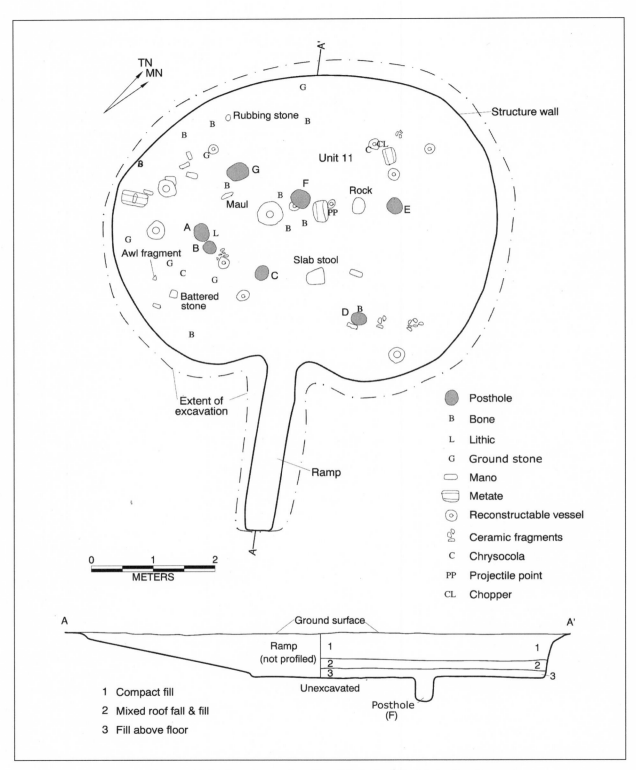

FIGURE 10.8. *Plan view and profile of Unit 11 at the McAnally site.*

TABLE 10.6
DEPOSITIONAL CONTEXTS WITHIN THE McANALLY SITE, UNIT 11

Unit (U-L-L)	Datum	Depth	Remarks
			Post-Occupational Fill and Superstructure (Analytical Context A)
11-1-1	G	23–38 cm	1 x 2 m trench at center of depression
11-1-2	G	0–70 cm	Wall and ramp trench on east side of unit
11-1-3	G	20–80 cm	1 x 1.5 m trench east-center of depression
11-1-4	G	24–40 cm	Polygon in SE quadrant
11-1-6	G	20–70 cm	Wall trench on south side
11-1-7	G	0–70 cm	Crescent-shaped locus on north and west sides (subsequently divided into loci 7 and 8)
11-2-1	G	38–53 cm	1 x 2 m trench at center of depression
11-2-4	G	40–55 cm	Polygon in SE quadrant
11-3-1	G	53–67 cm	1 x 2 m trench at center of depression
11-3-4	G	55–70 cm	Polygon in SE quadrant
			Collapsed Superstructure and Dark Organic Soil (Analytical Context C)
11-2-6	G	70–85 cm	Wall trench on south side
11-2-7	G	70–85 cm	Crescent-shaped locus on north and west sides (subsequently divided into loci 7 and 8)
11-4-1	G	67–82 cm	1 x 2 m trench at center of depression
1-4-5	G	70–84 cm	Subsumes former loci 2, 3, and 4
			Superstructure Down to Floor Surface (Analytical Context D)
11-3-6	G	85–97 cm	Wall trench on south side
11-3-7	G	85–100 cm	Truncated crescent along north wall
11-5-1	G	82–97 cm	1 x 2 m trench at center of depression
11-5-5	G	84–95 cm	Subsumes former loci 2, 3, and 4
11-3-8	G	85–95 cm	Wedge along west wall
			Subfloor to Sterile (Bedrock)
11-4-10	G	95–104 cm	Entire pithouse

Notes: Approximate depth is given in centimeters below datum. Datum G height above site datum = 9.90 m.

TABLE 10.7
ARCHITECTURAL FLOOR FEATURES IN THE McANALLY SITE, UNIT 11

I.D.	Plan View	Profile	Plaster	Length	Width	Depth	Remarks
Post A	Oval	U-shaped	Absent	30 cm	25 cm	23 cm	
Post B	Round	U-shaped	Absent	18 cm	Diameter	20 cm	Added to reinforce Post A?
Post C	Round	U-shaped	Absent	21 cm	20 cm	17 cm	
Post D	Oval	U-shaped	Absent	25 cm	20 cm	17 cm	
Post E	Oval	U-shaped	Absent	25 cm	18 cm	31 cm	
Post F	Oval	U-shaped	Absent	32 cm	30 cm	44 cm	
Post G	Oval	U-shaped	Absent	40 cm	30 cm	21 cm	

Note: Depth of feature is depth below floor surface.

TABLE 10.8
DEPOSITIONAL CONTEXTS WITHIN THE THOMPSON SITE, UNIT 1

Unit (U-L-L)	Datum	Depth	Remarks
		All Deposits (Analytical Context G)	
1-1-1	A	25–64 cm	1.00 x 0.75 m test trench
1-1-2	A	24–60 cm	Wall trench along east wall of pithouse
1-2-3	A	50–68 cm	Polygonal locus partially overlapping the ramp
1-2-5	A	50–84 cm	Polygonal locus extending into the ramp
		Post-Occupational Fill (Analytical Context A)	
1-1-4	A	29–40 cm	Wedge-shaped locus in NW quadrant
1-2-4	A	40–60 cm	Wedge-shaped locus in NW quadrant
		Pithouse Roof Fall to Floor Surface (Analytical Context D)	
1-3-4	A	60–79 cm	Wedge-shaped locus in NW quadrant
		Subfloor Testing to Sterile Bedrock	
1-4-6	A	N.D.	Wedge-shaped locus in NW quadrant

Notes: Approximate depth is given in centimeters below datum. Datum A height above site datum = 6.91 m. N.D. = no data.

FIGURE 10.9. *McAnally site, Unit 11, excavated to floor.*

another (Unit 11). Ceramics and radiocarbon dates indicate that Unit 8 may have been occupied during the second century A.D. Unit 11 was occupied during the sixth century A.D. Unit 11 produced an exceptionally large quantity of artifacts. Artifacts from the McAnally site are described in this chapter and in previous chapters.

THE THOMPSON SITE (NM Z:5:35)

The Thompson site (NM Z:5:35, University of New Mexico designation) is a Mogollon Early Pithouse period village located on a high, long knoll overlooking the east bank of the Rio Mimbres, west of Round Mountain peak. Surveyors estimated that the site contained 55 pithouse depressions (fig. 10.10)—an unusually large number for an early Mogollon village. Excavations in 1977 were designed to collect comparative samples from the southern end of the Mimbres Valley, as discussed in chapter 1.

It was also hoped that the soil would not be as hard as at the McAnally site and that more information would be recovered for the energy expended. Unfortunately, the soil was almost nonexistent; the site was incredibly shallow, with the pithouse depres-

sions having been literally hacked out of bedrock. Preservation was poor, and the deposits were sparse. It became clear that excavations would provide little information, given the limited amount of time and money available to us, and our efforts ceased after a few days. We wish to emphasize that the site has great information potential, but extensive sampling will be required to find locations that contain *in situ* floor assemblages or rich trash deposits.

(The question of which sites to work in future Early Pithouse research is an interesting one. Most sites are in locations that are inconvenient of access, yet one cannot avoid these locations and hope to understand the period. It might be possible, however, to find sites where the soils are neither exceedingly compact nor shallow. Perhaps the systematic auguring of a number of sites would be the first step in defining a useful universe of sites.)

The Mimbres Foundation staff excavated elements of seven pithouse depressions. None were excavated in their entirety because the deposits were shallow and the artifact densities in all locations were extremely low. No charcoal samples were available for radiocarbon dating. A few pieces of true San Francisco Red pottery were found, and they suggest that some of the pithouses may have been occupied during the

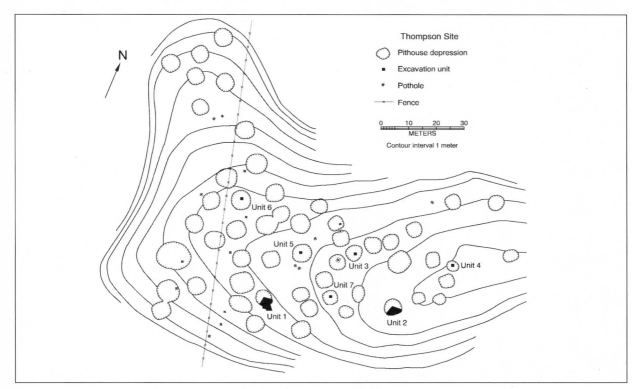

FIGURE 10.10. *Site plan for the Thompson site.*

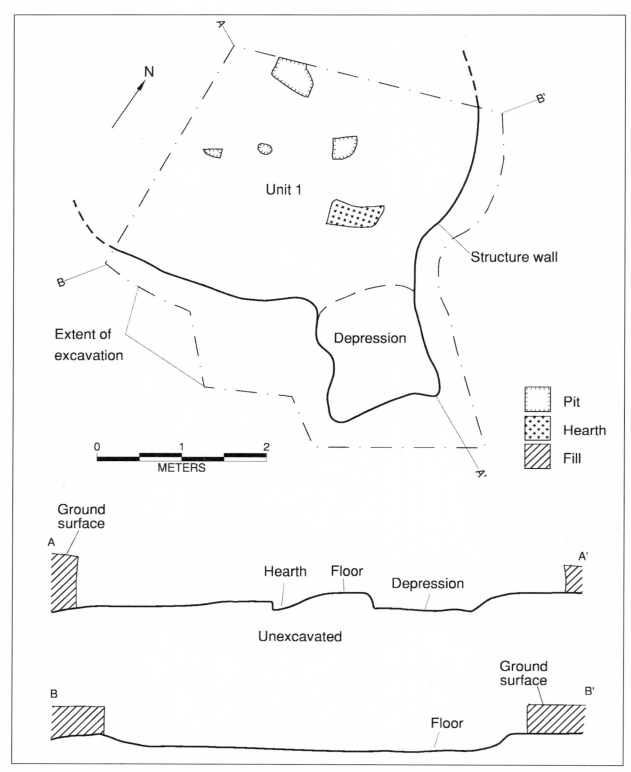

FIGURE 10.11. *Plan view and profile of the Thompson site, Unit 1.*

FIGURE 10.12. *Thompson site, Unit 1, excavated to floor.*

Georgetown phase (A.D. 550–700). Given the relatively large number of house depressions, it is possible that Thompson is a multicomponent site.

Unit 1

Unit 1 is a pithouse located west of the center of the village, approximately 3 vertical meters below the crest of the knoll. Approximately one-third of this pithouse was excavated down to the uneven bedrock surface beneath the floor. Artifacts found within the pithouse included projectile points, ground stone fragments, chipped stone debitage and cores, and potsherds. One flotation sample was removed from an ashy depression. Table 10.8 describes the depositional contexts of the different strata, and figures 10.11 and 10.12 show the plan view and profile of the excavated portion of the pithouse

Little is known of the construction of Unit 1 because little of the main chamber was excavated. The house was excavated down to the bedrock surface 0.50 to 0.75 m beneath the modern ground surface. The excavated portion revealed a curved wall with a possible ramp extending to the southeast. Where it joins the main chamber the ramp is 1.4 m wide. Since the ramp was not fully excavated, its length is unknown. Excavators found a clay-rich layer that varied from extremely thin to 3 cm thick, which may have been a plastered floor. Two postholes, two amorphous pits, and a probable hearth (an ash-filled depression) were located on the floor. Three other probable postholes were located along the walls of the ramp, but these were not excavated. Floor features located within Unit 1 are described in table 10.9.

Unit 2

Unit 2 is a very shallow pithouse (approximately 0.50 m beneath the modern ground surface) located immediately southwest of the crest of the knoll. Since the pithouse foundation was hacked into the andesite bedrock substrate of the hill, it is not surprising that the foundation was shallow. The few artifacts found within the pithouse included chipped stone flakes, Alma Plain potsherds, and a pestle. Approximately one quarter of the pithouse was excavated down to the uneven bedrock surface (figs. 10.13 and 10.14), revealing a curved wall but no ramp. The dimensions of the pithouse remain unknown. No chunks of roof material were found in the fill, and the floor was not plastered. Table 10.10 describes the depositional contexts of the fill strata.

The field crew described one floor pit as a "bedrock mortar." This feature (which may be a posthole) measured 10 cm in diameter and 4 cm deep. The sides were rough and irregular, and converged toward

TABLE 10.9
ARCHITECTURAL FLOOR FEATURES WITHIN THE THOMPSON SITE, UNIT 1

Plan View	Profile	Plaster	Length	Width	Depth	Remarks
Irregular	N.D.	Absent	> 35 cm	> 25 cm	95 cm	Floor pit
Irregular	N.D.	Absent	~ 25 cm	~ 25 cm	95 cm	Floor pit
Round	N.D.	Absent	~ 15 cm	Diameter	92 cm	Posthole
Irregular	N.D.	Absent	~ 15 cm	~ 15 cm	101 cm	Posthole
Rectangular	N.D.	Present	~ 60 cm	~ 25 cm	84 cm	Hearth

Notes: The depth of the floor feature is given in centimeters below datum A. Datum A height above site datum = 6.91 m.
N.D. = no data.

TABLE 10.10
DEPOSITIONAL CONTEXTS WITHIN THE THOMPSON SITE, UNIT 2

Unit (U-L-L)	Datum	Depth	Remarks
		All Deposits (Depositional Context G)	
2-1-1	B	36–76 cm	1.25 x 0.63 m test trench
2-1-2	B	36–82 cm	SW quadrant of pithouse
		Floor Surface	
2-2-2	B	82 cm	SW quadrant of pithouse

Notes: Approximate depth is given in centimeters below datum. Datum B height above site datum = 9.97 m.

the bottom. Two ash lenses were located on the floor, and their presence may be evidence of informal ("on-floor") hearths. So little of the room was excavated that we were unable to determine whether a formal hearth or a ramp was present, and we were also unable to assess the extent of a "raised bench" observed near the center of the room. Although some pithouses at other sites have benches along the walls, no others have been found to contain centrally located benches. The "bench" may be the margin of a collared hearth.

Units 3 through 7

All of the other units at the Thompson site were small test pits excavated to the bedrock surface as one level. Since these units were small, they provide no information about the presence or absence of floor or wall features, ramps, or the dimensions and surface areas of the pithouse chambers. Units excavated in these pithouses are described in table 10.11. Inspection

reveals that the depths of these pithouses varied from 0.40 to 0.80 m beneath the modern ground surface. Although all of the excavated units were initiated in order to retrieve datable charcoal specimens, no suitable specimens were recovered. Recovered artifacts included low frequencies of Alma Plain potsherds and chipped stone debitage, two shell beads, and a quartz crystal. Unit 5 had obvious signs of rodent disturbance.

Thompson Site Summary

In 1977, Mimbres Foundation staff excavated portions of seven pithouses at the Thompson site (fig. 10.15), but none of them in their entirety. Although artifact densities were very low, ceramics found in the test units were consistent with an Early Pithouse period occupation, with a possible Georgetown phase component also present. Because there were no charcoal fragments, no radiocarbon dates were obtained.

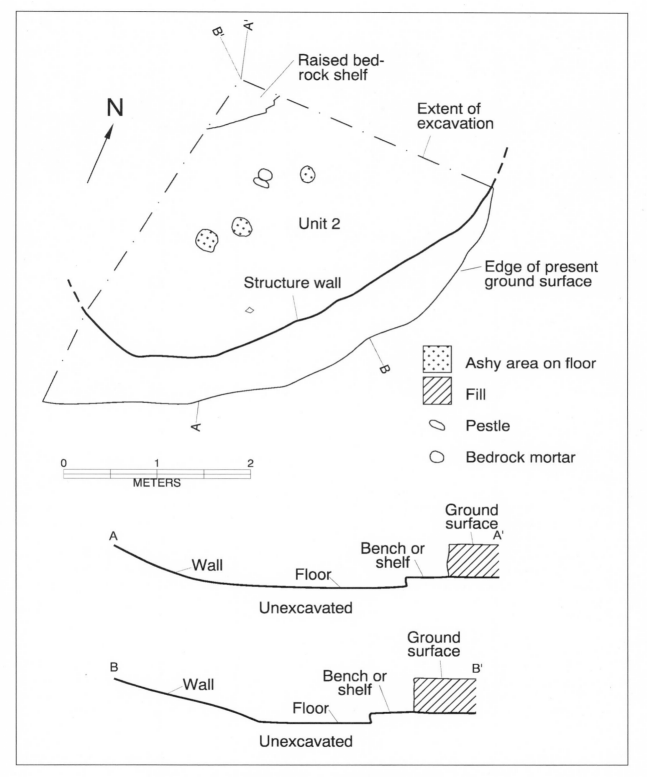

FIGURE 10.13. *Plan view and profile of the Thompson site, Unit 2.*

FIGURE 10.14. *Thompson site, Unit 2, excavated to floor.*

TABLE 10.11
DEPOSITIONAL CONTEXTS WITHIN THE THOMPSON SITE, UNITS 3 TO 7

Unit (U-L-L)	Datum	Datum Height	Depth	Remarks
		All Depositional Contexts (Analytical Context G)		
3-1-1	D	8.52 m	10–94 cm	64 cm diameter circle test pit
4-1-1	C	10.06 m	25–85 cm	50 x 50 cm rectangle test pit
5-1-1	E	7.86 m	15–90 cm	55 x 70 cm rectangle test pit
6-1-1	F	6.26 m	15–70 cm	50 x 50 cm rectangle test pit
7-1-1	G	8.38 m	20–62 cm	65 x 65 cm rectangle test pit

Notes: Approximate depth is given in centimeters below local datum. Datum height is given in meters above site datum.

CERAMIC DESCRIPTIONS AND SERIATION

Three types of potsherds were recovered at the McAnally and Thompson sites: San Francisco Red, Alma Plain, and a category to which we will refer as "Mogollon Early Red." Alma Plain includes all unslipped, unpolished, untextured brownwares, with a brown paste and a gray core with a white temper (Haury 1936b). Bowls are sometimes highly polished

on the interior surface, and jars are sometimes highly polished on the exterior. In differentiating between San Francisco Red and Mogollon Early Red, the ceramic analysts had to contend with typological issues surrounding the use of the term San Francisco Red raised by Shepard (1965) and Anyon and LeBlanc (1984:149–151).

The difficulty with the San Francisco Red type lies in the question "What, exactly, is meant by San Francisco Red?" The question arises because there

FIGURE 10.15. *Aerial view of the Thompson site, situated on the knoll overlooking the drainage, left of center.*

seems to have been a gradual developmental branching of San Francisco Red out of Alma Plain. The developmental sequence has not been adequately studied, and there is no formal typological definition of the intermediate type that we are calling Mogollon Early Red ("Miscellaneous Red" in Anyon and LeBlanc 1984). Roger Anyon (Anyon and LeBlanc 1984) examined red-painted wares from Galaz, Mattocks, McAnally, Thompson, and other Mimbres Valley sites. The developmental sequence from Alma Plain to San Francisco Red involved the production of bowls and jars with increasingly red slips and increasingly greater polishing and smoothing, and finally the production of bowls with dimpled exteriors and burnishing. Although Mogollon Early Red is found well into the Classic Mimbres period, its position at the start of the developmental sequence motivates our use of the adjective "early."

We initially thought to include any sherds that were part of this sequence in the category San Francisco Red, but this would add confusion rather than utility. Instead we chose to give the intermediate forms the name Mogollon Early Red because all had thin to modest red slips, slight to moderate polish, no dimpling, and no strong burnishing. The "Saliz vari-

ety" of San Francisco Red falls into our category of Mogollon Early Red. In contrast, the term "San Francisco Red" is reserved for vessels that have the following attributes: (1) thick red slips on bowl interiors and jar exteriors, ranging in color from orange-red to dark maroon; (2) slips that are smooth and highly polished; (3) light scoring on the interiors of jars; and (4) dimpling on the exteriors of bowls, with the result that the exterior slip may be unpolished and less evenly applied.

Although Mogollon Early Red is found throughout the Mimbres occupation of the Mimbres Valley (Anyon and LeBlanc 1984:149–162), it is clear that the effort to make vessels red came before the effort to burnish and polish them. Since the McAnally and Thompson sites contained few ceramics that could be classified as San Francisco Red, we suspect that San Francisco Red developed about the same time that the McAnally and Thompson sites were abandoned.

By inspecting the surfaces on the convex and concave sides of potsherds, the ceramic analysts were able to subdivide these into three categories: bowls, jars, and indeterminate pieces that were too small to classify. The distributions of the different types of ceramics and vessel forms from the McAnally and Thompson

TABLE 10.12
FREQUENCY DISTRIBUTION OF McANALLY AND THOMPSON SITE CERAMIC TYPES, BY EXCAVATION PROVENIENCE

Site	Unit (U-L-L)	Mogollon Early Red			Alma Plain			Total
		Bowl	Jar	Indeterminate	Bowl	Jar	Indeterminate	
McAnally	1-1-1	0	1	1	1	12	2	17
	1-2-1	0	0	0	0	9	0	9
	1-3-1	7	15	7	1	29	14	73
	1-4-1	1	11	1	2	24	2	41
	1-5-1	0	3	0	0	10	0	13
	1-6-1	0	3	0	0	1	1	5
Totals[a]		8	33	9	4	85	19	158
	2-1-1	0	1	0	0	2	0	3
	3-1-1	0	14	2	1	39	1	57
	3-1-2	0	1	0	0	1	2	4
	3-2-2	0	4	0	0	20	0	24
	3-3-2	0	3	0	0	29	12	44
	3-4-2	0	3	0	2	15	25	45
	3-5-3	0	6	7	0	44	10	67
	3-6-3	1	9	4	0	18	14	46
Totals[b]		1	40	13	3	166	64	287
	8-1-1	0	0	0	0	0	1	1
	8-1-2	0	0	0	0	0	1	1
	8-1-3	0	0	0	0	2	0	2
	8-1-6	0	1	0	0	1	0	2
	8-1-7	0	2	0	0	1	0	3
	8-1-8	0	2	0	0	6	0	8
	8-2-1	0	3	1	0	16	2	22
	8-2-2	0	2	1	0	7	1	11
	8-2-3	1	18	1	0	57	2	79
	8-2-4	0	4	0	0	18	0	22
	8-2-5	0	1	0	0	2	1	4
	8-2-6	0	0	0	0	5	0	5
	8-2-7	2	28	4	2	67	17	115
	8-2-8	3	6	3	0	65	4	81
	8-2-9	2	1	3	0	26	0	32
	8-3-1	3	3	0	1	21	1	29
	8-3-2	2	8	1	0	41	17	69
	8-3-3	4	24	6	0	85	11	130
	8-3-4	2	13	2	1	42	18	78
	8-3-7	4	15	4	0	53	39	115
	8-3-9	1	24	7	1	53	19	1 05
	8-4-1	1	5	2	0	8	4	40
	8-4-2	0	3	4	0	42	14	63
	8-4-3[c]	1	8	0	1	27	1	38
	8-4-4	0	18	1	0	57	2	78
	8-4-5	0	0	0	0	12	2	14
	8-4-7	6	16	2	2	81	21	128
	8-4-9	1	5	1	2	47	1	57
	8-5-1	3	0	0	0	60	3	66
	8-5-2	1	6	0	3	20	8	38
	8-5-5	0	1	0	0	10	1	12
	8-6-1	0	0	0	0	11	2	13
	8-6-10[d]	3	3	0	0	61	2	69
	8-6-11	0	1	0	0	4	0	5
Totals[e]		40	216	43	13	1,028	195	1,535

Continued on next page

TABLE 10.12 — *Continued*

Site	Unit (U-L-L)	Mogollon Early Red			Alma Plain			Total
		Bowl	Jar	Indeterminate	Bowl	Jar	Indeterminate	
McAnally, *cont.*	11-1-1	4	0	0	0	31	5	40
	11-1-2	0	3	0	0	33	0	36
	11-1-3	0	2	1	0	19	0	22
	11-1-4	1	4	0	0	45	10	60
	11-1-6	2	3	0	0	14	1	20
	11-1-7	2	26	4	1	207	2	242
	11-1-9	0	1	0	0	22	0	23
	11-2-1	0	1	1	0	16	0	18
	11-2-4	0	14	1	3	72	19	109
	11-2-6	0	7	0	1	29	1	38
	11-2-7	7	30	7	9	130	10	193
	11-3-1	0	4	2	0	42	2	50
	11-3-4	0	6	4	0	63	6	79
	11-3-6	1	25	0	1	73	32	132
	11-3-7	1	48	8	2	226	14	299
	11-3-8	2	8	3	2	66	9	90
	11-4-1	13	12	0	15	75	6	131
	11-4-5	6	75	14	9	189	65	358
	11-4-9[f]	1	23	0	0	8	0	32
	11-5-1	1	8	0	0	77	15	101
	11-5-5[g]	1	25	4	1	196	36	263
Totals[h]		42	325	49	44	1,633	243	2,336
Thompson	1-1-1	0	0	1	0	9	2	12
	1-1-2	0	2	2	0	22	0	26
	1-1-4	0	3	1	0	4	1	9
	1-2-4	3	12	0	4	48	2	69
	1-2-5	0	1	0	0	2	2	5
	1-3-4	3	15	3	1	81	3	105
Totals[i]		6	33	6	5	166	10	227
	2-1-1	0	0	0	0	2	0	2
	2-1-2	0	0	0	0	12	0	12
Totals		0	0	0	0	14	0	14
	3-1-1	1	1	0	1	22	0	25
	4-1-1	0	1	0	0	3	0	4
	5-1-1	0	0	0	0	6	2	8
	6-1-1	0	0	0	0	6	0	6
	7-1-1	0	0	0	0	6	0	6
	Other	0	16	0	16	0	0	32

[a] Seven red-slipped sherds from Unit 1 had modest polish.
[b] Eight red-slipped sherds from Unit 3 had modest polish.
[c] One true San Francisco Red sherd.
[d] One true San Francisco Red sherd. Not noted in the table is 1 white-slipped sherd from this U-L-L.
[e] Twenty-one other red-slipped sherds from Unit 8 had modest polish.
[f] One dimpled red-slipped sherd with poor polish.
[g] Vessel D from this U-L-L was slightly dimpled and had modest polish.
[h] Seventeen other red-slipped sherds from Unit 11 had modest polish.
[i] Two red-slipped sherds from Unit 1 had modest polish.

TABLE 10.13
FREQUENCY DISTRIBUTION OF McANALLY AND THOMPSON SITE CERAMICS, BY ANALYTICAL CONTEXT

Site	Unit	Analytical Context	Mogollon Early Red			Alma Plain			Totals
			Bowl	Jar	Indeterminate	Bowl	Jar	Indeterminate	
McAnally	1	A	0	1	1	1	21	12	36
	1	B	8	26	8	3	53	16	114
	1	C	0	6	0	0	11	1	18
	2	A	0	1	0	0	2	0	3
	3	C	1	40	13	3	166	64	287
	8	A	0	6	0	0	11	1	18
	8	B	8	55	10	3	219	24	319
	8	C	17	98	29	2	421	127	694
	8	E	12	55	4	8	306	37	422
	8	F	3	3	0	0	61	2	69
	8	G	0	0	0	0	11	2	13
	11	A	9	63	13	4	452	45	586
	11	C	26	124	21	34	423	92	720
	11	D	6	114	14	6	638	106	884
	11	F	1	23	0	0	0	8	32
Thompson	1	A	3	15	1	4	52	3	78
	1	G	3	18	6	1	105	7	140
	2	E	1	1	0	1	22	0	25
	2	G	0	0	0	0	14	0	14
	4	G	0	1	0	0	3	0	4
	5	G	0	0	0	0	6	2	8
	6	G	0	0	0	0	6	0	6
		G	0	0	0	0	6	0	6

sites are listed by provenience in table 10.12. In table 10.13, the frequencies of ceramic types and vessel forms are listed by their analytical units.

MISCELLANEOUS ARTIFACTS

Any excavation produces a number of aesthetically interesting objects whose presence in excavated deposits appears to be a consequence of prehistoric human use. Often their purpose, meaning, and use or function remain hidden to archaeologists, as in the case of several minerals and crystals found in McAnally site deposits. On the Thompson site, one *Olivella* shell bead and one shell ornament (fig. 10.16) were found. These miscellaneous artifacts were not used to address substantive questions of Upland Mogollon adaptations and resource use or other

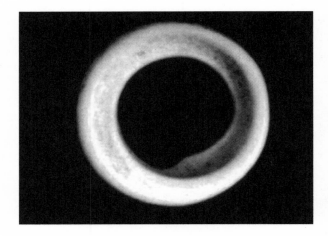

FIGURE 10.16. *Shell ornament from the Thompson Site, 3-1-1/1.*

TABLE 10.14
MISCELLANEOUS OBJECTS FROM THE McANALLY AND THOMPSON SITES

Site	Unit (U-L-L)	Description
McAnally	8-4-4/2	Worked antler tool (fig. 8.1)
	11-1-3/1	Chrysocolla (see 11-1-7/1 below)
	11-1-6/1	Chrysocolla (see 11-1-7/1 below)
	11-1-7/1	Chrysocolla (combined weight = 10.2 g)
	11-2-6/3	Worked sherd
	11-2-6/4	Bone awl fragment (unidentified species)
	11-2-7/5	Chrysocolla (see 11-2-7/7 below)
	11-2-7/7	Chrysocolla (combined weight = 0.5 g)
	11-3-7/1	Chrysocolla (weight = 7.5 g)
	11-4-5/2	Chrysocolla (weight = 4.2 g)
	11-5-1/3	Chrysocolla (from screen) (weight = 0.6 g)
	11-5-5/18	Worked sandstone slab (weight = 2.9 kg)
	11-3-8/10	Chrysocolla (weight = 0.1 g)
Thompson	1-3-4/4	Red hematite fragment
	1-2-4/2	Worked sherd (Mogollon Early Red)
	3-1-1/1	Shell ornament (fig. 10.16)
	3-1-1/2	Quartz crystal
	3-1-1/3	*Olivella* shell bead

aspects of their way of life. The miscellaneous artifacts are described and their depositional contexts are listed in table 10.14.

SUMMARY

From 1974 through 1977, Mimbres Foundation staff excavated one complete pithouse and elements of ten others at the McAnally (LA 12110) and Thompson (NM Z:5:35) sites. Ceramic assemblages from both sites and radiocarbon dates from the McAnally site are consistent with an Early Pithouse period (A.D. 200–550) occupation. As with most Mogollon Early Pithouse villages, the two sites are located on high knolls. Archaeologists noted the presence of 12 pithouse depressions on the surface of the McAnally site. The Thompson site had 55 surface depressions; test units revealed the presence of some true San Francisco Red potsherds, indicating that the Thompson site probably had a Georgetown phase (A.D. 550–700) occupation as well. This chapter has provided basic site plans, diagrams of pithouses, and descriptions of the depositional contexts from which artifacts were recovered.

11 Population Dynamics at the McAnally and Thompson Sites and Their Valleywide Context

Steven A. LeBlanc

The purpose of this chapter is to put the McAnally and Thompson sites into the context of the Mimbres Valley as a whole, with some reference to how this time period compares with the preceding and following periods. Many aspects of this analysis are admittedly little more than untested inferences. Nevertheless, they are a point of departure for testing ideas.

The Early Pithouse period may have begun with the rapid implementation of a new settlement strategy. Sites of the preceding Archaic period are exceedingly hard to find and must therefore have been much more ephemeral than the Early Pithouse sites. In contrast, Early Pithouse period sites are numerous in the Mimbres Valley; habitations were substantial and required considerable labor to build. Given the variation among sites in the number of pithouse depressions, some must have housed larger populations than are usually found among mobile foragers. Although it is pointed out in chapter 3 that the shift from the Archaic to the Early Pithouse period was not a simple change from foraging to farming, there must have been some form of qualitative change in overall adaptive strategy at this time.

Whatever particular form it took, the transition to the Early Pithouse period adaptation seems to have been quite rapid, not just for the Mimbres, but for the region as a whole. For example, although Archaic sites are more common in some portions of the Gila River

valley (Lekson 1992b), they are much smaller and more ephemeral than subsequent Early Pithouse period sites. Overall, there seem to be so many changes in settlement location, house form, and other aspects of material culture that I believe the transition included more than quantitative shifts in the reliance on agriculture or the degree of sedentism (LeBlanc 1982).

POPULATION DYNAMICS AT THE McANALLY AND THOMPSON SITES

In an effort to characterize Early Pithouse period settlement geography, it is useful to estimate the numbers of people involved. Based on the number of pithouse depressions that were observed among surveyed sites, the Thompson site is the largest known site of its time in the Mimbres Valley, and the McAnally site was near the median community size. In order to derive a static population estimate, one needs to know if a site was occupied continuously for the many years that it may have been used. It is also helpful to estimate that population growth rate. My approach to these problems is discussed below.

Early Pithouse period sites are almost evenly divided among the upper, middle, and lower valley locations, and they are rather evenly spaced. Based on sample survey, 73 percent of the Early Pithouse period sites had from 1 to 9 pithouse depressions, 20 percent had 10 to 24 depressions, and 7 percent had 25 or more depressions. The McAnally site, with 12 depressions, was larger than most sites, and the Thompson site, with 55 depressions, was quite large relative to the valleywide sample. It should be noted that publication of the locations of Early Pithouse sites found on survey has already resulted in their being looted, despite the lack of desirable artifacts in such sites. For that reason, our discussion does not include location maps.

Methods for Estimating Pithouse Longevity

Although estimating the absolute populations of sites requires many unsubstantiated assumptions, the exercise is useful for characterizing the range of variation in the intensity of site occupations. In order to estimate the number of pithouses that were used at any given time, we need to estimate the duration of site occupation (in years), the average use-lives of pithouses, and the population growth rate. Accurate estimates of the latter are already available; based on the number of sites and house depressions among sites, the population growth rate during the Pithouse periods ranged from 0.3 to 0.4 percent. If one assumes that the growth rate was higher when the population density was lower, a rate of 0.5 percent is indicated (Blake et al. 1986).

The most difficult problem is to determine how long individual pithouses were typically occupied. By comparing the Early Pithouse and Late Pithouse period populations, one can derive a reasonable relative population difference simply by assuming that the average pithouse use-life did not change much—an assumption that is somewhat counterindicated by the architectural study presented earlier in this volume. Therefore, in order to estimate the relative or actual size of a given community, one needs estimates, in years, of pithouse use-lives.

Information from the Late Pithouse period Galaz site is helpful because the use-life estimates from Galaz provided population figures that were consistent with independent estimates derived from mortuary data (Anyon and LeBlanc 1984), thereby lending credence to the approach used here to estimate the use-lives of Early Pithouse period structures and populations. At Galaz, the number of individuals on the site at any one time was derived from the size of the burial population and assumptions about mortality rates. Population estimates were also derived from the

number of pithouses, their sizes, and their approximate use-lives. When 25- to 40-year use-lives were assumed, the population estimates from the two different methods matched.

Based on ethnoarchaeological observations, however, Cameron (1990b) has questioned the assumption of comparably long pithouse use-lives; she suggests instead that pithouse use-lives did not exceed 15 years. Cameron's argument is based on how long it would take a pit structure to succumb to the elements and become essentially uninhabitable. I believe her estimate is in error for several reasons, the most important of which is that her analysis does not account for the increased longevity of house use-lives that would be imparted by maintenance or refurbishing. I believe the investment in excavating the pit, the desirability of particular locations (near family members, say), and the possession of rights to particular locations within the community are compelling enough incentives that refurbishing would have been relatively common, greatly extending the use-life of many structures. Diehl's architectural analyses in chapter 4 substantiate this belief. Cameron's estimate may provide an accurate gauge of the rate at which an abandoned house deteriorates, but it offers no direct information on the longevity of houses that were routinely used. For example, even low-intensity maintenance of exterior mud plaster, and the smoke from continued occupation, may prevent termite infestations or other forces that accelerate the pace of structure failures. So even houses that do not have obvious episodes of major reconstruction may be assumed to have longer use-lives than abandoned houses.

Refurbishing or remodeling of pithouses can sometimes be detected archaeologically. Dating such episodes may require a large number of tree-ring dates, and they may in turn be subject to a variety of interpretations. Nevertheless, an examination of a few structures from the southern Anasazi and Mogollon areas is instructive. At Allentown (Bannister et al. 1966; Roberts 1939, 1940), Structure 15 (House 4/32) was built around A.D. 853, remodeled around A.D. 873, and remodeled again in A.D. 1015. Pithouse 3, constructed in A.D. 937, was remodeled 11 years later. House 4 probably was constructed in A.D. 876 and may have been modified around A.D. 920. This gives refurbishing intervals of 11, 20, 42, and 44 years. At the Cerro Colorado site (Bannister et al. 1970; Bullard 1962), Structure 104 was apparently built in A.D. 653 and remodeled 14 years later, and it may have been slightly modified sometime thereafter. Structure 203 was built in A.D. 667 and modified after A.D. 691.

Structure 208 was probably built in A.D. 637 and remodeled after A.D. 653. Structure 405 was built in A.D. 676 and remodeled in A.D. 687. In this case, we have remodeling episodes 11, 14, 16, and 24 years apart. At the Early Pithouse period SU site (Bannister et al. 1970; Martin 1940, 1943; Martin and Rinaldo 1947), Pithouse G was built in A.D. 460 and remodeled after A.D. 481—a 21-year span. Finally, at the Galaz site (Anyon and LeBlanc 1984), Pithouse 29 was built in A.D. 859, remodeled in A.D. 870, and remodeled again after A.D. 893. Thus, at Galaz we have remodeling episodes at 11 and 23 years.

In summary, four sites that provide reasonable analogs for Early Pithouse structures provide evidence for possibly 11 remodeling episodes averaging 22 years apart. This is not far from Cameron's use-life estimate of 15 years, but the implications differ. If houses were remodeled on average every 20 years, *and then lived in for an additional 20 years before abandonment*, the average actual use-life of these pit structures would have been 40 years. Add another remodeling episode, and structure use-lives may increase to 60 years or more. It follows that population estimates that assume pithouse use-lives of 40 years are reasonably well supported by archaeological evidence.

A Population Estimate for the McAnally Site

The McAnally site had at least 12 pithouse depressions. Depression 5 is oblong, and it may represent two overlapped depressions. All of the other depressions were almost circular and were well separated. Thirteen is probably a safe upper limit for the number of houses. For the sake of comparison, if we follow Cameron in assuming that pithouses were occupied for no more than 15 years, then even if only a single pithouse was in use at one time, the site could not have been occupied for more than 200 years; halving this time span of total site occupation gives us only two structures in use at any one time. This in turn implies that only a small number of the sites in the valley were used at the same time, and most sites would have had only a single pithouse in use. Although this provides a theoretical minimum upon which to estimate the area population, one can make a series of reasonable assumptions to estimate the momentary population. For each of these scenarios, there is one aspect that is always the same: The community would have been small, close to what we typically associate with band-level organization, and would certainly have required mate exchange with

other communities.

Even though the Early Pithouse period lasted some 350 years, it is reasonable to assume that McAnally was occupied for only 200 of those years. I feel that the assumption is conservative, given the time span of radiocarbon dates that separate Unit 8 from Unit 11 (about 350 years). Let us also assume that pithouses were occupied for 40 years, and that the population grew by only 0.3 percent per year. Two pithouses could have been built initially and replaced every 40 years. These assumptions provide for the 12 observed pithouse depressions. But these assumptions must be incorrect because the resulting population seems too small: 10 people at any given time for the entire site, assuming occupancies of 4 to 5 people per house (Anyon and LeBlanc 1984:189–190).

At the other extreme would be the scenario in which no pithouse depression, once dug, ever went unused. Once built, the structure would be remodeled or completely rebuilt as needed every 40 years. Assuming the same 200-year occupation of the site and a 0.5 percent growth rate, the final population would be 2.7 times the initial population. Assuming 4 initial structures, with 12 in use at the end, the community grew from 16 to 20 occupants in the beginning to 48 to 60 at the end. Extending the site occupation to 350 years means that the initial population was housed in two structures. With the longer occupation interval, however, the initial population of the McAnally site seems much too small even for a "band-sized" social group that one would expect to find among the most highly mobile foragers—and the use of such substantial houses is quite inconsistent with the sorts of shelters built by very mobile groups (Diehl 1992; Gilman 1987).

A final, and perhaps more realistic, scenario assumes that 5 families initially occupied the McAnally site in 5 pithouses, and that the occupation lasted 300 years. Pithouse depressions were a big investment and would have been repeatedly reused and remodeled. Only a few pithouses were abandoned, but new ones were built. Over the 300 years, the population more than doubled, and 10 of the 12 depressions represent pithouses that were in use at the end of the occupation. This would result in a population estimate of 48 to 60 individuals.

A Population Estimate for the Thompson Site

The Thompson site presents a somewhat different picture, but the same scenarios that were described for the McAnally site may be applied. The pithouse depressions at Thompson, however, are shallow and would have been less costly to excavate; although this fact does not imply that the houses could not have been remodeled, their comparably low cost might have imposed less pressure to "recycle" house pits, and the Thompson site houses may have had briefer use-lives. Thus, a scenario of use-lives of 25 to 40 years for these structures is probably an upper limit. Assuming a 15-year use-life, and a 200-year site occupation, one may surmise that 4 structures were in use at any moment—yielding a momentary population of 16 to 20 people. Using 40-year house use-lives, one obtains a maximum population of about 40 people. With longer use-lives, one may conclude that 40 pithouses were in use at the end of the period, and one obtains a maximum population of around 200 people. The latter estimate, though plausible, seems extreme when compared with the populations of much larger Classic Mimbres period pueblos.

VALLEYWIDE POPULATION DYNAMICS

Population estimates for the valleywide Early Pithouse period are based on survey data alone. No burial data exist for independent assessment, as they do for some later periods. As discussed previously, the relative populations of different periods may be compared if one accounts for certain variables (Blake et al. 1986). The survey data were systematically collected and diligently recorded, however, so the information is accurate and, for the upper and middle valley sections at least, representative of the sampling universe. These data are discussed in detail in Blake et al. (1986) and are only summarized here.

Of the 500 recorded sites, 30 were assigned to the Early Pithouse period. We estimated that there were 86 Early Pithouse sites in the valley, given our sampling proportion. At the 30 identified sites, 221 pithouse depressions were recognized. From these we may estimate that there were 646 pithouses in the entire valley. In comparison, when the population peaked during the Mimbres Classic period, there were more than six times as many habitation rooms after adjusting for room-size differences and sampling biases. The Classic Mimbres period was, however, less than half as long as the Early Pithouse period. It would appear that the Early Pithouse period had between one sixth and one tenth the population of the Classic Mimbres period.

Turning these numbers into absolute population estimates is, again, methodologically risky, but the attempt may be made just the same. Assuming a pithouse use-life of 75 years and a 0.3 percent growth rate, Blake et al. (1986) estimated that there were initially 58 houses in the valley, and that this number grew to 166 by the end of the Early Pithouse period. If we assume that five people lived in each pithouse, we get an initial population of 290 people for the valley and a final population of 830. Using the more conservative house use-life estimate of 40 years reduces the initial valley population to 155 and the population at the end of the Early Pithouse period to 442. Interestingly, assuming a total valley population of 200 to 500 people, the valley's population was similar to that of many villages around the world. At the upper end of the range, then, the population size could have permitted biological endogamy with respect to other regions.

Also of note is the fact that there was no Early Pithouse period community within the valley (or elsewhere in the region, as far as we know) that was substantially larger than the Thompson site. That is, although there were sites twice the size of McAnally, and some possibly a bit bigger than Thompson, no known Early Pithouse period site was five or even three times larger than either of them. Moreover, no sites were so large as to suggest a different level of internal organization or the presence of a highly visible stratified control hierarchy.

There are, however, a number of very small sites of five pithouses or less. What do these sites represent socially? Because they are located in the same kinds of places (hilltops) as other residential sites, one cannot argue that they are special-purpose, nonresidential sites, and since they are not close to potentially arable land, they cannot be construed as "field houses" or the like. Furthermore, the artifact assemblages from the few excavated Early Pithouse period sites do not appreciably differ among sites (Diehl 1998). Were these sites occupied for comparatively brief intervals, and is this why they have fewer depressions on them?

It should be noted that Lekson (1992b) disagrees with my population assessment and argues that the population for all these periods was much smaller than the estimates given here. In fact, he argues that the population was only one quarter as large. Like Cameron, Lekson assumes house use-lives of 15 years. He thus derives an initial Early Pithouse period population of 58 people and an ending population of 166 people.

Lekson's estimates, which work out to an average

of about 100 people for the entire valley and its major tributaries, appear implausible. That such a small number of people would build, occupy, and abandon most of 86 sites in 400 years seems remarkable. It is even more remarkable if we expect people to live in groups of 20 to 25 people. The entire valley would have been initially occupied by two or three such groups, with only six in the valley at the end of the Early Pithouse period. This small number does not accord with the considerable evidence that there were far more than six communities at the beginning of the Georgetown phase. To reconcile Lekson's estimates with other data, one must assume that these very small Early Pithouse communities splintered into yet *smaller* communities around A.D. 550, or that there was a substantial and rapid population growth from immigration around that time.

Another line of reasoning also suggests that the argument for very low population densities is in error. The Mimbres Foundation scholars' estimates for the Early Pithouse, Late Pithouse, and Classic Mimbres periods all assume intrinsic growth rates that are reasonable. Moreover, if our estimates (Blake et al. 1986) for *any* period are correct, then they must *all* be approximately correct. Lekson's Early Pithouse period population estimate is quite inconsistent with our widely accepted estimates for the Classic Mimbres phase, and Lekson's model requires growth rates that far exceed what we expect on theoretical and empirical grounds.

We have considerable evidence that our Classic Mimbres phase population estimates are approximately correct. First, as documented in Anyon and LeBlanc (1984) for the Galaz site, the architectural data are closely corroborated by the burial data. If our village estimates are supported by independent data sets, why should our valleywide estimates be so far off? Second, every line of evidence points to significant environmental degradation and maximal resource utilization over the period of occupation. As Minnis (1985a) argues, this population estimate approaches the carrying capacity of the valley, and it explains the spread of farming hamlets and field houses to even the most agriculturally impoverished locations in the valley during the Classic Mimbres period. It seems unlikely that the population was one third to one fourth of the carrying capacity (as Lekson's figures imply), since under such circumstances one would not expect the intensification of agricultural production we have found through the use of marginal lands.

DISCUSSION

One can always deflect criticism or criticize another model by the refrain that "more data are needed," but we feel that it is important first to attempt to extract as much information as possible from the hard-won data available. In spite of all the assumptions required by our analyses of Mimbres Valley population dynamics, our effort helps paint a picture of the valley during the first millennium A.D.

Over a stretch of about 25 miles, sometime around A.D. 200, about 150 to 200 people founded six to eight communities in the Mimbres Valley—one community every 3 to 4 miles. Over the next 400 years, the population more than doubled, new sites were founded, and some old sites were abandoned. By the end of the Early Pithouse period there were at least a dozen concurrently occupied mid-sized communities, with some additional very small sites whose role is unclear. Shortly thereafter, a dozen or so new sites were established on the first terraces along this same stretch of river, and the hilltop locations were abandoned. The Late Pithouse period commenced with the shift in settlement locations.

Our scenario implies a high degree of community stability with a strong focus on the Mimbres River as a resource. It stands in radical contrast with Lekson's (1992b) highly mobile, minimal-farming adaptation model for this same time and place. Lekson's model is based on analogy with the historic Apaches, but it is inconsistent with archaeological data. The issues are clear-cut, and between these two models the implications are profound. From our perspective, it is apparent that the Early Pithouse period population was larger, less residentially mobile, and more dependent on agriculture than Lekson has proposed. Our model fits with the inferred major adaptive shift at the beginning of the Early Pithouse period and with documented (in this volume and elsewhere) increases in population, sedentism, and reliance on agriculture over the next millennium. These changes were significant and possibly not gradual. However, the Early Pithouse period subsistence economy seems to have marked the beginning of a new farming-oriented adaptation in the Mimbres Valley.

Appendix
Tree-Ring Dates from Upland Mogollon Pithouse Villages

Sample I.D.	Context	Interval of Occupation		Tree-Ring Date
		Upland Mogollon Synthesis	Local Phase Name	
	Bear Ruin		Forestdale Branch	
FST19	House 1	San Francisco	Forestdale	606vv
FST15	House 1	San Francisco	Forestdale	662vv
FST5	House 1	San Francisco	Forestdale	649vv
FST1	House 1	San Francisco	Forestdale	668vv
FST16	House 1	San Francisco	Forestdale	597vv
FST36	House 4	San Francisco	Forestdale	623vv
FST20	House 4	San Francisco	Forestdale	643vv
FST33	House 4	San Francisco	Forestdale	702vv
FST63	Kiva 1	San Francisco	Forestdale	657vv
	Bear Ruin		Forestdale Branch	
FST164	House 6	Early Pithouse	Hilltop	298vv
FST289	House 5	Early Pithouse	Hilltop	238vv
FST231	House 5	Early Pithouse	Hilltop	278vv
FST230	House 5	Early Pithouse	Hilltop	303r
FST332	House 5	Early Pithouse	Hilltop	307vv
FST261	House 5	Early Pithouse	Hilltop	321vv
FST260	House 5	Early Pithouse	Hilltop	322vv

Sample I.D.	Context	Interval of Occupation		Tree-Ring Date
		Upland Mogollon Synthesis	Local Phase Name	
	LA 5407		Gallo Mountain Vicinity	
HWS45	Feature 25	Early Pithouse	Unassigned	458vv
HWS48	Feature 25	Early Pithouse	Unassigned	470v
HWS46	Feature 25	Early Pithouse	Unassigned	497vv
HWS49	Feature 39	Early Pithouse	Unassigned	516r
HWS53	Feature 39	Early Pithouse	Unassigned	462r
HWS58	Feature 39	Early Pithouse	Unassigned	470v
HWS65	Feature 39	Early Pithouse	Unassigned	478vv
HWS63	Feature 39	Early Pithouse	Unassigned	492vv
HWS60	Feature 39	Early Pithouse	Unassigned	515r
HWS59	Feature 39	Early Pithouse	Unassigned	516r
HWS61	Feature 39	Early Pithouse	Unassigned	516r
HWS62	Feature 39	Early Pithouse	Unassigned	516r
HWS66	Feature 39	Early Pithouse	Unassigned	516r
HWS51	Feature 39	Early Pithouse	Unassigned	517r
HWS52	Feature 39	Early Pithouse	Unassigned	517r
HWS64	Feature 39	Early Pithouse	Unassigned	517r
HWS6	Feature 12	Early Pithouse	Unassigned	341vv
HWS25	Feature 12	Early Pithouse	Unassigned	390vv
HWS13	Feature 12	Early Pithouse	Unassigned	400vv
HWS20	Feature 12	Early Pithouse	Unassigned	414vv
HWS5	Feature 12	Early Pithouse	Unassigned	415vv
HWS11	Feature 12	Early Pithouse	Unassigned	418vv
HWS14	Feature 12	Early Pithouse	Unassigned	424vv
HWS17	Feature 12	Early Pithouse	Unassigned	434vv
HWS8	Feature 12	Early Pithouse	Unassigned	436vv
HWS16	Feature 12	Early Pithouse	Unassigned	437vv
HWS7	Feature 12	Early Pithouse	Unassigned	444vv
HWS18	Feature 12	Early Pithouse	Unassigned	449vv
HWS10	Feature 12	Early Pithouse	Unassigned	451vv
HWS23	Feature 12	Early Pithouse	Unassigned	465vv
HWS19	Feature 12	Early Pithouse	Unassigned	470vv
HWS21	Feature 12	Early Pithouse	Unassigned	472vv
HWS26	Feature 12	Early Pithouse	Unassigned	475B
HWS22	Feature 12	Early Pithouse	Unassigned	475B
HWS27	Feature 12	Early Pithouse	Unassigned	484B
	Galaz Ruin		Mimbres Branch	
MIM300	Unit 1	Three Circle	Three Circle	780vv
MIM312	Unit 1	Three Circle	Three Circle	786vv
MIM308	Unit 1	Three Circle	Three Circle	788vv
MIM305	Unit 1	Three Circle	Three Circle	805vv
MIM302	Unit 1	Three Circle	Three Circle	815vv
MIM296	Unit 1	Three Circle	Three Circle	816vv

Continued on next page

Sample I.D.	Context	Interval of Occupation		Tree-Ring Date
		Upland Mogollon Synthesis	Local Phase Name	
	Galaz Ruin		Mimbres Branch	
MIM298	Unit 1	Three Circle	Three Circle	820vv
MIM289	Unit 1	Three Circle	Three Circle	822vv
MIM310	Unit 1	Three Circle	Three Circle	828vv
MIM290	Unit 1	Three Circle	Three Circle	830vv
MIM287	Unit 1	Three Circle	Three Circle	831vv
MIM299	Unit 1	Three Circle	Three Circle	832vv
MIM288	Unit 1	Three Circle	Three Circle	833vv
MIM294	Unit 1	Three Circle	Three Circle	834vv
MIM318	Unit 1	Three Circle	Three Circle	834vv
MIM295	Unit 1	Three Circle	Three Circle	835vv
MIM304	Unit 1	Three Circle	Three Circle	841vv
MIM293	Unit 1	Three Circle	Three Circle	842vv
MIM292	Unit 1	Three Circle	Three Circle	843vv
MIM301	Unit 1	Three Circle	Three Circle	844vv
MIM313	Unit 1	Three Circle	Three Circle	848vv
MIM309	Unit 1	Three Circle	Three Circle	854vv
MIM311	Unit 1	Three Circle	Three Circle	854v
MIM297	Unit 1	Three Circle	Three Circle	858v
MIM314	Unit 1	Three Circle	Three Circle	858v
MIM291	Unit 1	Three Circle	Three Circle	858r
MIM324	Unit 1	Three Circle	Three Circle	858r
MIM306	Unit 1	Three Circle	Three Circle	858r
MIM448	Unit 18	Three Circle	Three Circle	788vv
MIM436	Unit 18	Three Circle	Three Circle	793vv
MIM445	Unit 18	Three Circle	Three Circle	808vv
MIM437	Unit 18	Three Circle	Three Circle	809vv
MIM446	Unit 18	Three Circle	Three Circle	837vv
MIM439	Unit 18	Three Circle	Three Circle	851vv
MIM450	Unit 18	Three Circle	Three Circle	851vv
MIM451	Unit 18	Three Circle	Three Circle	855vv
MIM442	Unit 18	Three Circle	Three Circle	866vv
MIM462	Unit 26	Three Circle	Three Circle	848vv
MIM460	Unit 26	Three Circle	Three Circle	852vv
MIM461	Unit 26	Three Circle	Three Circle	852vv
MIM471	Unit 29	Three Circle	Three Circle	825vv
MIM396	Unit 29	Three Circle	Three Circle	832vv
MIM418	Unit 29	Three Circle	Three Circle	832vv
MIM391	Unit 29	Three Circle	Three Circle	833vv
MIM413	Unit 29	Three Circle	Three Circle	836vv
MIM398	Unit 29	Three Circle	Three Circle	844vv
MIM381	Unit 29	Three Circle	Three Circle	849vv
MIM421	Unit 29	Three Circle	Three Circle	849vv
MIM426	Unit 29	Three Circle	Three Circle	851vv
MIM419	Unit 29	Three Circle	Three Circle	954vv
MIM378	Unit 29	Three Circle	Three Circle	855vv

Continued on next page

		Interval of Occupation		
Sample I.D.	Context	Upland Mogollon Synthesis	Local Phase Name	Tree-Ring Date
	Galaz Ruin		Mimbres Branch	
MIM424	Unit 29	Three Circle	Three Circle	856vv
MIM405	Unit 29	Three Circle	Three Circle	857vv
MIM377	Unit 29	Three Circle	Three Circle	858vv
MIM388	Unit 29	Three Circle	Three Circle	858vv
MIM401	Unit 29	Three Circle	Three Circle	858vv
MIM428	Unit 29	Three Circle	Three Circle	858vv
MIM393	Unit 29	Three Circle	Three Circle	859v
MIM411	Unit 29	Three Circle	Three Circle	859vv
MIM369	Unit 29	Three Circle	Three Circle	859r
MIM392	Unit 29	Three Circle	Three Circle	859r
MIM399	Unit 29	Three Circle	Three Circle	859r
MIM402	Unit 29	Three Circle	Three Circle	859r
MIM386	Unit 29	Three Circle	Three Circle	860vv
MIM420	Unit 29	Three Circle	Three Circle	860vv
MIM397	Unit 29	Three Circle	Three Circle	860r
MIM423	Unit 29	Three Circle	Three Circle	861vv
MIM425	Unit 29	Three Circle	Three Circle	861vv
MIM429	Unit 29	Three Circle	Three Circle	864vv
MIM406	Unit 29	Three Circle	Three Circle	866vv
MIM422	Unit 29	Three Circle	Three Circle	866vv
MIM374	Unit 29	Three Circle	Three Circle	868vv
MIM430	Unit 29	Three Circle	Three Circle	870vv
MIM370	Unit 29	Three Circle	Three Circle	870r
MIM375	Unit 29	Three Circle	Three Circle	870r
MIM379	Unit 29	Three Circle	Three Circle	880vv
MIM376	Unit 29	Three Circle	Three Circle	888vv
MIM407	Unit 29	Three Circle	Three Circle	892vv
MIM408	Unit 29	Three Circle	Three Circle	893vv
	Harris Village		Mimbres Branch	
GP601	House 4	San Francisco	San Francisco	801vv
GP647	House 10	Three Circle	Three Circle	736vv
GP673	House 10	Three Circle	Three Circle	843vv
GP645	House 10	Three Circle	Three Circle	846vv
GP646	House 10	Three Circle	Three Circle	854vv
GP651	House 10	Three Circle	Three Circle	858vv
GP667	House 10	Three Circle	Three Circle	860vv
GP676	House 10	Three Circle	Three Circle	861vv
GP657	House 10	Three Circle	Three Circle	869vv
GP678	House 10	Three Circle	Three Circle	870vv
GP641	House 10	Three Circle	Three Circle	870vv
GP675	House 10	Three Circle	Three Circle	873vv
GP640	House 10	Three Circle	Three Circle	874vv
GP661	House 10	Three Circle	Three Circle	875vv

Continued on next page

Sample I.D.	Context	Interval of Occupation		Tree-Ring Date
		Upland Mogollon Synthesis	Local Phase Name	
	Harris Village		**Mimbres Branch**	
GP680	House 10	Three Circle	Three Circle	876vv
GP631	House 10	Three Circle	Three Circle	876vv
GP657-1	House 10	Three Circle	Three Circle	876vv
GP626	House 10	Three Circle	Three Circle	877vv
GP682	House 10	Three Circle	Three Circle	877v
GP658	House 10	Three Circle	Three Circle	877v
GP660	House 10	Three Circle	Three Circle	877v
GP679	House 10	Three Circle	Three Circle	877r
GP666	House 10	Three Circle	Three Circle	877r
GP672	House 10	Three Circle	Three Circle	877r
GP677	House 10	Three Circle	Three Circle	877r
GP681	House 10	Three Circle	Three Circle	877r
GP665	House 10	Three Circle	Three Circle	877r
GP663	House 10	Three Circle	Three Circle	877r
GP664	House 10	Three Circle	Three Circle	877r
GP632	House 10	Three Circle	Three Circle	877r
GP671	House 10	Three Circle	Three Circle	877r
GP629	House 13	Three Circle	Three Circle	858vv
GP687	House 14	Unassigned	Unassigned	582
GP637	House 15	Three Circle	Three Circle	593vv
GP633	House 15	Three Circle	Three Circle	834vv
GP636	House 15	Three Circle	Three Circle	857r
GP635	House 15	Three Circle	Three Circle	859vv
GP634	House 15	Three Circle	Three Circle	861r
GP653	House 17	Three Circle	Three Circle	856vv
GP687	House 18	Unassigned	Unassigned	708vv
GP643	House 22	Unassigned	Unassigned	635vv
GP644	House 23	Three Circle	Three Circle	836vv
GP649	House 23	Three Circle	Three Circle	838vv
GP654	House 25	Georgetown	Georgetown	593vv
GP688	House 25	Georgetown	Georgetown	624v
GP650	House 26	Unassigned	Unassigned	716vv
GP690	House 28	Three Circle	Three Circle	608vv
GP656	House 28	Three Circle	Three Circle	624v
GP691	House 33	Three Circle	Three Circle	759vv
	SU Site		**Reserve/Pine Lawn Branch**	
SU47	House D^a	Early Pithouse	Pine Lawn	481vv
SU2	House G	Early Pithouse	Pine Lawn	350vv
SU1	House G	Early Pithouse	Pine Lawn	337vv
SU23	House G	Early Pithouse	Pine Lawn	418vv
SU24	House G	Early Pithouse	Pine Lawn	421vv
SU10	House G	Early Pithouse	Pine Lawn	432vv
SU18	House G	Early Pithouse	Pine Lawn	449vv

Continued on next page

| | | Interval of Occupation | | |
Sample I.D.	Context	Upland Mogollon Synthesis	Local Phase Name	Tree-Ring Date
	SU Site		Reserve/Pine Lawn Branch	
SU24B	House G	Early Pithouse	Pine Lawn	453vv
SU20	House G	Early Pithouse	Pine Lawn	455vv
SU11	House G	Early Pithouse	Pine Lawn	458vv
SU23-1	House G	Early Pithouse	Pine Lawn	460r
SU21A	House G	Early Pithouse	Pine Lawn	481vv
SU102	House N	Early Pithouse	Pine Lawn	400vv
SU140	House Q	Early Pithouse	Pine Lawn	373vv
SU173-1	House Q	Early Pithouse	Pine Lawn	386vv
SU126	House Q	Early Pithouse	Pine Lawn	388vv
SU186-1	House Q	Early Pithouse	Pine Lawn	413vv
SU131A	House Q	Early Pithouse	Pine Lawn	415vv
SU163	House Q	Early Pithouse	Pine Lawn	419vv
SU154-1	House Q	Early Pithouse	Pine Lawn	484vv
SU199	House S	Early Pithouse	Pine Lawn	477vv
SU237	House T	Early Pithouse	Pine Lawn	379vv
SU225	House T	Early Pithouse	Pine Lawn	450vv
SU250	House T	Early Pithouse	Pine Lawn	477v
SU226	House T	Early Pithouse	Pine Lawn	477vv
SU227	House T	Early Pithouse	Pine Lawn	478vv
SU245	House T	Early Pithouse	Pine Lawn	478vv
SU244	House T	Early Pithouse	Pine Lawn	482vv
SU258	House T	Early Pithouse	Pine Lawn	497vv
U209-1	House W	Early Pithouse	Pine Lawn	415vv
SU205	House W	Early Pithouse	Pine Lawn	436vv
SU262	House Z	Early Pithouse	Pine Lawn	448vv
	Turkey Foot Ridge		Reserve/Pine Lawn Branch	
SU429	House B	Three Circle	Three Circle	715vv[b]
SU408	House B	Three Circle	Three Circle	719vv
SU419	House B	Three Circle	Three Circle	732vv
SU404	House B	Three Circle	Three Circle	733vv
SU382	House B	Three Circle	Three Circle	759vv
SU442	House B	Three Circle	Three Circle	768vv
SU390	House B	Three Circle	Three Circle	768vv
SU397	House B	Three Circle	Three Circle	774vv
SU400	House B	Three Circle	Three Circle	777vv
SU414	House B	Three Circle	Three Circle	778vv
SU379	House B	Three Circle	Three Circle	778vv
SU410	House B	Three Circle	Three Circle	778v
SU516A	House E	San Francisco	San Francisco	725vv
SU525	House E	San Francisco	San Francisco	745vv
SU516B	House E	San Francisco	San Francisco	746vv
SU509	House E	San Francisco	San Francisco	747vv
SU526B	House E	San Francisco	San Francisco	748vv

Continued on next page

| Sample I.D. | Context | Interval of Occupation | | Tree-Ring Date |
		Upland Mogollon Synthesis	Local Phase Name	
	Turkey Foot Ridge		Reserve/Pine Lawn Branch	
SU517	House E	San Francisco	San Francisco	749v
SU524	House E	San Francisco	San Francisco	758vv
SU526A	House E	San Francisco	San Francisco	748vv
SU514	House E	San Francisco	San Francisco	761vv
SU511	House E	San Francisco	San Francisco	758vv
SU521	House E	San Francisco	San Francisco	773vv
SU519	House E	San Francisco	San Francisco	782vv
SU523	House E	San Francisco	San Francisco	783vv
SU488	House F	San Francisco	San Francisco	748vv
SU479-1	House F	San Francisco	San Francisco	770vv
SU486	House F	San Francisco	San Francisco	771vv
SU485	House F	San Francisco	San Francisco	772vv
SU479	House F	San Francisco	San Francisco	774vv
SU475A	House F	San Francisco	San Francisco	784vv
SU487	House F	San Francisco	San Francisco	788vv
SU500F	House H	San Francisco	San Francisco	768vv
SU489	House H	San Francisco	San Francisco	768vv
SU494	House H	San Francisco	San Francisco	780vv
SU500	House H	San Francisco	San Francisco	781vv
SU490	House H	San Francisco	San Francisco	783v
SU496	House H	San Francisco	San Francisco	786v
SU491	House H	San Francisco	San Francisco	787vv
SU541	House K	San Francisco	San Francisco	751vv
SU532	House K	San Francisco	San Francisco	767vv
SU537	House K	San Francisco	San Francisco	774vv
SU533	House K	San Francisco	San Francisco	775vv
SU559	House O	Three Circle	Three Circle	749vv
SU554A	House O	Three Circle	Three Circle	752vv
	Mogollon Village		Upper San Francisco River Area	
GP495	House 1	San Francisco	San Francisco	755vv
GP505c	House 2	Three Circle	Three Circle	786r
GP506	House 2	Three Circle	Three Circle	858vv
GP501	House 2	Three Circle	Three Circle	882vv
GP507	House 2	Three Circle	Three Circle	886vv
GP497	House 2	Three Circle	Three Circle	892vv
GP527	House 2	Three Circle	Three Circle	895vv
GP518	House 2	Three Circle	Three Circle	897r
GP516	House 2	Three Circle	Three Circle	897r
GP499	House 2	Three Circle	Three Circle	898v
GP514-2	House 2	Three Circle	Three Circle	898v
GP498	House 2	Three Circle	Three Circle	898r
GP500	House 2	Three Circle	Three Circle	898r
GP502	House 2	Three Circle	Three Circle	898r

Continued on next page

Sample I.D.	Context	Interval of Occupation		Tree-Ring Date
		Upland Mogollon Synthesis	Local Phase Name	
	Mogollon Village	Upper San Francisco River Area		
GP503	House 2	Three Circle	Three Circle	898r
GP504	House 2	Three Circle	Three Circle	898r
GP508	House 2	Three Circle	Three Circle	898r
GP509	House 2	Three Circle	Three Circle	898r
GP510	House 2	Three Circle	Three Circle	898r
GP512	House 2	Three Circle	Three Circle	898r
GP513	House 2	Three Circle	Three Circle	898r
GP514-1	House 2	Three Circle	Three Circle	898r
GP522	House 2	Three Circle	Three Circle	898r
GP523	House 2	Three Circle	Three Circle	898r
GP524	House 2	Three Circle	Three Circle	898r
GP526	House 2	Three Circle	Three Circle	898r
GP551	House 4	San Francisco	San Francisco	728vv
GP553	House 4	San Francisco	San Francisco	733vv
GP552	House 4	San Francisco	San Francisco	736v
GP511	House 4	San Francisco	San Francisco	736r
GP557	House 5B	San Francisco	San Francisco	736vv
GP5817	House 8	San Francisco	San Francisco	712vv
GP5816	House 8	San Francisco	San Francisco	743v
GP555	House 8	San Francisco	San Francisco	746r
GP554	House 8	San Francisco	San Francisco	748r

Abbreviations:

B = Bark is present.

r = Less than a full section is present, but the outermost ring is continuous around the available circumference.

v = A subjective judgment that the date is within a very few years of being a cutting date, although there is no direct evidence of the true outside on the specimen.

vv = There is no way of estimating how far the last ring is from the true outside.

a An Early Pithouse period house with mixed trash, including Three Circle phase trash.

b A Three Circle phase house built into the depression of a Georgetown phase house or San Francisco phase ceremonial structure. Old wood was reused during the final occupation of the house.

c This "r" date is a fairly obvious "old wood" outlier, given the other dates from this house.

References

Accola, Richard M.
1981   "Mogollon Settlement Patterns in the
        Middle San Francisco River Drainage,
        West-Central New Mexico." *The Kiva*
        46(3):155–168.

Adams, Jenny L.
1988   "Methods for Improving Ground Stone
        Artifact Analysis: Experiments in Mano
        Wear Patterns," in *Experiments in Lithic
        Technology*, edited by Daniel S. Amick and
        Raymond P. Mauldin, pp. 259–296. BAR
        International Series 528. Oxford, England.
1993   "Technological Development of Manos
        and Metates on the Hopi Mesas." *The Kiva*
        58(3):331–344.

Adams, Karen R.
1993   "A Regional Synthesis of *Zea Mays* in the
        Prehistoric American Southwest," in *Corn
        and Culture in the Prehistoric New World*,
        edited by Sissel Johannesson and
        Christine A. Hastorf, pp. 273–302.
        Westview Press, Boulder.

Ahlstrom, Richard N.
1985   "The Interpretation of Archaeological Tree
        Ring Dates." Ph.D. dissertation,
        University of Arizona, Tucson. Ann Arbor:
        University Microfilms.

Anyon, Roger
1980   "The Late Pithouse Period," in *An
        Archaeological Synthesis of South-Central and
        Southwestern New Mexico*, by Steven A.
        LeBlanc and Michael E. Whalen, pp.
        142–205.
1983   "Divergent Mogollon Evolution and the
        Development of Ceremonial Structures."
        M.A. Thesis, Department of Anthropology,
        University of New Mexico, Albuquerque.

Anyon, Roger, Patricia A. Gilman, and Steven A.
LeBlanc
1981   "A Reevaluation of the Mogollon-Mimbres
        Archaeological Sequence." *The Kiva*
        46(4):209–225.

Anyon, Roger, and Steven A. LeBlanc
1980   "The Architectural Evolution of Mogollon-
        Mimbres Communal Structures." *The Kiva*
        45:253–277.
1984   *The Galaz Ruin: A Prehistoric Mimbres
        Village in Southwestern New Mexico.*
        Maxwell Museum of Anthropology and
        the University of New Mexico Press,
        Albuquerque.

Arthur, John W.
1994   "Ceramic Function during the Early
        Pithouse Period in the Mimbres River

Valley." M.A. thesis, Department of Anthropology, University of Texas, San Antonio.

Bannister, Bryant, Elizabeth A. M. Gell, and John W. Hannah
1966 *Tree Ring Dates from Arizona N–Q: Verde–Showlow–St. Johns Area*. Laboratory of Tree-Ring Research, Tucson.

Bannister, Bryant, John. W. Hannah, and William J. Robinson
1970 *Tree-Ring Dates from New Mexico M–N, S–Z: Southwestern New Mexico Area*. Laboratory of Tree-Ring Research, Tucson.

Bartlett, Katharine
1933 *Pueblo Milling Stones of the Flagstaff Region and Their Relation to Others in the Southwest: A Study in Progressive Efficiency*. Museum of Northern Arizona Bulletin 3. Flagstaff.

Basehart, Harry W.
1974 "Mescalero Apaches Subsistence Patterns and Socio-political Organization," in *Apache Indians* 12:9–178. Garland, New York.

Beals, Ralph L., George W. Brainerd, and Watson Smith
1945 *Archaeological Studies in Northeast Arizona*. Publications in American Archaeology and Ethnology, vol. 44, no. 1. University of California Press, Berkeley.

Berkovitch, Fred B.
1991 "Social Stratification, Social Status and Reproductive Success in Primates." *Ethology and Sociobiology* 12:315–333.

Berman, Mary Jane
1978 *The Mesa Top Site: An Early Mogollon Village in Southeastern Arizona*. Cultural Resources Management Division Report 280. Department of Sociology and Anthropology, New Mexico State University, Las Cruces.
1979 *Cultural Resources Overview, Socorro Area, New Mexico*. USDA Forest Service, Southwestern Region, and USDI Bureau of Land Management, Albuquerque.

Bernstein, Irwin S.
1980 "Dominance: The Baby and the Bathwater." *The Behavioral and Brain Sciences* 12:419–457.

Bettinger, Robert L.
1991 *Hunter-Gatherers: Archaeological and Evolutionary Theory*. Plenum, New York.

Binford, Lewis R.
1980 "Willow Smoke and Dogs' Tails: Hunter-Gatherer Settlement Systems and Archaeological Site Formation." *American Antiquity* 45:4–20.
1990 "Mobility, Housing, and Environment: A Comparative Study." *Journal of Anthropological Research* 46:119–152.

Blake, Michael, Steven A. LeBlanc, and Paul E. Minnis
1986 "Changing Settlement and Population in the Mimbres Valley, Southwest New Mexico." *Journal of Field Archaeology* 13:439–464.

Bleed, Peter
1986 "The Optimal Design of Hunting Weapons: Maintainability or Reliability." *American Antiquity* 51:737–747.

Bluhm, Elaine A.
1960 "Mogollon Settlement Patterns in the Pine Lawn Valley, New Mexico." *American Antiquity* 25:538–546.

Boehm, Christopher
1993 "Egalitarian Behavior and Reverse Dominance Hierarchy." *Current Anthropology* 34:227–254.

Bradfield, Wesley
n.d. "Excavation Notes from the Cameron Creek Village (LA 190)." On file, Archaeological Records Management System, Laboratory of Anthropology, Santa Fe.
1931 *Cameron Creek Village: A Site in the Mimbres Area, Grant County, New Mexico*. School of American Research Monographs 1. Santa Fe.

Braun, David P.
1980 "Environmental Interpretation of Ceramic Vessel Use on the Basis of Rim and Neck Formal Attributes," in *The Navajo Project:*

Archaeological Investigations, Page to Phoenix 500 kV Southern Transmission Line, edited by Donald C. Fiero, Robert W. Munson, Martha T. McClain, Suzanne M. Wilson, and Anne H. Zier, pp. 171–231. Research Paper 11. Museum of Northern Arizona, Flagstaff.

1983 "Pots as Tools," in *Archaeological Hammers and Theories,* edited by A. S. Keene and J. A. Moore, pp. 107–134. Academic Press, New York.

1987 "Coevolution of Sedentism, Pottery Technology, and Horticulture in the Central Midwest, 200 B.C.–A.D. 600," in *Emergent Horticultural Economies of the Eastern Woodlands,* edited by William F. Keegan, pp. 153–181. Center for Archaeological Investigations, Occasional Paper 7. Southern Illinois University, Carbondale.

Bray, Alicia
1982 "Mimbres Black-on-White, Melamine or Wedgewood? A Ceramic Use-Wear Analysis." *The Kiva* 47:133–150.

Breternitz, David A.
1959 *Excavations at Nantack Village, Point of Pines, Arizona.* Contributions to Point of Pines Archaeology 13. Anthropological Papers of the University of Arizona 1. University of Arizona Press, Tucson.

Brinkman, Kenneth A.
1974 "*Juglans* L. Walnut," in *Seeds of Woody Plants in the United States,* coordinated by C. S. Schopmeyer, pp. 454–459. Agriculture Handbook 450. U.S. Forest Service, Government Printing Office, Washington, D.C.

Brody, J. J.
1977 *Mimbres Painted Pottery.* University of New Mexico Press, Albuquerque.

Brody, J. J., Catherine J. Scott, and Steven A. LeBlanc
1983 *Mimbres Pottery: Ancient Art of the American Southwest.* Hudson Hills Press, New York.

Bronitsky, Gordon, and Robert Hamer
1986 "Experiments in Ceramic Technology: The Effects of Various Tempering Materials on Impact and Thermal Shock Resistance." *American Antiquity* 51:89–101.

Brown, David E., editor
1995 *Biotic Communities: Southwestern United States and Northwestern Mexico.* University of Utah Press, Salt Lake City.

Brown, David E.
1995a "Great Basin Conifer Woodland," in *Biotic Communities: Southwestern United States and Northwestern Mexico,* edited by David E. Brown, pp. 52–57. University of Utah Press, Salt Lake City.

1995b "Madrean Evergreen Woodland," in *Biotic Communities: Southwestern United States and Northwestern Mexico,* edited by David E. Brown, pp. 59–65. University of Utah Press, Salt Lake City.

1995c "Plains and Great Basin Grasslands," in *Biotic Communities: Southwestern United States and Northwestern Mexico,* edited by David E. Brown, pp. 115–121. University of Utah Press, Salt Lake City.

1995d "Semidesert Grassland," in *Biotic Communities: Southwestern United States and Northwestern Mexico,* edited by David E. Brown, pp. 123–131. University of Utah Press, Salt Lake City.

1995e "Chihuahuan Desertscrub," in *Biotic Communities: Southwestern United States and Northwestern Mexico,* edited by David E. Brown, pp. 169–179. University of Utah Press, Salt Lake City.

Brown, David E., and Charles H. Lowe
1995 "Biotic Communities of the Southwest: A Supplementary Map," in *Biotic Communities: Southwestern United States and Northwestern Mexico,* edited by David E. Brown. University of Utah Press, Salt Lake City.

Browne, Jim
1940 "Projectile Points." *American Antiquity* 5:209–213.

Brumfiel, Elizabeth M., and Timothy K. Earle
1987 "Specialization, Exchange, and Complex Societies: An Introduction," in *Specialization, Exchange, and Complex Societies,* edited by Elizabeth M. Brumfiel and Timothy K. Earle, pp. 1–9. Cambridge University Press, Cambridge.

Bullard, William Rotch
1962 *The Cerro Colorado Site and Pithouse Architecture in the Southwestern United*

States Prior to A.D. 900. Papers of the Peabody Museum of Archaeology and Ethnology, vol. 44, no. 2. Harvard University, Cambridge.

Burton, Jeffrey F.
1991   *The Archeology of Sivu'uvi*. Publications in Anthropology 55. Western Archeological and Conservation Center, National Park Service, Tucson.

Bussey, Stanley D.
1973   "Late Mogollon Manifestations in the Mimbres Branch, Southwestern New Mexico." Ph.D. dissertation, University of Oregon. University Microfilms, Ann Arbor.
1975   *The Archaeology of Lee Village*. Center of Archaeological Study, Monograph 2. Las Cruces.

Cameron, Catherine L.
1990a "Pit Structure Abandonment in the Four Corners Region of the American Southwest: Late Basketmaker III and Pueblo I Periods." *Journal of Field Archaeology* 17:27–37.
1990b "The Effect of Varying Estimates of Pit Structure Use-Life on Prehistoric Population Estimates in the American Southwest." *The Kiva* 55(2):155–166.
1991   "Architectural Change at a Southwestern Pueblo." Ph.D. dissertation, Department of Anthropology, University of Arizona, Tucson.

Cann, R. L., M. Stoneking, and A. C. Wilson
1987   "Mitochondrial DNA and Human Evolution." *Nature* 325:31–36.

Carneiro, Robert L.
1981   "The Chiefdom: Precursor of the State," in *The Transition to Statehood in the New World*, edited by G. Jones and R. Krautz, pp. 37–79. Cambridge University Press, New York.

Cashdan, Elizabeth A.
1980   "Egalitarianism among Hunter-Gatherers." *American Anthropologist* 82:116–120.

Chapman, K. M.
1977   *The Pottery of Santo Domingo Pueblo: A Detailed Study of Its Decoration*. University of New Mexico Press, Albuquerque.

Chapman, Richard
1977   "Analysis of Lithic Assemblages," in *Settlement and Subsistence along the Lower Chaco River: The CGP Survey*, edited by Charles A. Reher, pp. 371–452. University of New Mexico Press, Albuquerque.

Ciolek-Torrello, Richard
1995   "The Houghton Road Site, The Agua Caliente Phase, and the Early Formative Period in the Tucson Basin." *The Kiva* 60(4):531–573.

Cordell, Linda S.
1997   *Archaeology of the Southwest*. Academic Press, New York.

Cordell, Linda S., and George J. Gumerman
1989   "Cultural Interaction in the Prehistoric Southwest," in *Dynamics of Southwest Prehistory*, edited by Linda S. Cordell and George J. Gumerman, pp. 1–17. Smithsonian Institution Press, Washington, D.C.

Cordell, Linda S., and Fred Plog
1979   "Escaping the Confines of Normative Thought: A Reevaluation of Puebloan Prehistory." *American Antiquity* 44:405–429.
1981   "Building Theory from the Bottom Up?" *American Antiquity* 46:198–199.

Cosgrove, Cornelius B.
1947   *Caves of the Upper Gila and Hueco Areas*. Papers of the Peabody Museum of American Archaeology and Ethnology, vol. 24, no. 2. Harvard University, Cambridge.

Cosgrove, H. S., and C. B. Cosgrove
1932   *The Swarts Ruin, a Typical Mimbres Site in Southwestern New Mexico*. Papers of the Peabody Museum of American Archaeology and Ethnology, vol. 15, no. 1. Harvard University, Cambridge.

Crabtree, Don E.
1972 *An Introduction to Flintworking.* Occasional Papers of the Idaho State University Museum 28.

Creel, Darrell
1989 "A Primary Cremation at the NAN Ranch Ruin, with Comparative Data on Other Cremations in the Mimbres Area, New Mexico." *Journal of Field Archaeology* 16:309–329.

Cutler, Hugh C.
1952 "A Preliminary Survey of Plant Remains of Tularosa Cave," in *Mogollon Cultural Continuity and Change: The Stratigraphic Analysis of Tularosa and Cordava Caves,* by Paul S. Martin, John B. Rinaldo, Elaine A. Bluhm, Hugh C. Cutler, and Roger Grange, Jr., pp. 174–183. *Fieldiana: Anthropology* 40.

Danson, Edward B.
1957 *An Archaeological Survey of West Central New Mexico and East Central Arizona.* Papers of the Peabody Museum of Archaeology and Ethnology, vol. 44, no. 1. Harvard University, Cambridge.

Dean, Jeffrey S., and William J. Robinson
1978 *Expanded Tree-Ring Chronology for the Southwestern United States.* Chronology Series 3. Laboratory of Tree Ring Research, University of Arizona, Tucson.

Deaver, William L., and Richard S. Ciolek-Torrello
1995 "Early Formative Period Chronology for the Tucson Basin." *The Kiva* 60(4):481–529.

Diehl, Michael W.
1992 "Architecture as a Material Correlate of Mobility Strategies: Some Implications for Archaeological Interpretation." *Behavior Science Research* 26(1–4):1–35.
1994 "Subsistence Strategies and Emergent Social Differences: A Case Study from the Prehistoric North American Southwest." Ph.D. dissertation, State University of New York at Buffalo. University Microfilms, Ann Arbor.
1997 "Rational Behavior, the Adoption of Agriculture, and the Organization of Subsistence during the Late Archaic Period in the Greater Tucson Basin," in *Rediscovering Darwin: Evolutionary Theory and Archaeological Explanation,* edited by C. Michael Barton and Geoffrey A. Clark, pp. 251–265. Archaeological Papers of the American Anthropological Association 7. Arlington, Virginia.
1998 "The Interpretation of Archaeological Floor Assemblages: A Case Study from the American Southwest." *American Antiquity* 63:617–634.
2000 "Some Thoughts on the Study of Hierarchies," in *Hierarchies in Action: Cui Bono?* edited by Michael W. Diehl, pp. 11–30. Center for Archaeological Investigations, Occasional Papers 27. Southern Illinois University, Carbondale.

Diehl, Michael W., and Patricia A. Gilman
1996 "Implications from the Designs of Different Southwestern Architectural Forms," in *Interpreting Southwestern Diversity: Underlying Principles and Overarching Patterns,* edited by Paul R. Fish and J. Jefferson Reid, pp. 189–193. Arizona State University Anthropological Papers 48. Tempe.

Duncan, Marjorie, Patricia A. Gilman, and Raymond P. Mauldin
1991 "The Mogollon Village Archaeological Project, 1991: Preliminary Report." Prepared for the USDA Forest Service, Silver City, New Mexico.

Dwyer, Peter D., and Monica Minnegal
1993 "Are Kubo Hunters 'Show Offs'?" *Ethology and Sociobiology* 14:53–70.

Earle, Timothy K.
1987 "Chiefdoms in Archaeological and Ethnohistorical Perspective." *Annual Review of Anthropology* 16:279–308.

Euler, Robert C., George G. Gumerman, Thor N. V. Karlstrom, Jeffrey S. Dean, and Richard H. Hevly
1979 "The Colorado Plateaus: Cultural Dynamics and Paleoenvironment." *Science* 205:1089–1101.

Fenenga, Franklin
1953 "The Weights of Chipped Stone Points: A Clue to Their Functions." *Southwestern Journal of Anthropology* 9:309–323.

Fish, Suzanne K.
1984 "Pollen Analysis of Samples from AZ CC:8:2 (ASU)," in *The Duncan Project: A Study of the Occupation Duration and Settlement Pattern of an Early Mogollon Pithouse Village*, by Kent G. Lightfoot, pp. 125–131. Office of Cultural Resource Management, Arizona State University, Tempe.

Fitting, James E.
1973 "An Early Mogollon Community: A Preliminary Report on the Winn Canyon Site." *The Artifact* 11(1&2):1–94.

Fontana, Bernard L., William J. Robinson, Charles W. Cormack, and Ernest E. Leavitt, Jr.
1962 *Papago Indian Pottery*. University of Washington Press, Seattle.

Foster, Michael S.
1982 "The Loma San Gabriel–Mogollon Continuum," in *Mogollon Archaeology: Proceedings of the 1980 Mogollon Conference*, edited by Patrick H. Beckett and Kira Silverbird, pp. 251–261. Acoma Books, Ramona, California.

Frisbie, Theodore R.
1982 "The Anasazi-Mogollon Frontier? Perspectives from the Albuquerque Area," in *Mogollon Archaeology: Proceedings of the 1980 Mogollon Conference*, edited by Patrick H. Beckett and Kira Silverbird, pp. 17–26. Acoma Books, Ramona, California.

Galinat, Walton C.
1988 "The Origin of Maiz de Ocho." *American Anthropologist* 90:682–683.

Gardner, P.
1991 "Foragers' Pursuit of Individual Autonomy." *Current Anthropology* 32:543–572.

Gatewood, John B.
1984 "Cooperation, Competition and Synergy: Information-Sharing Groups among Southeast Alaskan Salmon Seiners." *American Ethnologist* 11:350–370.

Geier, Clarence R.
1973 "The Flake Assemblage in Archaeological Interpretation." *The Missouri Archaeologist* 35(3).

Gilman, Patricia A.
1986 "Seasonality and Mobility in San Simon Pithouse Use," in *Mogollon Variability*, edited by Charlotte Benson and Steadman Upham, pp. 203–209. Occasional Papers 15. New Mexico State University Museum, Las Cruces.
1987 "Architecture as Artifact: Pit Structures and Pueblos in the American Southwest." *American Antiquity* 52:538–564.
1990 "Social Organization and Classic Mimbres Period Burials in the Southwest United States." *Journal of Field Archaeology* 17:457–469.
1995 "Multiple Dimensions of the Archaic-to-Pit Structure Period Transition in Southeastern Arizona." *The Kiva* 60(4):619–632.

Gilman, Patricia A., Raymond P. Mauldin, and Valli S. Powell
1991 "The Mogollon Village Archaeological Project, 1989." Manuscript prepared for the USDA Forest Service, Silver City, New Mexico.

Gladwin, Harold S.
1948 *Excavations at Snaketown, IV: Review and Conclusions*. Medallion Papers 38. Gila Pueblo, Globe, Arizona.

Goodyear, Albert C.
1989 "A Hypothesis for the Use of Crypto-crystalline Raw Materials among Paleoindian Groups of North America," in *Eastern Paleoindian Lithic Resource Use*, edited by Christopher J. Ellis and Jonathon C. Lothrop, pp. 1–9. Westview Press, Boulder.

Graybill, Donald A.
1973 "Prehistoric Settlement Pattern Analysis in the Mimbres Region, New Mexico." Ph.D. dissertation, University of Arizona. University Microfilms, Ann Arbor.

Gregg, Susan M., editor
1991 *Between Bands and States*. Center for Archaeological Investigations, Occasional Paper 9. Southern Illinois University, Carbondale.

Halbirt, Carl D.
1985 "Pollen Analysis of Metate Wash Samples: Evaluating Techniques for Determining Metate Function." M.A. thesis, Department of Anthropology, Northern Arizona University, Flagstaff.

Halley, David J.
1983 "Use Alteration of Pottery Vessel Surfaces: An Important Source of Evidence for the Identification of Vessel Function." *North American Archaeologist* 4(1):3–26.
1986 "The Identification of Vessel Function: A Case Study from Northwest Georgia." *American Antiquity* 51:267–295.

Hammack, Laurens C.
1966 *Diablo Highway Salvage Archaeology*. Laboratory of Anthropology Notes 41. Santa Fe.

Hard, Robert J.
1990 "Agricultural Dependence in the Mountain Mogollon," in *Perspectives on Southwestern Prehistory*, edited by Paul E. Minnis and Charles L. Redman, pp. 135–147. Westview Press, Boulder.

Harpending, Henry, and Alan Rogers
1990 "Fitness in Stratified Societies." *Ethology and Sociobiology* 11:497–509.

Hastorf, Christine A.
1980 "Changing Resource Use in Subsistence Agricultural Groups of the Prehistoric Mimbres River Valley, New Mexico," in *Modeling Change in Prehistoric Subsistence Economies*, edited by Timothy K. Earle and Andrew L. Christenson, pp. 79–120. Academic Press, New York.

Haury, Emil W.
1936a *The Mogollon Culture of Southwestern New Mexico*. Medallion Papers 20. Gila Pueblo, Globe, Arizona.

1936b *Some Southwestern Pottery Types*, Series IV. Medallion Papers 19. Gila Pueblo, Globe, Arizona.
1985 *Mogollon Culture in the Forestdale Valley*. University of Arizona Press, Tucson.

Haury, Emil W., and E. B. Sayles
1947 *An Early Pithouse Village of the Mogollon Culture*. Social Science Bulletin 16. University of Arizona, Tucson.

Hawkes, Kristen
1991 "Showing Off: Tests of a Hypothesis about Men's Foraging Goals." *Ethology and Sociobiology* 12:29–54.

Hayden, Brian
1976 "Australian Western Desert Lithic Technology: An Ethno-archaeological Study of Variability in Material Culture." Ph.D. dissertation, Department of Anthropology, University of Toronto.
1990 "Nimrods, Piscators, Pluckers, and Planters: The Emergence of Food Production." *Journal of Anthropological Archaeology* 9:31–69.

Hayden, Brian, and Rob Gargett
1990 "Big Man, Big Heart? A Mesoamerican View of the Emergence of Complex Society." *Ancient Mesoamerica* 1:3–20.

Hegmon, Michelle
1992 "Archaeological Research on Style." *Annual Review of Anthropology* 21:517–536.

Hegmon, Michelle, Margaret C. Nelson, and Susan Ruth
1998 "Abandonment, Reorganization, and Social Change." *American Anthropologist* 100(1).

Heidke, J., and Mark D. Elson
1988 "Tucson Basin Stucco-Coated Plain Ware: A Technological Assessment." *The Kiva* 53:273–285.

Herrington, Lavern C.
1979 "Settlement Patterns and Water Control Systems of the Mimbres Classic Phase, Grant County, New Mexico." Ph.D.

dissertation, Department of Anthropology, University of Texas at Austin.

Hibben, Frank C.
1938 "A Cache of Wooden Bows from the Mogollon Mountains." *American Antiquity* 4:36–38.

Hogg, Don Jack
1977 "Report on the Excavation of Three Mogollon Pit Houses on the Upper Mimbres River, New Mexico." M.A. thesis, Department of Anthropology, Eastern New Mexico University, Portales.

Huckell, Bruce B.
1988 "Late Archaic Archaeology of the Tucson Basin: A Status Report," in *Recent Research on Tucson Basin Prehistory: Proceedings of the Second Tucson Basin Conference*, edited by William H. Doelle and Paul R. Fish, pp. 57–80. Anthropological Papers 10. Institute for American Research, Tucson.
1995 *Of Marshes and Maize: Preceramic Agricultural Settlements in the Cienega Valley, Southeastern Arizona.* Anthropological Papers of the University of Arizona 59. University of Arizona Press, Tucson.

Huckell, Bruce B., Martyn Tagg, and Lisa W. Huckell
1987 *The Corona de Tucson Project: Prehistoric Use of a Bajada Environment.* Arizona State Museum Archaeological Series 174. University of Arizona, Tucson.

Hunter-Anderson, Rosalind
1986 *Prehistoric Adaptation in the American Southwest.* New York: Cambridge University Press.

Hunter-Anderson, Rosalind, and Yigal Zan
1984 "Proving the Moon Is Made of Cheese: The Structure of Recent Research in the Mogollon Area," in *Recent Research in Mogollon Archaeology*, edited by Steadman Upham, Fred Plog, David G. Batcho, and Barbara E. Kauffman, pp. 285–293. New Mexico State University Museum Occasional Papers 10. Las Cruces.

Jelinek, Arthur J.
1961 "Mimbres Warfare?" *The Kiva* 27(2):28–30.

Jewett, Roberta A., and Kent Lightfoot
1986 "The Intra-Site Spatial Structure of Early Mogollon Villages: A Comparison of Seasonal and Year Round Settlements," in *Mogollon Variability*, edited by Charlotte Benson and Steadman Upham, pp. 45–77. New Mexico State University Museum Occasional Papers 15. Las Cruces.

Jones, Bruce A.
1989 "Use-Wear Analysis of White Mountain Redwares at Grasshopper Pueblo, Arizona." *The Kiva* 54(4):353–360.

Kayser, David W.
1973 "Castle Rock Project: Archaeological Salvage along State Highway 32 in Agua Fria and Largo Creek Canyons, Catron County, New Mexico." Laboratory of Anthropology, Note 71. Museum of New Mexico, Santa Fe.

Keeley, Lawrence R.
1988 "Hunter-Gatherer Economic Complexity and 'Population Pressure': A Cross-Cultural Analysis." *Journal of Anthropological Archaeology* 7:373–411.
1996 *War before Civilization.* Oxford University Press, New York and Oxford.

Kelly, Robert L.
1983 "Hunter-Gatherer Mobility Strategies." *Journal of Anthropological Research* 39:277–306.
1992 "Mobility/Sedentism: Concepts, Archaeological Measures, and Effects." *Annual Review of Anthropology* 21:43–66.
1995 *The Foraging Spectrum: Diversity in Hunter-Gatherer Lifeways.* Smithsonian Institution Press, Washington, D.C.

Kent, Susan
1991 "The Relationship between Mobility Strategies and Site Structure," in *The Interpretation of Archaeological Spatial Patterning*, edited by Ellen Kroll and T. Douglas Price, pp. 33–89. Plenum Press, New York.

Kobayashi, Masashi
1994 "Use-Alteration Analysis of Kalinga Pottery: Interior Carbon Deposits of Cooking Pots," in *Kalinga Ethnoarchaeology: Expanding Archaeological Method and Theory*, edited by William A. Longacre and James M. Skibo, pp. 127–168. Smithsonian Institution Press, Washington, D.C.

Krugman, Stanley L., and James L. Jenkinson
1974 "*Pinus L.* Pine," in *Seeds of Woody Plants in the United States*, coordinated by C. S. Shopmeyer, pp. 598–638. Agriculture Handbook 450. U.S. Forest Service, Government Printing Office, Washington, D.C.

Lancaster, James
1983 "An Analysis of Manos and Metates from the Mimbres Valley, New Mexico." M.A. thesis, Department of Anthropology, University of New Mexico, Albuquerque.
1984 "Groundstone Artifacts," in *The Galaz Ruin: A Prehistoric Mimbres Village in Southwestern New Mexico*, by Roger Anyon and Steven A. LeBlanc, pp. 247–262. University of New Mexico Press and Maxwell Museum of Anthropology, Albuquerque.

Lanner, Ronald M.
1981 *The Pinyon Pine: A Natural and Cultural History*. University of Nevada Press, Reno.

Lawrence, W. G.
1972 *Ceramic Science for the Potter*. Chilton, Radnor, Pennsylvania.

LeBlanc, Steven A.
1975 *Mimbres Archaeological Center: Preliminary Report of the First Season of Excavation*. The Institute of Archaeology, University of California, Los Angeles.
1976a "Mimbres Archaeological Center: Preliminary Report of the Second Season of Excavation." *Journal of New World Archaeology* 1(6):1–24.
1976b "Archeological Recording Systems." *Journal of Field Archaeology* 3(2):159–168.
1982 "The Advent of Pottery in the Southwest," in *Southwestern Ceramics: A Comparative Review*, edited by Albert H. Schroeder,

pp. 27–51. Arizona Archaeological Society, Phoenix.
1983 *The Mimbres People: Ancient Painters of the American Southwest*. Thames and Hudson, London.
1997 "Modeling Warfare in Southwestern Prehistory." *North American Archaeologist* 18(3):235–276.
1998 "Settlement Consequences of Warfare during the Late Pueblo III and Pueblo IV Period," in *Migration and Reorganization: The Pueblo IV Period in the American Southwest*, edited by Katherine A. Spielmann, pp. 115–135. Arizona State University Anthropology Papers 51. Tempe.
1999 *Prehistoric Warfare in the American Southwest*. University of Utah Press, Salt Lake City.

LeBlanc, Steven A., and Michael E. Whalen
1980 "An Archaeological Synthesis of South-Central and Southwestern New Mexico." Manuscript on file, Bureau of Land Management, Albuquerque.

Lehmer, Donald J.
1948 *The Jornada Branch of the Mogollon*. University of Arizona Social Science Bulletin 17. University of Arizona, Tucson.

Lekson, Stephen H.
1988 "The Mangas Phase in Mimbres Archaeology." *The Kiva* 53(2):129–145.
1989 "Regional Systematics in the Later Prehistory of Southern New Mexico," in *Fourth Jornada Conference: Collected Papers*, edited by Meli Duran and Karl W. Laumbach, pp. 1–37. Human Systems Research, Las Cruces.
1990 *Mimbres Archaeology of the Upper Gila, New Mexico*. University of Arizona Anthropological Paper 52. University of Arizona Press, Tucson.
1992a "Archaeological Overview of South-western New Mexico." Manuscript prepared for the New Mexico State Historic Preservation Division, Project 35-88-3-120.004. Human Systems Research, Las Cruces.
1992b "The Surface Archaeology of South-western New Mexico." *The Artifact* 30(3):1–35.

Lerner, Shereen
1984   "Functional Interpretation of Black Mesa
       Ceramics," in *Papers on the Archaeology of
       Black Mesa, Arizona* 11, edited by Stephen
       Plog and Shirley Powell, pp. 87–101.
       Southern Illinois University Press,
       Carbondale.

Lightfoot, Kent G.
1984   *The Duncan Project: A Study of the
       Occupation Duration and Settlement Pattern
       of an Early Mogollon Pithouse Village.*
       Anthropological Field Studies 6. Office of
       Cultural Resource Management, Arizona
       State University, Tempe.

Lightfoot, Kent G., and Gary M. Feinman
1982   "Social Differentiation and Leadership
       Development in Early Pithouse Villages in
       the Mogollon Region of the American
       Southwest." *American Antiquity* 47:64–86.

Lightfoot, Kent G., and Roberta M. Jewett
1986   "The Shift to Sedentary Life: A
       Consideration of the Occupation Duration
       of Early Mogollon Pithouse Villages," in
       Mogollon Variability, edited by Charlotte
       Benson and Steadman Upham, pp. 9–44.
       Occasional Papers of the New Mexico
       State University Museum 15. Las Cruces.

Lischka, Leslie
1969   "A Possible Noncultural Bias in Lithic
       Debris." *American Antiquity* 34:483–485.

Longacre, William
1962   "Archaeological Reconnaissance in
       Eastern Arizona," in *Chapters in the
       Prehistory of Arizona I*, by Paul S. Martin,
       John B. Rinaldo, William A. Longacre,
       Constance Cronin, Leslie G. Freeman, Jr.,
       and James Schoenwetter, pp. 148–167.
       Fieldiana: Anthropology 53.
1964   "A Synthesis of Upper Little Colorado
       Prehistory, Eastern Arizona," in *Chapters
       in the Prehistory of Arizona II*, edited by
       Paul S. Martin, John B. Rinaldo, et al.,
       pp. 201–215. *Fieldiana: Anthropology* 55.

Lyons, David M., Sally P. Mendoza, and
William A. Mason
1994   "Psychosocial and Hormonal Aspects of
       Hierarchy Formation in Groups of Male
       Squirrel Monkeys." *American Journal of
       Primatology* 32:109–122.

Mabry, Jonathan B.
1998   *Paleoindian and Archaic Sites in Arizona.*
       The Center for Desert Archaeology,
       Tucson.

MacMahon, James A.
1988   "Warm Deserts," in *North American
       Terrestrial Vegetation*, edited by Michael G.
       Barbour and William D. Billings, pp.
       232–260. Cambridge University Press,
       New York.

Martin, Paul S.
1940   *The SU Site: Excavations at a Mogollon
       Village, Western New Mexico, 1939.*
       Anthropological Series, vol. 32, no. 1.
       Field Museum of Natural History,
       Chicago.
1943   *The SU Site: Excavations at a Mogollon
       Village, Western New Mexico, Second Season,
       1941.* Anthropological Series, vol. 32, no.
       2. Field Museum of Natural History,
       Chicago.
1967   "Hay Hollow Site." *Field Museum of
       Natural History Bulletin* 38(5):6–10.
1979   "Prehistory: Mogollon," in *Handbook of
       North American Indians*, vol. 9: *Southwest*,
       edited by Alfonso Ortiz. Smithsonian
       Institution Press, Washington, D.C.

Martin, Paul S., and John B. Rinaldo
1947   *The SU Site: Excavations at a Mogollon
       Village, Western New Mexico, Third Season,
       1946.* Anthropological Series, vol. 32, no.
       3. Field Museum of Natural History,
       Chicago.
1950   *Turkey Foot Ridge: A Mogollon Village, Pine
       Lawn Valley, Western New Mexico. Fieldiana:
       Anthropology* 38(2).

Martin, Paul S., John B. Rinaldo, and Ernst Antevs
1949   *Cochise and Mogollon Sites, Pine Lawn
       Valley, Western New Mexico. Fieldiana:
       Anthropology* 38(1).

Martin, Paul S., John B. Rinaldo, William A. Longacre,
Constance Cronin, Leslie G. Freeman, Jr., and
James Schoenwetter
1962   *Chapters in the Prehistory of Eastern Arizona,
       I. Fieldiana: Anthropology* 53.

Mauldin, Raymond P.
1991   "Agricultural Intensification in the
       Mogollon Highlands," in *Mogollon V*,
       edited by Patrick Beckett, pp. 62–74.

COAS Publishing and Research, Las Cruces.
1993 "The Relationship between Ground Stone and Agricultural Intensification in Western New Mexico." *The Kiva* 58(3):317–330.

McBride, Pamela
1989 "Paleoethnobotanical Analysis, SU Site," in *Final Descriptive Report: Archaeological Investigations at AR-03-06-06-157 and AR-03-06-06-162, Reserve Ranger District, Gila National Forest, Catron County, New Mexico.* Manuscript submitted to the USDA Gila National Forest, Silver City, New Mexico.

McGuire, Randall J., and Michael B. Schiffer
1983 "A Theory of Architectural Design." *Journal of Anthropological Archaeology* 2:277–303.

Mehringer, Peter J., Jr.
1967 "Pollen Analysis of the Tule Springs Area, Nevada," in *Pleistocene Studies in Southern Nevada*, edited by H. M. Wormington and D. Ellis, pp. 130–200. Nevada State Museum Anthropological Papers 13. Carson City.

Miksicek, Charles H.
1987 "Formation Processes of the Archaeobotanical Record," in *Advances in Archaeological Method and Theory*, vol. 7, edited by Michael B. Schiffer, pp. 211–247. Academic Press, New York.

Mills, Barbara
1984 "A Functional Analysis of Ceramics from the Anderson Site," in *Ladder Ranch Research: A Report of the First Season*, edited by Margaret C. Nelson, pp. 67–81. Technical Series, Paper 1. Maxwell Museum of Anthropology, Albuquerque.
1985 "'North American Cooking Pots' Reconsidered: Some Behavioral Correlates of Variation in Cooking Pot Morphology." Paper presented at the 50th Annual Meeting of the Society for American Archaeology, Denver.
1989 "Ceramics and Settlement in the Cedar Mesa Area, Southeastern Utah: A Methodological Approach." Ph.D. dissertation, University of New Mexico. University Microfilms, Ann Arbor,

Minnis, Paul E.
1980 "The Archaic in Southern New Mexico," in *An Archaeological Synthesis of South-Central and Southwestern New Mexico*, by Steven A. LeBlanc and Michael E. Whalen, pp. 64–102. Manuscript on file, Bureau of Land Management, Albuquerque.
1981 "Seeds in Archaeological Sites: Sources and Some Interpretive Problems." *American Antiquity* 46:143–152.
1985a *Social Adaptation to Food Stress: A Prehistoric Southwestern Example.* University of Chicago Press, Chicago.
1985b "Domesticating People and Plants in the Greater Southwest," in *Prehistoric Food Production in North America*, edited by Richard I. Ford, pp. 309–339. University of Michigan, Museum of Anthropology, Anthropological Papers 75. Ann Arbor.
1992 "Earliest Plant Cultivation in the Desert Borderlands of North America," in *The Origins of Agriculture*, edited by C. Wesley Cowan and Patty Jo Watson, pp. 121–141. Smithsonian Institution Press, Washington, D.C.

Minnis, Paul E., and Alan J. Wormser
1986 "Late Pithouse Period Occupation in the Deming Region: Preliminary Report of Excavations at the Florida Mountain Site (LA 18839)," in *Recent Research in Mogollon Archaeology*, edited by Steadman Upham, Fred Plog, David G. Batcho and Barbara E. Kauffman, pp. 229–249. New Mexico State University Occasional Papers, 10. Las Cruces.

Nelson, Ben A.
1980 "Cultural Responses to Population Change: A Comparison of Two Prehistoric Occupations in the Mimbres Valley, New Mexico." Ph.D. dissertation, Department of Anthropology, Southern Illinois University, Carbondale.
1985 "Reconstructing Ceramic Vessels and Their Systemic Contexts," in *Decoding Prehistoric Ceramics*, edited by Ben A. Nelson, pp. 310–329. Southern Illinois University Press, Carbondale.
1991 "Ceramic Frequency and Use-Life: A Highland Mayan Case in Cross-Cultural Perspective," in *Ceramic Ethnoarchaeology*, edited by William A. Longacre, pp. 162–181. University of Arizona Press, Tucson.

Nelson, Ben A., and Steven A. LeBlanc
 1986 *Short-term Sedentism in the American Southwest: The Mimbres Valley Salado.* Maxwell Museum of Anthropology and University of New Mexico Press, Albuquerque.

Nelson, Ben A., and Patricia A. McAnany
 1984 "The Mogollon Culture Area as a Frame of Reference for Predictive Modeling," in *Recent Research in Mogollon Archaeology*, edited by Steadman Upham, Fred Plog, David G. Batcho, and Barbara E. Kauffman, pp. 28–44. New Mexico State University Occasional Papers 10. Las Cruces.

Nelson, Margaret C.
 1981 "Chipped Stone Analysis in the Reconstruction of Prehistoric Subsistence Practices: An Example from Southwestern New Mexico." Ph.D. dissertation, Department of Anthropology, University of California, Santa Barbara.
 1984 "Food Selection at Galaz: Inferences from Chipped Stone Analysis," in *The Galaz Ruin: A Prehistoric Mimbres Village in Southwestern New Mexico*, by Roger Anyon and Steven A. LeBlanc, pp. 225–246. University of New Mexico Press, Albuquerque.
 1986a "Occupational History of Palomas Drainage, Western Sierra County, New Mexico," in *Mogollon Variability*, edited by Charlotte Benson and Steadman Upham, pp. 157–168. New Mexico State University Museum, Occasional Papers 15. Las Cruces.
 1986b "Chipped Stone Analysis: Food Selection and Hunting Behavior," in *Short-term Sedentism in the American Southwest: The Mimbres Valley Salado*, by Ben A. Nelson and Steven A. LeBlanc, pp. 141–176. University of New Mexico Press, Albuquerque.
 1991 "The Study of Technological Organization," in *Archaeological Method and Theory*, vol. 3, edited by Michael B. Schiffer, pp. 57–100. University of Arizona Press, Tucson.
 1999 *Mimbres during the Twelfth Century: Abandonment, Continuity, and Reorganization.* University of Arizona Press, Tucson.

Nesbitt, Paul H.
 1931 *The Ancient Mimbreños: Based on Investigations at the Mattocks Ruin, Mimbres Valley, New Mexico.* Logan Museum, Beloit College, Beloit, Wisconsin.

Ostrofsky, Benjamin
 1977 *Design, Planning, and Development Methodology.* Prentice-Hall, Englewood Cliffs, New Jersey.

Palmer, Craig J.
 1991 "Kin-Selection, Reciprocal Alliances and Information Sharing among Maine Lobstermen." *Ethology and Sociobiology* 12:221–235.

Parker, Kittie F.
 1990 *An Illustrated Guide to Arizona Weeds.* University of Arizona Press, Tucson.

Pase, Charles P., and David E. Brown
 1995a "Rocky Mountain (Petran) Subalpine Conifer Forest," in *Biotic Communities: Southwestern United States and Northwestern Mexico*, pp. 37–39. University of Utah Press, Salt Lake City.
 1995b "Rocky Mountain (Petran) and Madrean Montane Conifer Forests," in *Biotic Communities of the American Southwest, United States and Mexico: Desert Plants* 4(1–4):43–48. Boyce Thompson Southwestern Arboretum, Superior, Arizona.

Peebles, C. S., and Susan M. Kus
 1977 "Some Archaeological Correlates of Ranked Societies." *American Antiquity* 42:421–448.

Peet, Robert K.
 1988 "Forests of the Rocky Mountains," in *North American Terrestrial Vegetation*, edited by Michael G. Barbour and William D. Billings, pp. 64–101. Cambridge University Press, New York.

Pearsall, Deborah M.
 1989 *Paleoethnobotany: A Handbook of Procedures.* Academic Press, New York.

Plog, Fred
 1989 "Studying Complexity," in *The Sociopolitical Structure of Prehistoric*

Southwestern Societies, edited by Steadman Upham, Kent Lightfoot, and Roberta Jewett, pp. 103–125. Westview Press, Boulder.

Plog, Stephen
1977 "A Multivariate Approach to the Explanation of Ceramic Design Variation." Ph.D. dissertation, University of Michigan. University Microfilms, Ann Arbor.
1980 *Stylistic Variation in Prehistoric Ceramics*. Cambridge University Press, New York.

Price, T. Douglas, and James A. Brown, editors
1985 *Prehistoric Hunter-Gatherers: The Emergence of Cultural Complexity*. Academic Press, New York.

Rado, P.
1968 *An Introduction to the Technology of Pottery*. Pergamon Press, New York.

Rautmann, Alison E.
1993 "Resource Variability, Risk, and the Structure of Social Networks." *American Antiquity* 58:403–424.

Rice, Glen E.
1975 "A Systematic Explanation of Mogollon Settlement Pattern Changes." Ph.D. dissertation, University of Washington. University Microfilms, Ann Arbor.
1980 "An Analytical Overview of the Mogollon Tradition," in *Studies in the Prehistory of the Forestdale Region, Arizona*, edited by C. R. Stafford and G. E. Rice, pp. 9–40. Arizona State University Anthropological Field Studies 1. Tempe.

Rice, Prudence M.
1987 *Pottery Analysis: A Sourcebook*. University of Chicago Press, Chicago.

Rinaldo, John
1940 "Artifacts," in *The SU Site: Excavations at a Mogollon Village, Western New Mexico, 1939*, by Paul S. Martin, pp. 35–77. Anthropological Series, vol. 32, no. 1. Field Museum of Natural History, Chicago.

Roberts, Frank H. H., Jr.
1939 *Archaeological Remains in the Whitewater District, Eastern Arizona: Part I.* Bureau of American Ethnology, Bulletin 121. Smithsonian Institution, Washington, D.C.
1940 *Archaeological Remains in the Whitewater District, Eastern Arizona: Part II, Artifacts and Burials*. Bureau of American Ethnology, Bulletin 126. Smithsonian Institution, Washington, D.C.

Rocek, Thomas R.
1995 "Sedentarization and Agricultural Dependence: Perspectives from the Pithouse-to-Pueblo Transition in the American Southwest." *American Antiquity* 60:218–239.

Roth, Barbara J.
1992 "Sedentary Agriculturists or Mobile Hunter-Gatherers? Evidence on the Late Archaic Occupation of the Northern Tucson Basin." *The Kiva* 61:189–207.

Russell, F.
1908 "The Pima Indians," in *Twenty-sixth Annual Report of the Bureau of American Ethnology*, pp. 3–289. Smithsonian Institution, Washington, D.C.

Schiffer, Michael B.
1987 *Formation Processes of the Archaeological Record*. University of New Mexico Press, Albuquerque.
1988 "A Research Design for Ceramic Use-Wear Analysis at Grasshopper Pueblo," in *Pottery Technology: Ideas and Approaches*, edited by Gordon Bronitsky, pp. 183–205. Westview Press, Boulder.
1990 The Influence of Surface Treatment on Heating Effectiveness of Ceramic Vessels. *Journal of Archaeological Science* 17:373–381.

Schiffer, Michael B., James M. Skibo, Tamara C. Boelke, Mark A. Neupert, and Meredith Aronson
1994 "New Perspectives on Experimental Archaeology: Surface Treatments and Thermal Response of the Clay Cooking Pot." *American Antiquity* 59:197–217.

Schlanger, Sarah H.
1986   "Population Studies," in *Dolores Archaeological Program, Final Synthetic Report*, compiled by David A. Breternitz, Christine K. Robinson, and Timothy Gross, pp. 492–524. United States Department of the Interior, Bureau of Reclamation, Denver.
1991   "On Manos, Metates, and the History of Site Occupations." *American Antiquity* 56:460–474.

Schroeder, Albert H.
1979   "Pueblos Abandoned in Historic Times," in *Handbook of North American Indians*, vol. 9: *Southwest*, edited by Alfonso Ortiz, pp. 236–254. Smithsonian Institution Press, Washington, D.C.

Shafer, Harry J.
1982   "Classic Mimbres Phase Households and Room Use Patterns." *The Kiva* 48(1–2): 17–48.
1990   "Ten Years of Mimbres Archaeology." *The Artifact* 28(4):1–4.
1991a   "Archaeology at the NAN Ruin: The 1987 Season." *The Artifact* 29(3):1–43.
1991b   "Archaeology at the NAN Ruin: The 1989 Season." *The Artifact* 29(4):1–43.
1991c   "Classic Mimbres Architecture and Mortuary Patterning at the NAN Ranch Ruin (LA 15049), Southwestern New Mexico," in *Mogollon V*, edited by Patrick H. Beckett, pp. 34–49. COAS Publishing and Research, Las Cruces.
1995   "Architecture and Symbolism in Transitional Pueblo Development in the Mimbres Valley, Southwest New Mexico." *Journal of Field Archaeology* 22:23–47.

Shafer, Harry J., and Anna S. Taylor
1986   "Mimbres Mogollon Pueblo Dynamics and Mimbres Style Change." *Journal of Field Archaeology* 13:43–68.

Shepard, Anna O.
1965   *Ceramics for the Archaeologist.* Carnegie Institution of Washington, Publication 609. Washington, D.C.

Sims, Phillip L.
1988   "Grasslands," in *North American Terrestrial Vegetation*, edited by Michael G. Barbour and William D. Billings, pp. 266–286. Cambridge University Press, New York.

Sinopoli, Carla M.
1991   *Approaches to Archaeological Ceramics.* Plenum Press, New York.

Skibo, James M.
1992   *Pottery Function: A Use-Alteration Perspective.* Plenum Press, New York.

Smith, Watson
1973   *The Williams Site: A Frontier Mogollon Village in West-Central New Mexico.* Papers of the Peabody Museum of Archaeology and Ethnology, vol. 39, no. 2. Harvard University, Cambridge.

Speth, John D.
1972   "Mechanical Basis of Percussion Flaking." *American Antiquity* 37:34–60.

Stanislawski, M. B.
1978   "If Pots Were Mortal," in *Explorations in Ethnoarchaeology*, edited by Richard A. Gould, pp. 201–228. University of New Mexico Press, Albuquerque.

Stokes, Robert J.
1994   "A Critical Evaluation of the Mimbres-Mogollon Site Location Model: The Sapillo Valley Survey Project, 1993." Paper presented at the Annual Meeting of the Society for American Archaeology, Anaheim.

Stone, Tammy
1994   "The Impact of Raw-Material Scarcity on Ground Stone Manufacture and Use: An Example from the Phoenix Basin Hohokam." *American Antiquity* 59:680–694

Stuiver, M., and P. J. Reimer
1993   "Radiocarbon Calibration Program, Rev.3.0." *Radiocarbon* 35:215–230.

Tainter, Joseph A.
1982 "Symbolism, Interaction and Cultural Boundaries: The Anasazi-Mogollon Transition Zone in West-Central New Mexico," in *Mogollon Archaeology: Proceedings of the 1980 Mogollon Conference*, edited by Patrick H. Beckett and Kira Silverbird, pp. 3–9. Acoma Books, Ramona, California.
1984 "Perspectives on the Northern Mogollon Boundary Phenomenon," in *Recent Research in Mogollon Archaeology*, edited by Steadman Upham, Fred Plog, David G. Batcho, and Barbara E. Kauffman, pp. 45–74. Occasional Papers 10. New Mexico State University Museum, Las Cruces.

Torrence, Robin
1983 "Time Budgeting and Hunter-Gatherer Technology," in *Hunter-Gatherer Economy in Prehistory*, edited by Geoff Bailey, pp. 11–22. Cambridge University Press, Cambridge.

Trigger, Bruce G.
1989 *A History of Archaeological Thought*. Cambridge University Press, New York.

Tschopik, H., Jr.
1941 *Navajo Pottery Making: An Inquiry into the Affinities of Navajo Painted Pottery*. Papers of the Peabody Museum of American Archaeology and Ethnology, vol. 17, no. 1. Harvard University, Cambridge.

Turner, Christy G., III, and Laurel Lofgren
1966 "Household Size of Prehistoric Western Pueblo Indians." *Southwestern Journal of Anthropology* 22(2):117–132.

Upham, Steadman, Richard S. MacNeish, Walton C. Galinat, and Christopher M. Stevenson
1987 "Evidence Concerning the Origin of Maize de Ocho." *American Anthropologist* 89:410–418.

Upham, Steadman, Richard S. MacNeish, and Christopher M. Stevenson
1988 "The Age and Evolutionary Significance of Southwestern Maiz de Ocho." *American Anthropologist* 90:683–684.

USDA (United States Department of Agriculture)
1974 *Definitions and Abbreviations for Soil Description from the United States Department of Agriculture Soil Science Survey*. West Technical Service Center, Portland, Oregon.

Varien, Mark
1990 *Excavations at Three Prehistoric Sites along Pia Mesa Road, Zuni Indian Reservation, McKinley County, New Mexico*. Zuni Archaeological Program Report 233, Research Series 4. Zuni Pueblo, New Mexico.

Wallace, L.
1883 "A Buffalo Hunt in Northern Mexico," in *Sport with the Rod and Gun*, edited by A. M. Mayer. Century, New York.

Wendorf, Fred
1953 *Archaeological Studies in the Petrified Forest National Monument*. Museum of Northern Arizona, Bulletin 27. Flagstaff.
1956 "Some Distributions of Settlement Patterns in the Pueblo Southwest," in *Prehistoric Settlement Patterns in the New World*, edited by Gordon R. Willey, pp. 18–25. Viking Fund Publications in Anthropology 23. Wenner-Gren Foundation for Anthropological Research, New York.

West, Neil E.
1988 "Intermountain Deserts, Shrub Steppes, and Woodlands," in *North American Terrestrial Vegetation*, edited by Michael G. Barbour and William Dwight Billings, pp. 209–230. Cambridge University Press, New York.

Whalen, Michael E.
1980 "Human Adaptation to the Basin-and-Range Zone of the Mogollon Area," in *Mogollon Archaeology: Proceedings of the 1980 Mogollon Conference*, edited by Patrick H. Beckett and Kira Silverbird, pp. 179–189. Acoma Books, Ramona California.
1981 "Cultural-Ecological Aspects of the Pithouse-to-Pueblo Transition in a Portion of the Southwest." *American Antiquity* 46:75–92.

1994　*Turquoise Ridge and Late Prehistoric Residential Mobility in the Desert Mogollon Region*. Anthropological Papers 118. University of Utah Press, Salt Lake City.

Wheat, Joe Ben
1954　*Crooked Ridge Village (AZ W:10:15)*. University of Arizona Social Science Bulletin 24. University of Arizona Press, Tucson.
1955　*Mogollon Culture Prior to A.D. 1000*. American Anthropologist Memoir 82.

Whittlesey, Stephanie M.
1995　"Mogollon, Hohokam, and O'Otam: Rethinking the Early Formative Period in Southern Arizona." *The Kiva* 60(4):465–480.
1974　"Identification of Imported Ceramics through Functional Analysis of Attributes." *The Kiva* 40(1–2):101–112.

Willey, Gordon R., and Jeremy A. Sabloff
1993　*A History of American Archaeology*, 3rd edition. W. H. Freeman, New York.

Wills, W. H.
1985　*Early Prehistoric Agriculture in the American Southwest*. School of American Research Press, Santa Fe.
1988　"Early Agriculture and Sedentism in the American Southwest: Evidence and Interpretations." *Journal of World Prehistory* 2(4):445–488.
1989　"Patterns of Prehistoric Food Production in West Central New Mexico." *Journal of Anthropological Research* 45:139–157.
1991a　"Archaeological Investigations at AR03-06-06-157 & AR03-06-06-16, Reserve Ranger District, Gila National Forest, Catron County, New Mexico." Manuscript submitted to the USDA Gila National Forest, Silver City, New Mexico.
1991b　"Organizational Strategies and the Emergence of Prehistoric Villages in the American Southwest," in *Between Bands and States*, edited by Susan A. Gregg, pp. 161–180. Center for Archaeological Investigations, Occasional Paper 9. Southern Illinois University Press, Carbondale.

1992　"Plant Cultivation and the Evolution of Risk-Prone Economies in the Prehistoric American Southwest," in *Transitions to Agriculture in Prehistory*, edited by Anne Birgitte Gebauer and T. Douglas Price, pp. 153–176. Prehistory Press, Madison, Wisconsin.
1993　"Recent Evidence for the Introduction of Maize to the American Southwest from Mesoamerica." *Revista de Arqueologica Americana* 7:83–97.
1996a　"The Transition from the Preceramic to the Ceramic Period in the Mogollon Highlands of Western New Mexico." *Journal of Field Archaeology* 23:335–359.
1996b　"Archaic Foraging and the Beginning of Food Production in the American Southwest," in *Last Hunters, First Farmers*, edited by T. Douglas Price and Anne Birgitte Gebauer, pp. 215–242. School of American Research Press, Santa Fe.

Wills, W. H., and Bruce B. Huckell
1994　"Economic Implications of Changing Land-Use Patterns in the Late Archaic," in *Themes in Southwest Prehistory*, edited by George J. Gumerman, pp. 33–52. School of American Research Press, Santa Fe.

Woodbury, Richard B., and Ezra B. W. Zubrow
1979　"Agricultural Beginnings," in *Handbook of North American Indians*, vol. 9: *Southwest*, edited by Alfonso Ortiz, pp. 43–60. Smithsonian Institution Press, Washington, D.C.

Woosley, Anne I., and Allen J. McIntyre
1996　*Mimbres Mogollon Archaeology: Charles C. Di Peso's Excavations at Wind Mountain*. University of New Mexico Press, Albuquerque.